Joseph Masters

The Priest in Absolution

Part I

Joseph Masters

The Priest in Absolution
Part I

ISBN/EAN: 9783744764353

Printed in Europe, USA, Canada, Australia, Japan

Cover: Foto ©Lupo / pixelio.de

More available books at **www.hansebooks.com**

THE

PRIEST IN ABSOLUTION:

A MANUAL FOR SUCH

AS ARE CALLED UNTO THE HIGHER MINISTRIES

IN THE ENGLISH CHURCH.

PART I.

"Cur baptizatis, si per hominem peccata dimitti non licet? In Baptismo utique remissio peccatorum omnium est. Quid interest utrum per pœnitentiam, an per lavacrum hoc jus sibi datum sacerdotes vindicent? Unum in utroque mysterium est."—AMBROS. DE PŒNIT. I. 8. p. 400, ed. Ben.

LONDON:
JOSEPH MASTERS, ALDERSGATE STREET,
AND NEW BOND STREET.
1866.

ADVERTISEMENT TO THE READER.

In the Apostles' Creed we believe "the Forgiveness of sins." This is apparently limited in the Nicene Confession to the "One Baptism." Baptism conveys to and assures the penitent of the remission of all sins previously committed. In this Sacrament the Priest is the ministerial agent of God, and it is his duty, in the case of all of riper years offering themselves for Baptism, to make sure that they truly repent. Hence even the catechumens of John the Baptist were baptized in the river Jordan, "confessing their sins." When the Priest admits applicants to Baptism or rejects them, he thereby remits or retains their sins. There can be no more well-founded objection to saying that the Priest forgives sin in Baptism, than in saying that the physician cures and heals.

But is there no balm in Gilead?—is there no spiritual physician for relapse into sin after Baptism? Whatever theories people may form for themselves, the commission of Absolution involves this restorative power, and is given to Priests of the English Church, the commission being of a universal character, and not confined to Baptism. Nay, if compared with the formula of the Roman Church, the English Ritual would seem the more prominently to set before the Priest as his great work that of binding or loosing. In the Roman Church the duty of offering the great Unbloody Sacrifice for the sins of mankind is more particularly set before candidates for the Priesthood. Yet the Eucharistic Sacrifice is only one way whereby the pardon of sin is set forth and exhibited. In the English Church it has been thought enough to put before the clergy in a more general manner, as the one abiding thought of their lives, that they receive the Holy Ghost for the remission and retention of sins, howsoever administered by them, and that, as dispensers of God's Holy Word and Sacraments, they are henceforth to devote themselves to the one object of standing between the living and the dead, by awakening the soul to a sense of its responsibilities and shortcomings, by leading it to sure and certain trust in the mercy of God, and by supplying it with all means of grace, whereby it may be kept in the way of eternal life.

As every one, then, who receives the Order of Priesthood in the English Church is endued with authority to forgive or retain sins, it becomes of the utmost consequence that English Priests should apply themselves to diligent study in order that they may the better know when to forgive and when to retain. In the Visitation Office the Priest is required, after examining the sick person as to his spiritual and temporal affairs, to move him to make a special confession of his sins, if he feel his conscience troubled with any "weighty[1]" matter. On which Bishop Sparrow suggests that all sin may be considered a weighty matter. Those, at any rate, who, with eternity so close at hand, do not so consider it, are indeed much to be pitied, unless they have had this serious regard of sin before that awful moment arrives, and have already anticipated the motion of the Priest to urge them to Confession. Moreover, the Priest is after such Confession to absolve the sick person, "if he humbly and heartily desire it[1]." These words, "humbly and heartily," point to the special conditions under which Absolution is to be given or withheld. Persons who regard Absolution as being entirely a corrupt following of the Apostles, cannot, of course, humbly and heartily desire it. But to be able to form a judgment as to the fitness of persons to receive Absolution, demands of the Priest no little thought, preparation, and experience.

And not only is the Priest ordered to move the sick to Confession of sin with a view to Absolution; but he is

---

[1] See Rubric in the Visitation Office.
[2] Rationale on the passage.

to invite all, whose consciences, without being so moved, are disquieted, to come to him, or to some other discreet and learned Minister of God's Word, and open their griefs, that by the Ministry of God's Holy Word they may receive the benefit of Absolution[3]. Here, again, Absolution is set before the people as the end and object of opening griefs. And this disposes of such notions as that men may confess their sins to one another with the same profit as to the Priest. No one but the Priest is empowered to apply the Absolution and Remission of sins, or to exclude from Absolution and Remission of sins. The benefit of Absolution is not to be imparted by the Priest solely upon the opening of griefs; there must be also the humble and hearty desire of receiving it on the part of the person troubled in conscience, or it must be kept back. To learn, therefore, when sins are to be remitted or retained, should form an important part of the studies of candidates for the Priesthood, lest they hereafter, through neglect or abuse of the gift bestowed upon them by the laying on of hands, be rejected by Him in Whose stead they were sent forth to beseech men to be reconciled to God.

[3] See Exhortation, "when the Minister giveth warning for the celebration of Holy Communion."

CONTENTS.

CHAPTER I.

HINTS FOR THE PRIEST IN HEARING CONFESSIONS.

		PAGE
1.	The Office of the Priest who hears Confession	1
2.	The Priest as a Spiritual Father	2
3.	His readiness to Minister	3
4.	The Priest as a Spiritual Physician	5
5.	The Priest as a Theologian	7
6.	The Priest as a Judge	9
7.	Precautions necessary to be taken	10

CHAPTER II.

HINTS FOR THE PRIEST WHILE A CONFESSION IS BEING MADE.

1.	Hints for the Priest in examining the Penitent	22
2.	Hints for examining and admonishing the Penitent	26
3.	How Penitents should be disposed to Grief and Resolutions	30
4.	How different Persons should be stirred up to Sorrow	37

CHAPTER III.

WHAT KIND OF PENANCE SHOULD BE ENJOINED UPON PENITENTS?

The Confessor is bound to enjoin some Penance 40

		PAGE
I.	Things to be observed in fixing proportionable Acts of Penitence	40
II.	The Kind of Acts of Penitence to be enjoined	41
III.	When a lighter Penance than usual may be imposed	44
IV.	Unsuitable Penances	45
V.	When a Penance enjoined by one Priest may be changed by another	47
VI.	In Cases of Doubt the Priest should lean to the milder Course	47

CHAPTER IV.

HOW AND WHEN ABSOLUTION SHOULD BE GIVEN.

I.	Form of Absolution	48
II.	The Form of Absolution Authoritative	50
III.	Absolution not to be given dependent on some Future Condition	51
IV.	Absolution to be given to any one Rightly Disposed	51
V.	Absolution should by right be given absolutely, sometimes with some Present Condition	51
VI.	What should be done if the Penitent, after having been absolved, add a fresh Mortal Sin which he had omitted to mention?	53
VII.	What should be done if the Confessor has forgotten the Sins confessed before he gives Absolution?	53
VIII.	Absolution from Censures, though anterior to Absolution from Sins, does not include Fulfilment of Penance or Amendment of Life	55
IX.	No Half Absolution to be given on account of the Concourse of Penitents	55
X.	Absolution cannot be validly given to a Person who is not present to receive it	56
XI.	Absolution may be given from Venial Sins to a Person rightly disposed	57
XII.	What should be done if the Person thinks he may relapse	57

CHAPTER V.

WHEN AND HOW ABSOLUTION SHOULD BE REFUSED OR DELAYED.

	PAGE
I. When Absolution is to be delayed, and what are the Signs of Indisposition for it?	59
II. When Absolution should be refused?	62
III. What if the Penitent conceals a grievous Sin, of which the Priest has been made aware by the Confession of the Partner in the Sin?	64
IV. If Absolution is refused, it should be done gently	66

CHAPTER VI.

HOW PENITENTS OUGHT USUALLY TO BE DIRECTED TO A DEVOUT OR REALLY CHRISTIAN LIFE?

I. In what consists a truly devout Life?	67
II. He should instil into himself a Thought of the great Importance of his last End	68
III. Great Horror of Sin	69
IV. By urging the Thought of the Vanity of the World, and the Constancy of Eternity	70
V. By suggesting Means of attaining to Virtue—	70
First—A high idea of Virtue	70
The Second is an ardent and strong Desire thereof	71
The Third is constant Prayer	72
The Fourth, a constant effort to advance	74
The Fifth, to walk in God's presence	74
The Sixth, to propose to ourselves Christ as our example	74
VI. Acts of Faith, Hope, and Charity frequently to be made	75
VII. Also of Humility	76
VIII. We should learn to do all with a right Intention	77
IX. The Penitent should be instructed as to general and particular Self-examination	77
X. Confession and Communion to be devout and frequent	78
XI. Summary of Counsels to be given by Priests in order to lead a Religious Life	79

CHAPTER VII.

WHETHER, WHEN, AND HOW ERRORS AND FAILURES INTO WHICH THE PRIEST FALLS IN ADMINISTERING HIS OFFICE MAY BE AMENDED?

	PAGE
I. What should be done if he has not Absolved a Penitent rightly disposed, who has committed Mortal Sin?	82
II. What if he has omitted to inquire the Number and Class of Sins?	84
III. What if he has neglected to admonish him in regard to Restitution?	85
IV. What if he has Obliged or Released from Obligation to Restore through some Innocent Mistake?	86
V. What if through Culpable Error or Malice?	88
VI. What if he has ordered the thing which ought to be restored to be given to the Poor?	89
VII. Whether it is necessary, before Correcting a Mistake, to ask the Penitent's Leave	89
VIII. What the Priest should do when he reflects upon the Confessions which have been made to him	90
IX. General Directions in concluding this part of the Manual	91

THE PRIEST IN ABSOLUTION,

&c.

CHAPTER I.

HINTS FOR THE PRIEST IN HEARING CONFESSIONS.

(1) *The Office of the Priest who hears Confession.*

THE Priest when called to hear confession should "magnify his office" by considering the importance of this ministry to individual souls, whereby such as have been guilty of heinous offences against God, are, if contrite, cleansed from the guilt of sin, and delivered from due punishment. He should call to mind the solemn time, when on his admission to the Priesthood, the Bishop said to him in the words of CHRIST, "Whose sins thou dost forgive, they are forgiven; and whose sins thou dost retain, they are retained:" and by doing so impress upon his own mind the great need he has of illumination and sanctification by the HOLY GHOST, lest through any fault on his part, he "strengthen the hands

of the wicked," or " make the heart of the righteous sad."
And in order to become the more able duly to minister to
souls diseased in the Sacramental rite of Absolution, he
should consider the different functions which the Priest
discharges, according to the condition of the various cases
which come before him; and he will thus learn his need
of a more than common holiness, to which he will never
attain, if he be not a man of prayer and meditation. He
has to direct the consciences of others without erring on
the side of rigour or laxity; he has to probe wounds
without being stained by them; he has to deal with
women and with youths; and listen to the recital of the
most shameful falls without deriving any injury therefrom; he has to use firmness with great people without
yielding to any respect of persons, and to minister to the
ills of the poor with as great a care as to those of the
rich. He must, in a word, be full of charity, gentleness,
and wisdom.

(2) *The Priest as a Spiritual Father.*

As the Priest is the Spiritual Father of his people
generally, so does he especially discharge this function in
the ministry of Absolution. No love is more pure, more
honourable, more strong, more unwearied, more disinterested, more careful, more liberal, more prudent, more
patient than that of a father. Such should be the character of the Priest's relations to those who open their
griefs to him, as being his spiritual children.

(3) *His readiness to Minister.*

Hence, "*he ought never to refuse his ministry to any one.*" He ought to be always ready to minister to poor and rich alike, on all days and at all hours, remembering that, if he should send any away without seeing them, he may be quenching the smoking flax, and so an opportunity may be lost to some soul at the critical point of its life. Cases, whether unknown or known, should be received with alacrity, lest, for want of a speedy remedy, the soul relapse into the state of self-complacency or despair, from which an impulse of Divine Grace had roused it. If it be impossible to receive them at the time, he should fix a day and hour for their reception, however inconvenient to himself, and do what he can to persuade them to come back at the time appointed. Having an ardent desire for the salvation of souls, and especially of those who come to open their griefs, he will pray GOD to co-operate in their conversion and spiritual progress. He will receive them with the love of a father, bearing with their ignorance, stupidity, weakness, slowness, and other imperfections, never giving their cases up while he can aid and succour them with any hope of their amendment. "The pastoral charge," as says St. Bernard, "is not of strong, but of weak and feeble souls; for the strong can walk well enough by themselves, but the weak must be carried." To be a good confessor it is not needful to be a great theologian, or an experienced ascetic, but rather must he be filled with charity, not with any kind of charity, but the charity of a father, or good pastor, and not of a hireling. Now this qualification of a Priest, though more easy in appearance, is in reality the most difficult; for it binds him to three things : (1) the acquisition of sound morality as a judge, and of great skill as a physician : (2) to make good use of these qualities to ensure the profit of the applicant: (3) to take upon him a large part of the fatigue, that just as the sheep in receiving all the benefits of the fold, and of the shepherd's care, are not tempted to hate him, or to flee away from him, never to return, so the soul, through being drawn by the charity of the Priest, which changes the bitterness of the confession into sweetness, often returns to him, and thereby is kept faithful to God. Thus the Priest should receive all who come to him for assistance in the difficulties attending the spiritual life with great readiness, taking care not only never to send them away through disgust of the trouble, but also never to show by words or manner that he does not listen to them willingly. Rather should he produce in their minds a persuasion that he receives a sensible consolation and singular delight in the trouble which he takes for the good and consolation of their souls Love for souls alone will enable the Priest to devote himself heartily to this arduous ministry. One who was most devoted to this work, never would allow persons to be sent away without seeing them, and forbade strictly such excuses as, "He is lying down to rest," or "He cannot be seen." "Do you not know," said he, "that I do not wish to have a moment or hour to myself?" Another, equally inflamed with zeal for the salvation of souls, travelled upwards of one hundred miles to receive the confession of an old man, who had expressed himself to one of his friends, as anxious for this blessing, but unwilling to make his confession to any one else. At all times the Priest, who realizes the fact that he is a father of his people, should have before him the picture which our blessed LORD sets before us in the Gospel, of the loving and affectionate manner wherewith the father of the prodigal greets and presses to his heart the son who "was dead and is alive again, was lost and is found."

(4) *The Priest as a Spiritual Physician.*

As the Priest should have impressed upon him the character of a father, so should he add to this the skill of a physician; else though he has the desire of saving souls, he will not know how to do it. It is for this that the study of ascetic as well as of moral theology is so necessary. This study is specially required, in order to become acquainted with the best remedies to be applied to particular cases of temptation. The duty which devolves on a Priest in his character of a physician, to probe the spiritual wounds of his patients, renders it desirable that he should be very cautious in receiving to confession those with whom he lives on terms of familiarity, lest any thing occur to lower him in their eyes, or create a difficulty in their own minds. But if he does receive such persons, it is an additional motive for preserving a careful discipline over his own life, lest he lose the esteem or confidence in which he ought to be held by them. Two evils result from the want of such care; an uneasiness in the minds of those who have made him the depository of their sins, while they are in his presence; and the danger of any defects in his character being discovered by too close observation, which might render him less valued. In the case of sickness, the Priest should abstain from pressing his ministry, if he have reason to think that at such a crisis the penitent may wish for other advice; and it is important that the soul should have liberty to apply wherever it feels most confidence. Even when in time of health penitents address themselves to another Priest on any particular occasion, he must be careful not to express dissatisfaction, or to make inquiries about it. Rather must he endeavour so to acquit himself, that they shall have no reason to seek elsewhere for the aid and consolation which they require. The Priest, however, is not precluded from admonishing especially the young and thoughtless, if he finds that they, without good reason, or out of mere caprice, withdraw from his direction. Care must be taken in the case of the poor, lest they mix up their temporal and their spiritual needs, by taking the opportunity of asking for alms, and so learn to avail themselves of the ministry of Absolution only for the sake of their bodily wants. It is better, if need occur, that the Priest relieve them through a third person, than that he should himself minister to their aid. In the case of rich persons, he must be careful, when imposing the necessity of almsgiving, not to ask them to give to any object, lest he bring his ministry into discredit, or dislike. In short, the Priest should avoid interference in all temporal matters as much as possible; the only exception to the rule being in the case of his being actually consulted, and feeling obliged to give advice.

(5) *The Priest as a Theologian.*

But not only does the Priest need to acquire the skill of a physician, he also must be a theologian. In order to form a right decision upon a particular case, a knowledge of moral theology is indispensable. He must (1) be able to distinguish between sins unto death and sins not unto death; between what in the nature of sin is grievous, and what is comparatively trivial, so as not to confound one with the other. He must (2) be acquainted with the principles upon which he has to decide how far the particular sin is tinged by the circumstances of the case, so as to remove it from one class to another. (3) He must know what special circumstances render it obligatory to make restitution in the instance of thefts or scandal. (4) He must be able to discover what is the immediate source or occasion producing the evil, and what are at least the best remedies. (5) He must know in what state the penitent ought to be. (6) He must be acquainted with the most usual penances to be enjoined, and also with the remedies most commonly applied. (7) He should be able to distinguish cases which reasonably admit of doubt as to the course to be pursued, and those which allow of an easy solution, so as not to feel embarrassment, but to be able at once to give a decision, or to reserve the case for further inquiry or deliberation. This knowledge of moral theology must be directed by discretion, else the Priest will be wrecked on the shoals either of laxity or severity, and lead those to whom he ministers to presumption or despair. This discretion must be exercised and attained, (1) by carefulness in putting questions: (2) by defining what is allowed and what is forbidden, what is of precept and what of counsel: and (3) by ascertaining the state of the penitent's mind, so as to decide on giving, or withholding, Absolution. To this end the Priest must use prayer for enlightenment in his studies: he must also guard himself against taking up theories, or sticking to one authority. The great point is to avoid the extremes of laxity or severity. Thus in a case where there is danger of formal sin, severity is of more use than laxity; while even in a case, where there is a risk of material sin, much prudence is required. In all cases the decision should be influenced mainly by the spiritual need and profit of the penitent. A lax system of moral theology, by excessive indulgence to human weakness, does not render the law sufficiently felt and respected; a severe system, by causing the yoke of the law to become too burdensome, gives occasion to human frailty to abandon both law and law-giver. It is in avoiding both of these dangers that a sound moral theology is best exhibited. A severe moralist will only take account of the smallest reason in favour of the law, and disregard the particular case to which it is to be applied; while the lax moralist will avail himself of the least reason in favour of the individual, without any regard to the precepts against which it militates. When the penitent knows, and is aware of the obligation under which he lies, it is impossible to dispense with it. It becomes the duty of the Priest to supply motives for rousing him to fulfil his duties, and not to dispense with them. In case of doubt it is best to be silent, or to advise a middle way, or to give the best counsel he can without making the penitent incur an obligation. Thus the moral theologian must never forget that he is also a physician. One rule of safety is to be cautious of prescribing what he would not carry out himself. And, as it is impossible to settle a cut-and-dry course for every one, it is best to inculcate duties only in the abstract; as for example to urge almsgiving in general, without specifying the particular acts of self-denial to be performed in order to be able to give alms, although the Priest should be prepared, if asked for advice, to suggest the most suitable mode. Meanwhile a vast knowledge of moral theology is not required for ordinary dealings with souls. Although no Priest should neglect the study of it, he must look to experience and common sense, as his main guide in determining the cases which commonly come before him.

(6) *The Priest as a Judge.*

To the knowledge of a moral theologian must be added the decision of a judge. As the physician is bound to use the best remedies, so is the judge obliged to give the safest decisions. He must not decide in opposition to Holy Scripture, or to Catholic Canons rightly interpreted, or manifest reason. He must go on something more than probability in cases of right or fact, of what is lawful and what is valid. Where opinions are equally balanced, he may follow that which most approves itself to his own mind in the case before him. And generally speaking in a conflict of probabilities, some reasons being more or less apparently conclusive, it will not always be best to take that which seems most probable, as the ground of decision, without regarding the special case under consideration, else there would be a danger of making our LORD's yoke heavier to the individual than he can bear.

(7) *Precautions necessary to be taken.*

Having spoken of the qualifications to be sought for in the Priest as a Confessor, let us consider the precautions he should take both on account of himself, and of those to whom he ministers. He must have a pre-eminent regard for this part of his ministry, and take all possible pains to acquire the fitting qualifications; he must not relinquish its duties for human reasons, nor for ill-grounded spiritual motives. The most necessary qualifications are that he have the love of a father, the skill of a physician, the knowledge of a theologian, and the decision of a judge. Though love is not enough without skill and knowledge, yet without paternal love all is in vain, since the possession of that quality alone makes this ministry pleasant to himself and profitable to his penitent. Many cases require but little knowledge or skill, but all require love for aiding the penitent and sustaining him through his confession. The Priest must have the skilful adroitness of a physician, in order to direct the moral knowledge of which it is the strength, the aid, the enrichment, the perfection and complement. He must also have an acquaintance with ascetic knowledge, which, distinguishing between speculative and practical theology, shows us what rule of morality in the exercise of the holy ministry is most useful to the glory of God and the sanctification of souls; that is to say, neither too lax nor too rigid a rule, but one prudent and discreet. Such knowledge is the strength and aid of morality, because to the understanding of the matters, which are the subject of inquiry, it adds the adroitness, discernment, and reserve necessary for discovering and perceiving the whole amount of the mischief, and for applying the necessary remedies, without going too far, so as to do harm to the patient. If the Priest be called upon to declare and decide in his character of theologian, he would learn how best to avoid the twofold rock of rigour and laxity: sometimes by safe language, sometimes by a wise silence, at other times by using some reproof, or by being content with simple counsels. But it is above all in his capacity as judge, in remitting or retaining sins, that skilful adroitness supplies the Priest with means for bringing the sinner into a right state for receiving Absolution to his soul's health, or for submitting to have it refused him without danger to his soul. It is the wealth and enrichment of morality, because of the motives, examples, and experiences which it puts at the Priest's disposal; it gives him numberless ways of making the performance of the most arduous duties easier to the penitent, and enables him to find the fit remedy for every malady of the soul; in short, it renders penitence more conformable and useful, whether to repair the past, or to secure against the future. This is not all; for while the simple knowledge of morals secures the right absolving of the sinner, ascetic theology conducts him to perfection; hence the need of this latter study in order to possess the skill of the physician. Moral theology must always be attended to, and for needful proficiency in such studies there is required much prayer, a teachable and impartial mind, and diligent reading.

The Priest must bear a high esteem for this part of his ministry. To be convinced that none is more useful to souls, and even to his own, will animate him so as never to neglect it, nor to fulfil it with negligence. In order to impress on his own mind the necessity of striving to realize in himself the charity of a father, the skill of a physician, the knowledge of a theologian, and the precision of a judge, the Priest should consider that nothing is more pleasing to JESUS CHRIST than this ministry to souls, and that it is the greatest exercise of love and patience towards them; that nothing more evidences love to our neighbour, as being a more incessant and less attractive labour than that of preaching, and that nothing is more beneficial to the Priest himself, both in regard to GOD or his neighbour. In regard to GOD it is a co-operation with Him in the work of man's salvation, not merely by disposing to certain states of mind, but by actual production of them in the case of such as are rightly disposed. To this we may add the gratitude of those who profit by this ministry towards the spiritual fathers of their souls, manifested in their continual intercessions on behalf of them as being their counsellors in doubts; consolers in trials, sickness, and death; aids in relapses; in short, helpers to attain eternal life.

But this ministry is fruitful to the Priest himself in specially contributing to his sanctification. It demands of him frequent mortification, in curtailing his favourite occupations or recreations; in producing fatigue of body, and anxiety of mind. He must practise a lively charity, and great patience in receiving and assisting such as have recourse to him. In short, the truths which he inculcates on others, the reproofs which he administers to their faults, the encouragements which he gives to virtue, are all useful to him, and "turn into his own bosom." This profit he will have if he does not dread the trouble, not from week to week as in preaching, nor *daily* as in celebrating; but, it may be, often in the day, and under most urgent and difficult circumstances to the penitent. Then too there is less danger of vainglory than if he were preaching to a numerous and brilliant auditory. For in this case the labour is known only to GOD, to the Priest, and to the confessed. Sometimes in lieu of praise, he incurs only blame, which must be endured in silent waiting for the result, without the power of self-defence by breaking the seal of confession; sometimes he suffers great inconveniences by having to minister to the sick; or he requires much deliberation so as to give advice in cases of conscience—all these being frequent means of sanctification for the Priest. Some have conceived that he performs in this ministry all the spiritual works of mercy; consolation of the afflicted, instruction of the ignorant, counselling of the doubtful, conversion of the sinner, preservation of the righteous, and conducting of them to perfection, filling them with zeal, and rendering them useful to others. Neither mere human motives, nor ill-conceived spiritual reasons, should hinder the Priest from discharging his functions: nothing, in short, but the necessity of life or the care of health; and even these might well be sacrificed to the glory of GOD, where souls are at stake. Indolence often asserts itself under the protest of the responsibilities attached to them, or under that of health, and the love of popularity under the cloke of dreading temptations and failures. If want of knowledge is pleaded, it should be borne in mind that in ordinary cases only a common-place kind of information is requisite. Few confessions require special study, and when these occur, the special point may be reserved for investigation.

To avoid mistakes, (1) an experienced Priest should be consulted as to the mode of putting questions. Care should be taken to avoid putting secondary questions instead of primary. For example, if a person confesses evil thoughts, the first thing to ask is whether they were consented to or indulged in. If not, there is an end of the matter. The great point is to be practical; to question about probable and likely, rather than about possible and rare evils. So, also, care should be taken to become acquainted with the most useful advice, and the most suitable penances to be given. (2) After discharging his functions the Priest should examine himself, repairing, if possible, any fault, or at the worst humbling himself, but not losing heart at any defect. Thus he will learn how to manage better on a future occasion. (3) In difficulties ascetic theology is more useful than moral theology for solving a knotty point. But the knowledge of both is a material help to further the cure of the penitent: especially in dealing with young and virtuous persons, or sinners whose cases require immediate Absolution, also with the sick; with persons who are in great danger of sinning, or who are not alive to it; and with such as relapse.

When the Priest has learnt how to put questions discreetly, how to absolve without error, and how to retain sins without loss to the penitent, provided he has the charity of a father, he need not think of relinquishing this ministry. To avoid the ministry of Absolution on account of the temptations into which it may bring the minister is unreasonable, because the holy fear, which the Holy Spirit inspires in the soul, is one preservation against falls, accustoming him to gain the victory over himself, in order to render him more sympathizing with others, and more adroit in guiding them. If the confessor did not fear, there would be reason to fear for him. One might rather dread the idea of his becoming ever proof against such alarms in a ministry, wherein he must needs be likely to fall if he fear not its perils nor seek to obviate them by suitable precautions: for it must be allowed it has its rocks. The confessor then should fear, and his fear should only end with his life: "Blessed is the man who feareth always." But his fear must have its limits, so as not to make him fall into dejection and abandon his functions. Rather should it lead him on the contrary to hope more and more, and to forearm himself by self-distrust, by suitable precautions, and by trust in GOD. His hope will not be in vain. All the while that he exposes himself to danger for a motive so holy, and with the prospect of assisting men in becoming reconciled to GOD, and takes care to use suitable precautions, he will find GOD's words come true:—"GOD is faithful, and will not suffer you to be tempted above that ye are able, but will with the temptation also make a way to escape." He that shrinks from the trials incident to the discharge of his duties, must look to lose the triumphs and rewards which are in store for the valiant conquerors in the warfare of grace.

Zeal for his own sanctification may tempt the Priest to relinquish this ministry. Doubtless, his own sanctification ought to be his first duty; yet one result of sanctification should be the desire of the sanctification of others. True sanctity is the best of all sciences. It furnishes the experience of virtues to be practised and of vices to be combated, and puts one in the best condition of giving instruction to others. Possessed of this sanctity, the Priest will obtain from GOD the efficacious blessing of His Word, so that he may reach the hearts of penitents, soften, encourage, and sanctify them. Filled with the Spirit of GOD, he will often obtain immediately and by a few words what others, less fervent, will not effect by long discourses often repeated. Thus he may be able in a little time to be useful to a great number of souls, while a lukewarm Priest is scarcely, after a long time, able to be useful to any one. Let, then, the Priest aim specially and continually at his own sanctification. The Apostles were thus zealous, though filled with the Holy Ghost and confirmed in grace. Hence they obtained the appointment of the seven deacons, with the view that they might the better "attend to prayer." They who are inferior to the Apostles in grace and virtues must all the more need prayer of a more continued and frequent character. And all the more saintly that the Priest becomes, will he become useful to others in leading them to true holiness. And, besides, a Priest is bound by his office to labour for the sanctification of others. Not in vain, nor to be hidden in the earth, has the sublime talent of the power of the keys been committed to him. To make this profitable to others, especially in confession, is a powerful means of his own sanctification. He should labour to be discreet—he should not neglect any of his duties, but know how to unite them prudently while labouring in turn for his own sanctification and for that of others. He should try to find more time for all his duties, by curtailing sleep or pleasant occupations, and all that is foreign to the obligations of his calling, which is that of labouring for himself and for others. Thus he will find time for prayer, and yet be always ready to receive confessions. At certain times he may, for his soul's good, suspend this ministry, in order to go into retreat, in order that he may re-animate the vigour of his zeal for souls.

And this ministry above all aids him who ministers to become holy. The Priest should above all things labour to make all his duties useful to himself by purifying his intentions, so as to direct all to the glory of GOD, and to the salvation of souls alone, and not to respect of persons. He should entertain great trust in GOD, distrusting his own wisdom and prudence. Hence, on entering on this duty, he should lift up his heart to GOD with the intention of washing His people in the most precious blood of CHRIST our SAVIOUR. He should pray for light and grace to avoid all mistakes in his judgments and penances; and for help to overcome difficulties without giving offence; and to cleanse others so as not to be soiled himself. He should arm himself with a firm resolve to observe the rules of patience and meekness, and form an intention of absolving penitents only as their state requires, absolutely or conditionally, as seems just and right without partiality. He should go to his duty with ready mind and joy because GOD vouchsafes to make use of him as a worker together with Himself in the care of such souls as are sent to him to be directed, instructed, or delivered from the captivity of sin. He should pray for the true conversion of those to whom he ministers. The fifty-first Psalm may be well said before hearing a confession, with a prayer of this sort:—

"O LORD GOD ALMIGHTY, be merciful to me a sinner, that I may worthily thank Thee for having made me, out of Thy great mercy, unworthy as I am, a minister of the Priest's office, and hast appointed me to be the humble means of praying and making intercession to our LORD JESUS CHRIST for sinners, and for such as return to penitence. Wherefore, O LORD, our Governor, who wouldest all men to be saved, and come to the knowledge of the truth; who wouldest not the death of a sinner, but rather that he should be converted and live, receive my prayer which I offer for Thy servants who have come to repentance, and grant them the spirit of compunction, that they may flee out of the snares of the devil by which they are bound, and return to Thee by making hearty acts of penitence, through the Same JESUS CHRIST our LORD. Amen."

When the penitent kneels down, the Priest should pray heartily thus:—

"GOD be in thy heart and in thy lips, that thou mayest make a good confession of all thy sins, to His Glory, and thy salvation, in the name of the FATHER, and of the SON, and of the HOLY GHOST."

And to conclude, the Priest must be disinterested. If any thing is given to him, he should bestow it on the Church or poor. "Never touch the purse of your penitent," said an experienced Priest. "I seek not yours, but you," must be ever his motto. He must not be mixed up with wills: and never expose himself to the dangers of avarice, the pest of old age. For further encouragement the Priest should bethink him of the recompense awaiting him at the hands of his Master, if he improves this talent entrusted to him, whereby he exercises not only spiritual, but also corporal works of mercy. He not only teaches the ignorant, recalls wanderers to the right road, abates causes of disagreement, consoles the sorrowful, advises the doubtful, powerfully entreats GOD in behalf of those whose safety is imperilled, but he also redeems those who are enslaved in sure captivity, sets free such as are tied and bound with the chain of their sins, covers the naked with the robe of Grace, refreshes with spiritual meat and drink the hungry and fainting. These are labours which GOD will recompense in the Great Day. To these we may add the reward due to extraordinary patience, gentleness, self-abnegation in grievous troubles, and difficulties such as arise through ill-instructed penitents, hardened, refractory, and abandoned sinners, so they be united with a sincere zeal for GOD'S glory and with charity to souls.

CHAPTER II.

HINTS FOR THE PRIEST WHILE A CONFESSION IS BEING MADE.

If a penitent, and especially one somewhat uninstructed, does not mention when he last confessed, the Priest should inquire about it, and whether he fulfilled the penance which was enjoined him, and if not, whether he neglected it knowingly and wilfully?

It does not seem expedient in all cases to ask as soon as penitents begin their confession to what condition of life they belong, lest the Priest appear to be influenced by curiosity, or they be put out by it. When occasion offers, in the mention of some sin, or it seems necessary or expedient for completing the examination, the Priest shall ask kindly what evil he has done since the last confession; if he observe fear in the penitent, he must encourage him not to be ashamed to speak the truth for his soul's sake, and permit him first to set forth the result of his self-examination; if he cannot explain himself sufficiently, or it be plain he has not examined himself as he ought, the Priest must not therefore at once dismiss the uninstructed person with Absolution; but gently rouse him, and aid him with various questions, going over the subjects, in which such persons usually fail. Then the Priest should suggest the mode of well examining himself: for example, what ill he has done in thought, word, and work; what he has omitted at home; in Church, privily, openly, in this or that time, against God, himself, his family, and other neighbours; for ill-instructed persons, if dismissed at once without Absolution, either will not return to confession, or will instantly go to some one else, irritated and far from being corrected, since many are incapable of examining themselves as they ought; but if any one is found to be guilty of grievous sins in different particulars, and can only tell the number by conjecture, he must be reminded of the duty of diligent self-examination, and sometimes ought to be dismissed with suggestions how to do so, that he may duly examine his conscience and come back soon, unless circumstances perchance require otherwise.

If the penitent omit what ought to be added, and make his confession from a written paper, he should immediately be asked about it; but if from memory, and the Priest thinks that he can sufficiently recollect it, he should defer inquiry to the close of the confession; but if he fears he may forget it, he may let him add one or more details of sin, and then inquire, lest afterwards the penitent be obliged to repeat his confession with fresh confusion and trouble; when he has satisfactorily answered the inquiry, the Priest should recall to mind the last-mentioned detail, and bid the penitent proceed from that point; for so he will be brought back again to the former train of thoughts from which a divergence has been made.

Should the penitent in his confession begin to disclose the sins of others, he should be warned to confess his own, but to be silent about those of others lest he should injure them, so that it become a humble confession of his own sins (as it should be), and not an accusing of others. If he introduce impertinent matter, or as it were compose a history, he should be told that it is enough to confess his sins so far as relates to their kind and number, without mentioning the occasion and cause. Sometimes, however, it may be of use, if it be observed that the full narration tends to the confession of a particular sin, to inquire whether he finds himself guilty of sin in this or that matter. Lastly, if he express some things too coarsely, or indecently, he should be instructed how to express himself more decorously, yet so as to express the kind of sin.

The Priest should take care not to give signs by hands, feet, eyes, or any bodily motion, so as to give a bystander any suspicion that any thing extraordinary is being related in confession; whatever he hears, he should give no sign of wonder or indignation, though the penitent alone might notice it; for else he will be deterred from relating the rest. For the same reason he should not chide before the end of the confession and examination: but in order to unravel more grave offences, rather on this account deal more gently with him, and encourage him to expel all the poison and obtain peace.

(1) *Hints for the Priest in examining the Penitent.*

It is not necessary to examine those who often confess and seldom commit grievous sin, and who it is evident know all that relates to a perfect confession; whence as a rule members of Brotherhoods and Sisterhoods, Ecclesiastics, and others who are versed in theology, should not be cross-examined, unless some thing requiring explanation seems to have been omitted by them; for then and not else it is presumed, and justly presumed, that they either do not understand or do not perceive their duty. If it is necessary to question the penitent, it is best to do it with respect to age, nature, condition, sex, and occupations, and only concerning those things which seem likely to have been committed by the penitent. On the subject of chastity it is specially necessary to proceed with caution, lest haply the penitent be taught what as yet he knows nothing about, and it is best for him to be ignorant of. Should he deny sins of thought, he should not be questioned about acts, unless he be perchance very uninstructed; for persons often do not realize that thoughts are sins, at any rate unless they willed to proceed to acts; whence ordinarily such ought to be questioned about works, then about words, and lastly about thoughts. If the penitent confess wilful thoughts, he should be questioned about conversations, looks, touch; if he confess these, he should be questioned whether perchance any thing worse has been committed, or at any rate lusted after, or willed to be committed, if shame or fear had not held him back; for some are so uninstructed that except they be thus questioned they remain silent, thinking it enough to give the Priest an opportunity of questioning them by their dropping hints. Finally, the nature and number of sins should be asked. In questioning, the Priest should not be too minute, but cautious and discreet. Though the

Priest is bound to question the penitent (if, as is likely, he either does not open his conscience or has not searched deeply into it), according to the common and practical rule; yet he must not be curious or too minute in questioning, lest he either render penance hateful to himself or to penitents, of which CHRIST would have him beware, or cause danger of spiritual ruin. And it is best that the Priest should sometimes less perfectly understand the sins than expose himself or the penitent to scandal, or render penance itself odious. Whence, 1st, He should be slow to ask about those circumstances which the penitent cannot speak of without very great shame, and the Priest can understand by other adjuncts or words. Hence he should not question any one who confesses incest, in whatever degree it may have been committed, because it is seldom in the first degree, and does not probably differ in its other degrees. Nor should he question married persons about conjugal duty, unless he has reason to think that they have sinned in excess: and in this case he may inquire whether they be unanimous, whether the husband is faithful to the wife, the wife obedient to her husband; and so he will easily detect whether they have "defrauded one the other:" if the wife confesses any improprieties of intercourse, let not particular questions be put; but in general, whether "procreation of children" has been thereby hindered. 2ndly, A sick person, who is less capable or disposed to attend, should be more leniently questioned than another: also he who feels burdened with many sins than he who has fewer, because the questioning should be adapted to the age of each penitent. 3rdly, Nor should the penitent ordinarily be asked with what conscience he proceeded to this or that, for this would be too serious a thing for the Priest to do; and it might be presumed generally speaking that he felt the object to be intrinsically bad; except when circumstances advise otherwise, because, as I have said, ill-instructed persons often do not feel the wickedness of "*morose delectation*" in a foul object. The same may be said of foul conversation, and what are called jokes. Finally, the Priest should take care not to render confession liable to the laughter and scoffs of others, by allowing it to degenerate into narrative and loquacity. As the penitent in examining his own conscience is not supposed to go into every possible detail, but to apply such a moderate degree of diligence, such as sensible persons are wont to use in matters of great moment according to their capacity, so the Priest in questioning the penitent is only supposed to use a moderate and usual degree of it, considering both the circumstances of the penitent, and the time elapsed since the last confession: and this because, when a penitent has not confessed for a long time, there is need of proportionally greater diligence than if a less time has elapsed. The reason of this is, that the penitent is under special and primary obligations, since he is his own accuser and witness in the tribunal of penitence; but the Priest, as being judge, is only liable in default of the penitent, whose defects he should supply, in order that a full and perfect judgment may be attained. Hence some infer that the Priest is not obliged to use greater diligence than the penitent, generally speaking, provided he knows how to examine himself; the reason being, that if either the penitent or the Priest is obliged to use greater diligence than usual or than what is wont to be exercised by diligent persons in matters of great moment, Penance might become too burdensome and tedious, and expose penitents to continual and numberless anxieties. The Priest, however, should not be deterred by the authority of any penitent; but when he judges it necessary he should question even nobles after the fashion of the confessor, who, after hearing the confession of the Emperor Charles, said, "Thou hast confessed Charles's sins, now confess the Emperor's;" for penitents are all alike guilty in this sacred tribunal. The Priest is judge in the place of GOD; and CHRIST did not make one law for rustics and plebeians, and another for nobles and grandees, but willed that all should be under the same obligation.

(2) *Hints for examining and admonishing the Penitent.*

Penitents either should, or at least may be profitably taught and reminded of, in the first place, what are the chief truths necessary to be known: secondly, what is requisite for a worthy reception of the Absolution and the Eucharist: thirdly, how to lay aside the errors under which they labour at any time: fourthly, the obligations which they have perchance contracted of restoring character, or of compensating injuries. If the Priest notice that the penitent is undoubtedly ignorant of the truths necessary to be known, such as the Trinity in Unity, the Incarnation, and Rewards and Punishments, or of the requisites for Absolution or the Eucharist, he should defer him to another day, till he gets better instructed; or if it be inexpedient for him to be sent away without

Absolution, the Priest after hearing what is most essential, as far as possible, and having due regard to circumstances, should teach him what is most necessary; and if he can well judge and sufficiently discern that he has faith about necessary points, and elicit from him acts of faith, hope, charity, and contrition, after having counselled him to get better instructed, he may give him Absolution.

3. If the Priest observe that something is taken by the penitent for sin which is not sin, or for deadly which is not unto death, he should show him the truth, lest he sin from a mistaken conscience. Similarly, if the penitent through vincible ignorance think something to be no sin which is really sin—he must undoubtedly be taught the contrary: as also if he think so through invincible ignorance, and there be hope of doing him good; except a grievous injury impend thereby on some other person, on which account the penitent might be left to run the risk of material sin. But if no benefit could be reasonably hoped for therefrom, he may be left awhile in blameless error, lest he be drawn from material into formal sin. But persons are rightly counselled respecting the foulness of pollution—those at least who seem to be ignorant of it—because often ignorance is not invincible, but joined with fear or doubt; often also so vicious a habit is contracted, that, even when at last they acknowledge its baseness, they are corrected only with the greatest difficulty; nay, they even lead others astray, persuading them there is no sin in it. When it is doubtful whether admonition is likely to benefit or do harm to one or the other labouring under invincible ignorance, the hope of doing good must be balanced with the fear of doing harm, and if

hope prevails the admonition should be given. If one thus circumstanced questions the Priest about any thing in regard to which his conscience is disquieted, the truth should be disclosed to him generally speaking; because when he is doubtful or anxious about the matter, and himself questions the Priest, the latter, unless he disclose the truth, will appear by silence to approve his conduct. But the Priest must take care not to say more than is necessary if no advantage is hoped for. For example, a person bound by the simple vow of chastity has contracted a valid marriage, and then inquires if he may lawfully render due benevolence to his wife; the answer must be given in the affirmative, and nothing be said about the duty of not being the first to urge it, because else the person would be drawn from material into the imminent danger of formal sin. I say, generally speaking, because if the knowledge of the truth were likely to be of serious harm, the Priest would have to act as though he had not heard what was said; or must say that there is no need to treat of this point. Meanwhile he may do as he trusts will not offend GOD, because in such a case to disclose the truth to the penitent would be like presenting him with a sword with which he might hurt himself or his neighbour severely. Lastly, if it is hoped that the penitent, though he is not for the present disposed to receive instruction with benefit, is likely to be disposed at another time, the instructions should be deferred, and he may be told, "Take heed not to sin, else thou mayest do what thy conscience approves as lawful; I shall take another opportunity to speak to thee more at large." The reason of all this is, that the light of nature warns us that we must avoid offending GOD as much as possible, and that we must not do good or avert a less ill, if it be foreseen that graver consequences will flow therefrom; for this would not be to consult for the honour of GOD and salvation of souls, but rather to do them injury; whence St. Augustine said, "If I knew it would not profit thee, I would not advise nor alarm thee."

(4) Penitents should be stirred up to lead a Christian life, each suitably to his capacity and disposition. It is proper to exhort all, (1) above all things to battle against the sin in themselves which is most scandalous, dangerous, and the root of all others, or into which they fall oftenest, or which most impedes their progress, and disquiets their mind: if any thing untoward happen, to resolve to amend it night and morning, frequently make acts of contrition, and implore continually aid from GOD, confessing their own weakness and inconstancy. (2) They should be taught every morning to preface their actions with a right intention of pleasing GOD, and renew it every now and then through the day, especially before such acts as are more important or exalted. (3) At every striking of the hour or oftener they should call to mind the presence of GOD, by adoration, praise, and acts of love, or of thanksgiving for benefits, or of trust in Him. (4) It will be some times useful to contrast their own life with that of CHRIST, and set Him before them as a pattern in their actions, both in prosperity and adversity. So a Priest advised one who sought some instructions from him, to meditate on these few heads:—CHRIST lived in the greatest want, and I live in the greatest abundance; CHRIST in hunger and thirst, and I in exquisite luxuries; CHRIST was naked, and I am clothed with costly garments; CHRIST was in pains, and

I am in pleasures." And these thoughts influenced him so much, that a little while after, when at a rich banquet one of these four points came into his mind, he was forced to depart from the table shedding tears, and to seek solitude wherein he might the more freely have conversation with GOD and himself. It is useful also to take some point from the life of the Saint whose festival is being kept, and propose it for the imitation of penitents.

(5) Such admonitions should be such for the most part as do not seem so much a finding fault, especially if the penitents are old or of great dignity, or are somewhat timid or small-minded, or easily irritated: for these will easily either lose courage, or be provoked, and scarce receive fault-finding without impatience and disdain. Hence the Priest in his fault-findings should be rather chary than profuse, kind rather than severe, but more exacting when admonitions can or ought to be given to those who are of a more hardened nature, and think too little about their soul's health, especially if a kind admonition has had no effect, so that his strictness be after the unbosoming of sins, and be such that the penitent may understand that it proceeds out of a desire for his salvation.

(3) *How Penitents should be disposed to Grief and Resolutions.*

Although most penitents, especially youths, uninstructed persons, and great sinners, should be stirred up to supernatural grief and serious resolutions; yet when sufficient indications of these are present the Priest need not

trouble himself further. The indications are as follows :—
(1) If the penitent says, "After I committed the sin I immediately felt sorry, or had a great battle with myself to confess the sin—or, alas! I am a wretch and a great sinner." (2) If at the outset he accuse himself of more grievous sins, or of what he had omitted before in confession, or endeavour anxiously to reveal all thoroughly, both as to number and nature of sins. (3) If he say of his own self, "I will avoid occasions of sin," or, "I will restore what I took away, and satisfy other obligations," or, "Enjoin me a heavy penance." The reason of this is, that when, notwithstanding the natural reluctance which a man feels to put himself to shame, there is extraordinary anxiety to make a good confession, it is rightly presumed, unless there be evidence of any other motive, that such a one is supernaturally moved to sincere grief, and wishes for amendment. It is not to be taken as a sign of insufficient sorrow in all cases if the penitent smiles, for persons of a joyous temperament smile often even on serious occasions, and others smile out of nervousness.

2. Though the Priest may rightly presume in ordinary cases respecting adults who appear to be well instructed, that they are duly disposed, and that the serious confession of sins is a sign of sorrow, yet it is expedient to stir them up to renew their sorrow; yes, and to question young persons and less-instructed persons, before they have begun to confess, whether they have elicited sorrow and resolution to amend : because some, as experience teaches, when questioned, reply that they have forgotten it, or thought it enough to elicit it when with the Priest; and though this is true, yet it is hardly

likely that they can instantly feel sorrow and resolution to amend. Hence if it is found that the penitent has not previously elicited an act of sorrow, with resolution to amend, he is to be counselled that in future, after self-examination, he should effect this before coming to the Priest, and motives for sorrow should be set before him, and he should be stirred up to it; and time should be given that he may secretly elicit it himself, because should the Priest only lead the way in words, it may easily happen that the penitent may recite them with him without inward sincere grief and serious intention. When he seems duly disposed he should be directed to accuse himself afresh in general, though this is not absolutely required; because while the penitent waits for Absolution he really petitions for it, and continues to confess himself guilty, and thus there is sufficient sorrow to precede confession. If the penitent say that he has before confession elicited an act of sorrow with purpose of amendment, the Priest may rest satisfied, unless circumstances give rise to a different persuasion; he may also direct him to renew his sorrow by way of penance. Besides this he should exhort and instruct, in regard to the means of amendment to be used, those especially who are more ignorant or guilty of graver sins, or who have too often fully and deliberately fallen back into the same venial sins.

3. Motives for sorrow should be set before penitents adapted to the special capacity of each: for all persons are not alike moved by the same things. Hence the Priest should have different motives ready for suggestion: such for instance as, first, loss of grace and of eternal life; or, if the sin is venial, a retarding of bliss, and failure to obtain increase of grace, and hence a consequent danger

of a grievous fall—" For whoso despises little things shall fall by little and little :" how by that loss man, from being the child of GOD becomes His enemy, and the slave of the devil; from being an heir of heaven, a beggar, naked, and the fuel of hell. Secondly, the most heavy pain of hell, by which, GOD as a most just judge punishes sins, specially those which are mortal, eternally; and what greater folly can be conceived than that man for some short-lived gain, earthly dross, base and trifling pleasure such as is common to brutes, or for momentary earthly honour, should deprive himself of so many good things, and consign himself to eternal pains, and to the eternal wrath of GOD, and eternal shame before GOD,—to a sort of eternal necessity of cursing his parents, and the day of his birth; so that it has been well said, that there are only two necessary prisons in the world, one of heretics, into which they ought to be sent who do not believe; the other of fools, into which they should be cast who believe that by sin they are alienated from GOD, their sole and chief good, and sentenced to eternal miseries and torments, and yet are not afraid to sin. Thirdly, the foulness of sin consisting, first, in the fact that sin is the highest ingratitude against GOD, man's Creator and Benefactor : secondly, that it is immense impiety and rebellion against a most loving Father : thirdly, that it is enormous irreverence and disobedience towards a sovereign LORD : fourthly, that it is a mean esteem and contempt of GOD, since He is neglected and has the meanest creatures preferred to Him : fifthly, that it is a wrong done to GOD, since it is an abuse of the things of the LORD GOD contrary to His will : sixthly, that it is a dishonour offered to GOD, by denying the worship and subjection due to His

Supreme Majesty; as the Apostle saith, " By breaking the law dishonourest thou GOD : " seventhly, that it is the effect of pride, through which the sinner refuses to be subordinate, saying, " I will not serve : " eighthly, that it is desertion of a loving SAVIOUR and a going over to the devil His enemy. But this foulness of sin is increased by the consideration that sin is committed in the sight of GOD, and is committed at the very time when GOD preserves the sinner and grants him being, cherishes, surrounds him with benefits, invites him paternally to Himself, and promises and wills to grant him salvation : that the sinner perverts GOD's condescension in thus dealing with him into an occasion of casting contempt on Him and destroying himself, and makes GOD to serve by his sins; that he is a reproach to CHRIST, who redeemed his soul at so high a price, while the devil exults that CHRIST is regarded with such indifference by those whom He has numbered with His Church, and willed to be members of His mystic Body. And this foulness of sin, as it is abominable to GOD, renders the sinners, whom it infects, equally loathsome to Him—" Their abominations were according as they loved [1]."

The fourth motive for sorrow is the benefits conferred by GOD—such as creation, translation from nothingness to existence, preservation, and continued production, at the cessation of which at any moment, men would return to nothing; Redemption by the Blood and ignominious Death of the Son of GOD; the incorporation into Him by Baptism, whereby man is admitted to the friendship of GOD, and becomes a son of GOD, of which blessing so many are

[1] Hosea ix. 10.

deprived, and therefore are like to perish everlastingly; education by Catholic parents, for lack of which thousands are lost, who, had they been thus blessed, would have probably served GOD better; forgiveness of sins so often repeated; the constant love of GOD, whereby He has recalled the wanderer, brought back and received the prodigal, clothed him in the robe of grace, has so far sustained and cherished him; admission to the Eucharistic Table so often repeated, and innumerable other benefits wherewith GOD has so encompassed the Christian, that which way soever he look back they meet his eyes.

It is good sometimes to inquire of the penitent, What benefit GOD derives from man? Nothing. What does man derive from GOD? Every thing. Has GOD ever done thee any ill? Never. Art thou not shameless in that thou dost so dishonour GOD? art so ungrateful to Him? It is also useful if the confessor recounts the special benefits received by the penitent, as Nathan the prophet recounted them to David on his fall, when desiring to show him the foulness of his sins, he said, "Thou art the man, thus saith the LORD GOD of Israel, I anointed thee to be king over Israel, and delivered thee out of the hand of Saul, &c. Wherefore hast thou despised the commandment of the LORD, to do evil in his sight?" Moreover GOD's benefits are enhanced by the consideration of the infinite dignity of the donor, of the infinite love with which they are bestowed, of the unworthiness of the creature on whom they are bestowed, and by the thought of the greatness of the gifts themselves, so as to present man's ingratitude in the blackest character.

The fifth motive is GOD Himself, in that He is the Being above all not to be offended, most deserving of our worship, honour and love: the mean esteem and contempt of Whom is the only ill, even sin: an ill all the more grievous in that He Who is offended is of infinite dignity and majesty. And further we must consider Who it is that is offended, meanly esteemed and despised —by whom, and on account of what, with what aids, where, when? What the Father for His satisfaction has exacted from His Incarnate Son, who did no sin, but took on Him ours, that He might blot them out? What pains GOD, Whose nature is beneficence, inflicts on the impenitent in this world and in the next? It is at the close of the confession that the Priest should redouble his efforts to make the penitent understand the greatness and number of his faults, and thus the miserable lost state in which he is, but always with charity. He may use strong expressions in order to bring the penitent to himself, so long as they are dictated by compassion and charity. "My son, is not this the life of a reprobate? What ill has CHRIST done to you that you should treat Him thus? If He had been your mortal enemy, could you have treated Him worse? GOD who died for you! Ah, if you died to-night, this moment, where would you be? whither would you go? what would you get for all your sinful indulgences? Hell in your heart, and hell for eternity. Yet be of good cheer; there is time to put an end to sins; give yourself up to GOD; it is enough to have offended Him in the past. I will help you all I can; come to me whenever you can. Strive to become holy and you will be happy." One Priest used always to try to make the sinner feel the difference betwixt the happiness of those who live in a state of grace, and the misery of those who live separated from GOD.

(4) *How different Persons should be stirred up to Sorrow.*

Of these motives the Priest should first propose what seems most to fit in with the capacity and state of the penitent: for some are most drawn by love, others by fear. Those who are more advanced in virtue and who endeavour to progress, are easily stirred up by the consideration of the immense benefits bestowed on us by GOD. The less instructed and more hardened must be first alarmed at the thought of punishment, and roused to sorrow thereby: then drawn on to sincere love and grief for having offended so great a benefactor; finally, to the love of GOD for His own sake, and to sorrow for having offended and contemned Him, with a resolve for His sake not to sin in future. It is good to set before them all the labours, toils, passion, and death of CHRIST. What they were? How great? With what end? With what love He did, and suffered these things? Lo! what thy Saviour did and bare for thee, though He had no need of thee, and what is the return which thou hast made Him? Circumstances may be taken advantage of; such as the festival, which especially commemorates GOD's special mercies; the object for which one has sinned—the good, advantage, or pleasure, or human respect. It may be urged on the penitent—"Thou couldest love so short-lived a good; so petty, so worthless, so changeable. How much more oughtest thou to love GOD, the only good, in respect of whom all other things are but a shadow!" Appeal to his faith—"Thou canst not imagine any thing better than GOD, and dost thou not love Him? Whatever thou lovest, thou lovest with the view that it may be well with thee;

but consider whether any thing can be better with thee than to possess GOD, the universal good? 'Eye hath not seen, nor ear heard, neither hath it entered into the heart of man to conceive what God hath prepared for them that love Him;' and dost thou not love so kind and liberal a GOD, &c., nor grieve at having offended Him?" &c. It must be remembered that sorrow for sin must be preceded by at least virtual hope and faith: since none can be sorry for their sins who do not in some degree believe GOD to be a rewarder of the just and unjust, and that He is outraged by sin.

Thus, after suitable remonstrances or warnings the Priest ought to get the penitent into a fit state for Absolution, by causing him to elicit a good act of contrition or of firm resolve. It must be observed that few penitents, especially if ignorant, take care to make an act of contrition before confession. Some confessors are content to inquire of them, "*And now do you ask pardon for all this?*" and "*Do you repent of all this?*" which is not a true act of contrition, and without any more ado they give Absolution. Such is not the conduct of good confessors: they apply themselves with all their powers to excite in such penitents as are burdened with mortal sins, a true repentance and sincere abhorrence of evil. They begin with making them elicit some degree of sorrow. "Ah! my son, where ought you to be now? In hell, alas! in fire, desperate, and forsaken by the whole world and by GOD for ever. Do you then repent of having offended GOD, on account of the hell which you have deserved?" It is to be observed that it is not enough to repent of sin because we have thereby deserved hell, but we must repent of having offended GOD because we have merited hell. After this the Priest should lead on the penitent to feel sorrow, not only because of the dreadful consequences of his sin, but because he has sinned against so much love, and done despite against such vast grace and unceasing mercy. He may cause the penitent to elicit such acts of contrition as the following: "My son, what hast thou done? Thou hast offended GOD who is infinitely good; thou hast failed in respect to Him; thou hast refused to obey Him; thou hast despised His grace; and now, since thou hast offended a GOD who is goodness itself, repent thereof with all thy heart; abhor more than aught else the outrages which you have offered Him," &c.

CHAPTER III.

WHAT KIND OF PENANCE SHOULD BE ENJOINED UPON PENITENTS?

The Confessor is bound to enjoin some Penance.

THE Priest must impose some act of penitence on the penitent, greater or less in proportion to the sins confessed; since he ought, as judge, to obtain some reparation for the injured party. He must take care not to connive, or appear to connive at sins, by dealing too indulgently with penitents, and he should enjoin penances, not only for the purpose of protecting renewed life or of healing infirmities, but also by way of punishment, in order to impress upon penitents the enormous guilt of sin. But the difficulty which often occurs is to decide what is in proportion to this or that penitent, or to this or that sin.

I.

These things should be observed in fixing proportionable Acts of Penitence.

(1) The Priest should pay attention to the class of sins in fixing the act of penitence, so that it shall be duly proportioned, suitable and not too light.

(2) He should have regard to the ability of the penitent, so as not to impose what is too heavy and easily evaded.

(3) He should see that the act enjoined be at once such as may avenge or correct the former mode of life, as well as preserve from relapses. For the Priest should, as a judge, punish offences, but, as a physician, heal the sick so far as he can prevent a relapse; and though the quality of the offence should be taken into account, yet much more should the nature, condition, and advantage of the penitent be attended to.

II.

The Kind of Acts of Penitence to be enjoined.

These may be enjoined by way of punishments[2].

(1) Fasting, abstinence from particular meats and drinks, and some act of mortification of the flesh.

(2) Prayer and some particular religious exercise.

(3) Alms and some act of benevolence to one's neighbour, whence may be imposed various kind offices, and so charity is exercised, and alms become most efficacious; thus every penitent may be encouraged to do all that he can to repair his errors by bringing forth living fruits of repentance.

(4) Simple inward acts of Faith, Hope, and Charity may be enjoined, meditation upon death, judgment, hell, &c.

---

[2] Jeremy Taylor, iv. 9. Holy Living. "True repentance is a punishing duty, and acts its sorrow."

(5) Works also may be enjoined: thus, if one accused himself of negligence in time of Holy Communion, or during public or private prayers, it might be enjoined him to do this several times with more devotion. But it is always expedient to add something not enjoined, in order that the penance may partake more of the nature of "revenge[3]."

(6) Penances most opposite to the sins committed should be enjoined, such as alms on rich misers and fraudulent persons; yet the Priest must beware of any wish that the alms should be given to him or his. In like manner, upon unclean persons, drunkards, gluttons, &c., there should be imposed fasting, sackcloth, discipline, less comfortable beds or less sleep, less delicacy in food. Again, envious, passionate, and hateful persons should have assigned them works of charity towards those whom they dislike, such as to pray for them, pay respect to them, or aid them as far as they can. For faults are cured by their opposites, and it is a useful remedy against all sin, that whereinsoever a man has transgressed therein he should abstain from even lawful indulgences.

(7) Those who have scarcely any leisure for prayer, or who are bound to say many prayers, ought not to have long prayers imposed upon them, but rather some few acts to be performed with fervour and in a state of grace, which are of more use than many things done lukewarmly and in a state of sin. Such things, therefore, as to confess on certain festivals, daily read a portion of a religious book, or meditate (if capable of doing

---

[3] 2 Cor. vii. 11.

so) for a quarter of an hour, or longer on some mystery by which they are most likely to be moved, or on some subject by which they are most likely to be alarmed, such as the Passion of our LORD, judgment, death, hell, the grievousness of sin, CHRIST's love towards the human race, &c.; or even to resolve every morning to watch until their next confession against a particular sin, for the honour of the most Holy Trinity and our crucified LORD: to examine conscience every evening, lament any lapse into sin, resolve amendment, and seek for grace; or after lying down, to think that they may die and rise no more from their bed; what sentence the wicked must expect, and to what place they must be consigned, what suffering they must endure there for ever; to say in rising, "I begin this day which GOD has given me to work out my salvation, perhaps I shall have no to-morrow, and this life may come to an end, and then eternity!" The Priest may enjoin some one or other of these penances as may seem most suitable to the case before him, and he will find by experience their utility. Thus, a vain girl who grew no better by various penances imposed on her, was led to amend her life by this short precept: "As often as thou washest thyself say to thyself, 'This flesh will one day be food for worms.'" A youth entangled in pleasures of the flesh was corrected by being told, "When thou liest down at night, think if thou wouldst for the empire of the world lie motionless for thirty years on this bed, though strewn with roses. If not, what madness to consign thyself for a brief pleasure to everlasting torment!" A rough soldier was softened by a Priest saying to him, "I give thee this ring off my own hand, that by wearing it thou mayest as often as thou lookest on it remember eternity." It may also be enjoined to meditate daily on some text of Holy Scripture, such as, " What shall it profit a man, if he gain the whole world, and lose his own soul ? " " They spend their days in wealth, and in a moment go down to the grave." " Which of you can dwell with everlasting burnings ?" or, " All ye that pass by, behold and see if there be any sorrow like unto my sorrow." " Because I called and no man regarded, I also will mock at your calamity."

III.

When a lighter Penance than usual may be imposed.

A lighter penance than what otherwise might be given may be imposed.

(1) If the penitent seems very contrite.

(2) If the penitent is too weak, or so weak that a heavier penance would be very difficult of performance. Hence a dying person can only be enjoined to take his pains as penance, or to utter a short ejaculatory prayer, or even only to put it up in silence.

(3) When there is reason to fear that the penitent may omit a heavy penance, or betake himself to a less suitable Priest, or fall into despair, in which case it is best to commend him to GOD's mercy on the fulfilment of a light penance.

(4) When a special advantage may be hoped for by lenient dealing with the penitent, so as to induce him to a more frequent use of the Sacraments.

(5) When the penitent is known to be in the habit of performing acts of repentance.

(6) When the penitent is told beforehand to prepare himself for censure and to receive it patiently.

(7) When the penitent is urged to be reconciled to his neighbours, to make restitution, to avoid the next occasion of sin—which are all acts of sufficient penance.

(8) When the penitent is ready to perform what is enjoined by way of advice; for example, to discharge his daily duties with more exactness, what is thus fulfilled under the cover of mere counsel may be taken as part of penance.

(9) If the Priest take a part of the penance on himself and so move the penitent to shame and grief, to frequent the Sacraments, to lead a Christian life, and, by consequence, to more penitential acts. But if a lighter penance than ordinary is enjoined, the penitent should be admonished that it is done for sufficient reasons to rouse him to voluntary punishment, and to strive for amendment more diligently, and so draw him to regular confession; for otherwise the penitent will not sufficiently regard the weight of his sin, when he finds it so lightly punished by his Priest.

IV.

Unsuitable Penances.

Amongst unsuitable penances we reckon (1) that which is made up of too many different kinds, such as fasting, different prayers, &c., because the penitent may easily forget them, or else perform them in a perfunctory manner. (2) That which is after the fashion of the ancient Canons, according to which a seven years' penance was enjoined for any deadly, scandalous sin—consisting of a bread and water fast on the Wednesday and Friday in every week, though Absolution had been already given. We say this, because that extreme rigour is no longer convenient, as it would give occasion to heretics to misrepresent penance as homicidal, and render it odious to penitents, and so deter them from confession, and because such severity was relaxed in the later ages of the Church. (3) That which by being imposed on the penitent may cause him to commit a further sin by exposing him to the peril of a grievous lapse. (4) That which is perpetual, because it is immoderate. (5) That which is public and grievous is ordinarily inconvenient, because contrary to the practice of the Church, and might easily engender the suspicion of a grievous sin, or cause dissensions. I say *ordinarily*, because occasions may arise when it may be necessary to enjoin a public penance in order to remove a notorious scandal. And in such cases the seal of confession is not violated by such an injunction of the Priest, because the duty of removing scandal arises from another point of view, and the penitent is supposed to consent when he ought to do so. Thus it is right to order a slanderer to ask forgiveness of the slandered. (6) Such as long prayers imposed on persons of little leisure, severe bodily chastisements on those of delicate constitution, long separations of married persons, because they are ill-proportioned to the strength, station, and condition of penitents.

V.

When a Penance enjoined by one Priest may be changed by another.

If a penitent remembers something grave which he had forgotten, or has fallen into some sin which he feels is an obstacle to Communion, and returns after being absolved, and needs a fresh Absolution, a fresh penance may need to be enjoined; except the first seems sufficient, and the Priest enjoins it on him anew. If the penitent seeks to have a different penance to what another Priest has enjoined, he should not be yielded to, unless his former confession was made confusedly and indistinctly, so as not to be understood, or some manifest change in his condition had occurred, rendering the penance no longer possible or suitable.

VI.

In Cases of Doubt the Priest should lean to the milder Course.

If a doubt arises in regard to the sufficiency of the penance, the Priest should lean to the milder course, as being less perilous, as the physician should begin with the milder and less powerful medicines.

Sometimes it is well to ask the penitent what penance he can best perform, and if he be found ready to perform it, it is expedient that it be one which lasts somewhat long, for half or a whole month, in order that sins may not be forgotten, that the habit be abolished, and the design of extirpating it be nourished.

CHAPTER IV.

HOW AND WHEN ABSOLUTION SHOULD BE GIVEN.

I.

Form of Absolution.

IN order that the Priest may proceed regularly, he is formally obliged to use at least such words as these in Absolution :—" I absolve thee from thy sins, in the name of the FATHER, ✠ and of the SON, and of the HOLY GHOST. Amen."

These may be prefaced by the rehearsal that " Our LORD JESUS CHRIST, Who hath given authority to His Church to absolve all those who truly repent and believe in Him, He, of His great mercy, forgive thee thy sins, and by His authority committed unto me, I absolve," &c. Or by the prayers : " The LORD ALMIGHTY have mercy on thee, and forgive thee all thy sins, and bring thee to everlasting life. Amen." " The LORD ALMIGHTY and Allmerciful vouchsafe thee pardon, absolution, and remission of all thy sins. Amen." At the conclusion may be added : " The Passion of our LORD JESUS CHRIST be to thee for remission of sins, increase of grace, and reward of eternal life. Amen." (1) During the utterance of all or any of these words, the Priest should raise his right hand over or towards the penitent. (2) In the case of frequent or brief confessions, or if there be many come to confess, or any other reasonable cause, the absolution may be begun at the words "Our LORD JESUS CHRIST," &c., omitting the preceding and succeeding paragraphs. The words should be said in a low tone, lest, if his custom were to speak more audibly, a bystander should observe whether or no the Absolution was given. Whether the Absolution should be given with bare or covered head depends on the custom of the place. In Germany it is given with bare head, to denote the authority of Christ; elsewhere with covered, to signify that of the Confessor in his quality of judge. Before giving Absolution the Priest should try above all to get at the origin and causes of the spiritual malady of the penitent. Some confessors are content to ask the nature and number of sins: if they see the penitent rightly disposed they give him Absolution; otherwise they send him away unabsolved—saying, "Go away, I cannot give you Absolution." Such is not the conduct of experienced Priests. They begin by inquiring into the beginning and grievousness of the evil: they ask about the frequency and duration of the sin,—when, with whom, where, how, in order to be better able to counsel and rebuke the penitent, dispose him for Absolution, and apply to him suitable remedies. Having thus inquired, the Priest becomes acquainted with the origin and gravity of the offence, and gives the necessary admonitions. For while as father he has to listen with benevolence to the confessions of his penitents, he is nevertheless as a physician obliged to warn them and rebuke them according to their needs, especially if they confess seldom and are loaded with mortal sins. This duty extends to all—however elevated in rank, ecclesiastical or civil, whenever they confess grave faults with too little contrition. The Priest thus deals more with individual souls in this ministration than in preaching. He ought never to grudge the time employed, nor even mind how many penitents may be waiting their turn, for it is more useful to hear a few good confessions than a number of bad ones. We may remark here how reprehensible is the conduct of those who, when they find a penitent not rightly disposed, send him away there and then, through fear of giving themselves any trouble. All the more that a penitent comes without the proper dispositions the Priest is bound to do his utmost to get him into the proper state for Absolution, by representing to him the wrong he has done to God, the danger of punishment, &c. It matters little that others who may be waiting go away: the Priest will only have to render an account to God of the penitent before him, if he fail in regard to him, and not of others.

II.

The Form of Absolution Authoritative.

The essential form of Absolution is not to be put forth after the manner of a prayer, but as by authority, being a judicial act. Christ did not say, "whosesoever sins ye pray to be forgiven," but "whosesoever sins ye remit, they are remitted."

III.

Absolution not to be given dependent on some Future Condition.

Absolution is not to be given subject to some future contingency; as e. g. " I absolve thee, if within three days thou makest restitution;" for the effect of the Sacraments is not to be held in suspense : yet Absolution may be given subject to some present condition.

IV.

Absolution to be given to any one Rightly Disposed.

The Priest is bound to absolve a penitent who makes a proper confession and is rightly disposed, as he ought also even when in doubt as to his state, if he can on consideration decide in favour of the penitent. The reason of this is that the penitent has acquired by his confession a right to be absolved, and ought not to be deprived of it by any doubt if it can be resolved in his favour.

V.

Absolution should by right be given absolutely, sometimes with some Present Condition.

When there is no reasonable doubt of the necessary requisites for Absolution, the penitent should be absolved without any condition; but with some condition if there be doubts which cannot be solved, and if either some necessity or great benefit to the penitent so require. The reason of the first is that he, if rightly disposed, has a right to Absolution; of the second, that thus we provide for the respect due to the Sacrament and for the soul's health of the penitent. Conditional Absolution should be given; first, when there is some doubt as to the exercise of reason, or as to sufficient right disposition or grounds, and when though no certainty can be had, yet there is a necessity or wise reason for Absolution. Secondly, if a dying person shows doubtful signs of penitence. Thirdly, if there be a reasonable doubt as to contrition or efficacious purpose of confessing mere venial sins, or mere doubtfully deadly sins, so that it is not certain that he has even sinned venially, or that he acknowledge himself so to have sinned. And if the penitent bring mere doubtfully venial sins, and there be no other grounds of decision, it seems that Absolution ought not to be given, even with conditions, lest, by giving it unnecessarily, disrespect be offered to the Sacrament. For the penitent then has no right to Absolution, because he brings no necessary definite grounds for it, and care must be taken for due respect to the Sacrament. But if there should be in any wise fear lest perhaps he be in deadly sin, he should be absolved conditionally, and then there would be no peril of irreverence, provided that he appears to be in a state of contrition, to excite which the priest should labour. Further, the condition may be expressed in words: such as, if thou be not already absolved; if thou art alive (to a dying man); if thou art able to receive it (to infants or insane); if thou art rightly disposed.

VI.

What should be done if the Penitent, after having been absolved, add a fresh Mortal Sin which he had omitted to mention?

If the penitent after Absolution come to add a fresh mortal sin, which he had omitted through forgetfulness, with renewed contrition, he should be absolved afresh. If it be doubtfully mortal, he should be bidden to accuse himself again in general terms of the sins before spoken of, or add again an undoubted venial sin; unless, indeed, the doubtfully mortal were certainly venial; but if he bring only venial sins, he should be dismissed without a second Absolution, because it seems contrary to the respect due to the Sacrament to repeat it there and then without necessity, and the penitent could not reasonably object to its non-repetition. But in the case of a second Absolution, the Priest should not lift his hand or openly make the sign of the Cross if there is any danger of bystanders observing him, and thinking that the penitent was guilty of mortal sin.

VII.

What should be done if the Confessor has forgotten the Sins confessed before he gives Absolution?

If, after the confession is made, the Priest has forgotten the individual sins of the penitent, so that he remembers none of them in particular, which often happens when only venial sins are brought to him, he may absolve, provided that he so far realizes the state of the penitent, as to give the proper penance which he had decided upon while the confession was going on. For it is enough for Absolution that the Priest have had at some time a distinct knowledge of the sins, though afterwards he may be somewhat confused as to the state of the penitent, which arises from the fact that he remembers only that many or few sins of a distinct kind were revealed, or none but venial, but there is no reason why he should not require that the last-mentioned venial sin be repeated to him. A similar case would arise if the Confessor were overwearied, unwell, or distracted; if then he were uncertain whether the penitent had only spoken of venial sins, he should inquire about more grave kinds of sin, especially such as men of his class are likely to fall into; but he should not do this to an excessive degree, lest the Sacrament become distasteful, and for this reason, in order to take away any disgust, the Priest should kindly say that he had laboured under some infirmity, been distracted, or wearied. If he knows the state of the penitent's conscience to be good, whether it be after the confession of one venial sin, or of the sins of a whole life, he may give Absolution. We should notice, however, that the Priest who thus allows himself to be overtaken by sloth or distraction sins grievously, when he thereby fails to understand the faults of the penitent, and obliges him to rehearse his sins afresh to his great annoyance.

VIII.

Absolution from Censures, though anterior to Absolution from Sins, does not include Fulfilment of Penance or Amendment of Life.

Absolution from ecclesiastical censures, though it ought to precede Absolution from sins, at least where there is a reasonable ground of fear that some excommunication is due to the more grievous sins which the penitent confesses, does not necessarily presume that penance has been fulfilled, or that amendment of life is proved to the satisfaction of the Priest. As a rule no one liable to excommunication can be admitted to the benefits of any Sacrament. But when the penitent acts with good faith, and is not aware of his sin exposing him to censures, and the Priest has the power of removing them, he may be absolved from sin, and so from excommunication. In the early discipline we find that persons were admitted to the Holy Eucharist before they had completed their term of penance; hence the Absolution which was given to them at its close was not so much Sacramental as reconciliatory, since they had been sacramentally absolved before they finally were absolved in token that their penance had been fulfilled.

IX.

No Half Absolution to be given on account of the Concourse of Penitents.

Absolution should not be given to any one who has not confessed all his mortal sins, because there happens to be a great number of penitents waiting to confess who may go away. Nor must half-absolutions be given to those who have ill digested their confessions, for want of time to hear them go over them again. It is better to hear fewer confessions, and to see that those who make them are well instructed and disposed, than to absolve many in a bustle who are less disposed, with small hope of amendment. But when there is a moral or physical impossibility of a complete confession, and Absolution is necessary, as when a dying man seems at the point of death before he has completed his confession, or if when the Priest comes he finds that a general confession should be made, and when he has with him the viaticum, and feels that he cannot protract the confession without giving offence to those in attendance, and causing disgrace to the penitent, he may absolve one who has made an imperfect confession; only he should take care to secure afterwards the completion of the confession.

X.

Absolution cannot be validly given to a Person who is not present to receive it.

Absolution cannot lawfully or validly be given to any one absent, but only to persons present, at least morally so. For the form of Absolution consists of formal words, which can only be used to a person present, as "I absolve thee." But confession may be made by letter or otherwise to an absent Priest, in order to receive Absolution from one present. And Absolution from ecclesiastical censures may be given in writing. *Morally present* is added, because, though the case may be extremely rare, a person may be out of sight, and mixed with a crowd, and yet be within reach of hearing, and so long as the Priest and penitent can have oral communication, Absolution may be given.

XI.

Absolution may be given from Venial Sins to a Person rightly disposed.

Absolution may be given to a penitent rightly disposed, though he has only confessed venial sins. For venial sins are a sufficient ground for exercising the power of Absolution, and the penitent by confessing them has acquired a right to receive it, as well as the increase of grace, which is always conferred, whenever the Sacrament is duly applied for. Such persons, however, should be exhorted to arouse in themselves sincere grief and resolutions, and reminded that by often relapsing into the same venial sins they add to their past life a still more grave character, and that such sins are committed with greater deliberation, in that they have already received grace in order to correct them, and that they should therefore the more detest them, and resolve to watch against them, and so the utmost pains be taken to reverence and profit by the Sacrament.

XII.

What should be done if the Person thinks he may relapse.

No one should be deemed to be not rightly disposed for Absolution because there may be grounds for thinking that he may relapse, or even if he himself thinks so; because that fear and opinion may arise from the possibility of a change in his present goodwill, not from any real defect in his present disposition. Hence that opinion, as being an act of the understanding, may co-exist with sincere grief and resolution. Therefore the Priest should examine whether that opinion of the penitent proceeds from an actual inclination to sin, or from despair, or timidity, or rather from consciousness of infirmity, increased by frequently repeated acts. Whatever be the cause, the Priest should strive to heal the disease by suggesting means, by encouraging confidence, and arousing a spirit of humility before God, so as to walk in His presence and implore His aid with more fervent prayer. But the Priest must take care not to propound dangerous suppositions as to what the penitent would do in such and such circumstances, and whether he would refuse to sin though at the risk of suffering this or that evil. It is sufficient that he now is sincerely sorry, and means for the future to sin no more.

CHAPTER V.

WHEN AND HOW ABSOLUTION SHOULD BE REFUSED OR DELAYED.

I.

When Absolution is to be delayed, and what are the Signs of Indisposition for it?

ABSOLUTION must be delayed, (1) if the Priest has any doubts as to the case admitting of his pronouncing it, and there is no pressing necessity for doing so.

(2) If he has good grounds for doubting that the penitent is rightly disposed, and cannot satisfy his doubt, and there is no necessity to absolve—for else the Sacrament would be exposed to the danger of being made of null effect. The signs of a doubtful disposition are, if the penitent, contrary to promise, has not resisted the last occasion of sin: if he has engaged himself to remove a scandal, renew a friendship, restore what was another's, or to satisfy other grave obligations, and has not kept his promises when he might have done so.

(3) Generally speaking, if after long omission of confession and frequent relapses, the penitent appears to have examined his conscience in a negligent manner:

because there is then great danger lest he should be wrongly absolved without having made a full confession. I say generally speaking, because if the penitent be uninstructed, or cannot examine himself better, or cannot come back again, he should be aided in his confession, and absolved if he be considered rightly disposed.

(4) If the penitent be a notorious sinner, e. g. a usurer, or infamous fornicator, the public Absolution should be put off until it is quite clear that he had amended his life, because else the faithful would be scandalized; yet he might be absolved in private if duly disposed, but the Communion should not be given publicly to him.

(5) If, taking all things into consideration, it seems better for the penitent that his Absolution be deferred, so that he may entertain a great horror of his sins, and acquire a deeper sense of their wickedness, and be more strengthened against relapses; that greater grief and firmer resolution may be conceived; and that he may be more tied down to use the prescribed means, make restitution to others and compensation for injuries, and fulfil other obligations. The Priest may *sometimes* defer Absolution *for a short time*, though the penitent seem rightly disposed, at any rate if he is *not altogether unwilling*. The reason of this is that the Priest is the physician of the soul, and so can use the means which, in his wisdom, he may judge to be useful for its spiritual health; as he may enjoin what tends to its preservation in grace, or exact the previous fulfilment of some act of penance. He who is duly disposed has indeed the right to be absolved, but not in all cases, of immediate Absolution; just as a Catechumen has no claim to

receive baptism immediately, but at such time as in the judgment of the Priest shall seem expedient. I have said *sometimes*, because Absolution should be deferred but seldom in the case of a person rightly disposed; and care should be taken not to defer it when Communion cannot be put off without giving rise to remark, or a danger is foreseen of the person being driven to confess the same sins to another Priest, because thereby an unjust burden is imposed on him; or lastly, if he is exposed to the danger of dying without Absolution, or cannot come back again for a long period. I have said *for a short time*, that is, for eight or more days, because a longer delay ought not to take place in the case of one rightly disposed, when it is uncertain if he have perfect contrition, and be unlikely to incur the peril of damnation. I have said *if the penitent be not unwilling*, for if he were altogether unwilling, and could not be brought into such a state of mind as to acquiesce, he ought to be absolved; for else he would be irritated or go to some other Priest, or not return soon to confession. But he whose Absolution is deferred should be excited to frequent acts of charity and contrition, so as to acquire thence greater strength against temptations, and that by being better disposed he may afterwards receive fuller grace. Penance should be also enjoined, and he should be reminded that there is no need for him to confess afresh the sins he has just laid open if he return to the same Priest; for that Priest, though he does not remember them distinctly, can absolve him from those sins, provided he has already imposed a suitable penance and imposes a further one.

II.

When Absolution should be refused?

Absolution should be refused to any one who is clearly indisposed for it. First, if he will not restore the property of others, or make compensation for injury caused to their goods, whether of fortune, fame, or honour, when he is able. And I add this last reservation because if he is unable at present, it is sufficient if he has the will to do it, and engages to do it, and to seek the fitting opportunity to do it.

(2) If he will not condone an offence committed against himself, and if he threatens tremendous vengeance, or wishes to delay reconciliation to his neighbour longer than he ought to the scandal of others; or is unwilling to do what he ought so as to avoid mortal sin, e. g. pay his servants their wages, or dress as modesty requires.

(3) If he retains the will to do any plainly forbidden act, as e. g. to take part in a duel, whenever the opportunity offers.

(4) If he knows any thing likely to cause serious loss or injury to another, and is unwilling to take suitable means to avert it; e. g. if he knows that any one is in danger of being seriously led astray, and does not take care that the parties who are interested in the thing being hindered or put right are made aware of it. The reason of this is that such persons are in actual grievous sin, not being in such charity with their neighbours as to be willing to do them good.

(5) Generally speaking, if the penitent is ignorant of the means necessary to be known for Salvation, and cannot be now instructed in them; as for instance, if he be ignorant of the mystery of the Most Holy Trinity, the Incarnation, &c., because faith in these holy mysteries is probably the foundation of justification. I said at first, *generally speaking*, because at the point of death a person who is ignorant of the mystery of the Most Holy Trinity may receive conditional Absolution, if he cannot be instructed, for it is probable that it is not of the means necessary to be known for Salvation. I said secondly, *and cannot be instructed;* for if he can, he should be instructed, or if time does not permit he should be reminded to take diligent pains to be instructed. This point is clear enough. A greater difficulty consists in the case of habitual sinners, or of persons placed in close proximity to temptation. The Priest is then obliged to warn those who are in blameable ignorance of any one of their obligations. If this ignorance be not their fault, and if it relate to things necessary to salvation, he ought always to draw the penitent out of it; but if it relate to other matters, even to the Divine commands, and if the Priest judges that the drawing the penitent's attention to it might be injurious to him, he ought to pass by it and let the penitent alone, because it is better to avoid running the risk of formal than of material sin, since GOD punishes the latter only. But this applies only to cases where it is difficult or impossible to make amends, or put the thing to-rights. And specially in cases where some injury would accrue to the state, the Priest is bound to prefer the common good to that of the penitent.

Hence it is right to warn princes and prelates if they are ignorant of their obligations, and persons who are known as zealous professors of religion. And if the penitent inquires as to this or that, the Priest is bound to tell the truth.

III.

What if the Penitent conceals a grievous Sin, of which the Priest has been made aware by the Confession of the Partner in the Sin?

If the Priest has learnt from the confession of another person that the penitent has committed a certain sin, which he has not yet confessed, nor does now confess —such as, for instance, if a betrothed man confesses that he has not confessed since Easter, but has committed sin with his betrothed since Low Sunday; while she, on the other hand, says that she has not confessed since Easter, but makes no mention of the sin, the Priest may question her after the customary manner in such cases; e. g. whether she has no further grief, whether nothing has happened since her being engaged which could burden the conscience, for the Priest has not lost, through the knowledge acquired by him in administering the Sacrament, the right of putting questions in the customary manner. And this I add because he has no right to use that knowledge for an extraordinary examination. But if the betrothed woman denies the commission of the sin, there is some dispute as to what course should be taken by the Priest. Some think that conditional Absolution should be given, because the woman deserves as much credit as her accomplice, and so has right to be absolved. Others allow this if there is reasonable ground of excuse—such as want of recollection that it had taken place since her last confession, or that through her stupidity she thinks that such an act might take place without sin, because she considers herself already, in the sight of GOD, to be his wife, &c. But if such a judgment cannot be arrived at, and the Priest is sure that the sin has been committed and yet not been confessed, it is held that she ought not to be absolved, but that the Priest, having given the usual admonition respecting the honourably entering into matrimony as being the main hope of looking for happiness in that condition, and respecting diligent preparation for confession, should enjoin the *Misereatur* to be said, and to dismiss her without Absolution. By these means it is believed the Sacrament is preserved from being invalidly ministered, both because a person who accuses himself with the consequent shame to himself is rather to be believed than a person who may perchance deny through fear of confusion, and because the Priest, by giving Absolution, would do her no good, and so no gain nor confusion results to her. But if the Priest learn, apart from confession, from others, that the sin was committed within two days (for example) after her last confession, he ought rather to believe the penitent. But if the credit of the witness was greater, and circumstances were against the penitent, Absolution ought not to be given absolutely.

IV.

If Absolution is refused, it should be done gently.

When Absolution must be refused to any one, it should be done gently, and it should be demonstrated to the penitent that such a course is necessary for his salvation and for that of the Priest; that the latter has no greater powers than those which GOD has conferred upon him, and that were he to attempt to absolve, he would effect nothing; and lest the penitent be alarmed the penitence imposed should not be too severe, but should be partly suggested by way of advice; and the Priest should say that he would pray for him, and should further admonish him that, should he go to any other Priest, he would have to confess the same sins, and that he must not at present go to Communion. The penitent should be kindly advised to wait for a short time, in order to excite in himself feelings of greater sorrow for sin, which may be the beginning of a real conversion; to this end he should be told to perform some penance, or some acts of devotion and of resolution against sin; and to think every day seriously of death, hell, or eternity, and to utter ejaculatory prayers when tempted. But if the penitent should remonstrate that death may find him unabsolved in the mean time, he should be told, that the danger was greater in absolving him unprepared than in leaving him to acquire true sorrow for sin. Should he sin in the interval less than usual, he may be absolved, since the least sign of resistance is an evidence of contrition and amendment.

CHAPTER VI.

HOW PENITENTS OUGHT USUALLY TO BE DIRECTED TO A DEVOUT OR REALLY CHRISTIAN LIFE?

I.

In what consists a truly devout Life?

EVERY one may be instructed in this matter in proportion to their several states, conditions, and capacities. A truly devout life does not consist in long vocal prayers, nor in long remaining in churches, nor in feelings of piety, as some women mistakingly imagine; but in avoiding sin and living suitably to their condition, and in doing what they have to do from a right intention, or from a supernatural motion of virtue, specially of love to GOD and to their neighbour, having the will of GOD, who needs not our goods, as the cynosure of their own will. For what devotion would there be in a matron spending all the time, which was due to her children and domestic affairs, in church; in a daughter, whose proper duties lay in labouring at home, and aiding her parents in preparing victuals and other necessaries, in visiting churches, or in occupying herself at home with holy reading or prayer? GOD, the Great Father of the Christian family, distributes duties, and assigns to each his station and functions; and he who conforms himself to His Holy Will with greatest love and reverence, leads the most devout life; and no work is good but such as is conformable to the Divine Will. The LORD CHRIST assuredly did not less please His Father by leading a private life for thirty years, by labouring in the workshop of His foster father, and by obeying His mother, than He did afterwards by preaching the Kingdom of GOD and working miracles.

II.

He should instil into himself a Thought of the great Importance of his last End.

He should have a conception of the great importance of his last end. Man was created in order that he might, in this his mortal life, praise and reverence the LORD his GOD, and by serving Him at last be saved. All other things created by Him upon earth are for the sake of man, to aid him towards the end for which he was created. These thoughts should be deeply impressed upon penitents in moving them to a fervent desire of attaining their end. Whatsoever a man does, whatsoever he suffer that does not tend thither, must be counted as lost. He that fails to reach that end— good were it for that man if he had not been born. Further, the penitent should have put before him, the manifold, easy, and pleasant means which GOD has given man for the attainment of his end; yea, how He has ordained all things, whether prosperous or adverse, to work together for good to them that love GOD. And therefore the man is inexcusable who despises or abuses the riches of the goodness of GOD. Finally, he should be urged to become entirely indifferent, and receive at the hand of GOD, with the same willing and grateful mind, adversity and prosperity, since he is ignorant what most conduces to his end, health or sickness, riches or poverty, honour or neglect and contempt.

III.

Great Horror of Sin.

He should conceive great detestation and horror of all sin, especially of deadly sin, by considering its wickedness, which, though it passes all human understanding, will yet become more apparent, if, first of all, (1) the pains are considered by which GOD, the just avenger, visited one single mortal sin in the case of the fallen angels and Adam, and still punishes mortal sins for ever in hell. Secondly, the satisfaction which He exacted of His Only Begotten Son, Who took on Him our sins and purged them away. For He did not deem it sufficient to perform one act of obedience, though that were of infinite value, but He willed to be born a beggar, and, abandoned by men, to live poor and as it were unknown, to endure reproaches, contempt, and calumnies, and even to undergo the ignominious death of the cross between two thieves. Thirdly, Who it is That is offended, dishonoured, and despised by mortal sin, and by whom and for what object, and under what circumstances; such as in the very presence of GOD, and at the very time when He gives man life through the desire of His Salvation, and nourishes and sustains him.

IV.

By urging the Thought of the Vanity of the World, and the Constancy of Eternity.

He should consider the inconstancy of all things which the world offers, the shortness of life, the certainty of death, the uncertainty of the time of its occurrence; the happiness or misery of eternity to come. "What shall it profit a man if he gain the whole world and lose his own soul?" It will profit nothing a man to be rich, or full of pleasures and honours—nothing to have been a prince, a king, or monarch of the whole world. Thus will the penitent be led to attain to the love of spiritual poverty, and his mind be wrenched from earthly things.

V.

By suggesting Means of attaining to Virtue.

First—A high idea of Virtue.

He should have general means of attaining to virtue suggested to him; such as, first, a high esteem of virtue, for virtue is the substance of Christian life, the dignity, beauty, honour, ornament, and nobility of rational beings. If this be wanting, all other things are of no avail; if a man have this, it raises him to the likeness of God; for it makes him prudent, just, brave, temperate, mild, patient, kind, and merciful, and adorns him with other perfections; whence a sort of beautiful likeness to God and imitation of His perfections results; yea, rather he is a son of God, and the son resembles the Father. " God's likeness in us," says S. Augustine concerning the Creation, "is to be seen in our habits, that as God, who created man in His own image and likeness, is Love, good and just, patient, and mild and merciful, and the other characteristics which are read of God, so man was created to have love, to be good, just, patient, mild, and pure and merciful; so that the more a man has such virtues in him, the nearer he is to God, and the greater is the likeness he bears to his Creator. But if any one, which God forbid, through the bye-ways and cross-roads of vice and crime degenerates and wanders from this most noble likeness of his Creator, then it happens to him, as it is written, ' Man being in honour, hath no understanding.' " But who can unfold how great the excellence is which likeness to God confers on man? " I said, ye are gods, and ye are all the children of the Most Highest." Wouldest thou be one of them? Follow after virtue.

The Second is an ardent and strong Desire thereof.

The second general means is an ardent, strong, and efficacious desire of virtue. Ardent, so that one is drawn towards it as a hungry man to food, or as a thirsty man to drink. "Blessed are they that hunger and thirst after righteousness, for they shall be filled." Strong, so as to lift up the heart against difficulties, and confirm it by the pursuit of virtue: for such as dread these difficulties will not attain solid virtue. "They wish," says S. Gregory (Moral. vii. 12), "to be humble, but so as not to be looked down upon; to be contented with what they have, but not to be in poverty; to be chaste, but without having to emaciate their bodies; to be patient, but without having to experience insults; and when they seek to gain virtue, they look to escape the labours of virtue; what is all this but ignorance how to play the warrior in the battle-field, and to desire warlike triumphs in cities?" Lastly, efficacious desire, which extends to the practice of external operations, and despising the criticisms of men and one's own comforts, seeks not for spiritual consolations to the neglect of the substance of virtue, like the child who licks the butter from the bread and neglects the bread; but for constant and firm virtues, which never fail them on any occasion, place, or time. "God," says S. Jerome (Ps. lxxx.), "gives not by measure, but according to the disposition of our heart."

The Third is constant Prayer.

The third general means is constant and humble prayer, or petition for virtue, for virtue is God's chief gift, which is only won by prayer; but God wills to be recognized as the Author thereof, and to be compelled by a sort of importunity, that we may learn to recognize it as a gift, adore the Source of it, and show ourselves grateful, and when this happens it is to our benefit, and not to God's. And hence God so often exhorts us to prayer: " Ask, and ye shall receive; seek, and ye shall find; knock, and it shall be opened unto you " (Matt. vii.). " Men ought always to pray, and not to faint " (Luke xviii.). " Whatsoever ye shall ask the Father in My Name, He will give it you" (John xvi. 23). Prayer should be put up with confidence, so as to be made in the name of Christ, relying on His merits, not on our own, and with humility referring our requests to the glory of God, that the Father may be glorified in the Son, otherwise the request is not made in the Name of Christ. Further, the mode of asking for gifts of grace is threefold: for they may be asked for generally, after the manner of David, " O learn me true understanding and knowledge " (Ps. cxix.); or particularly, in special prayer, during this week, or this whole month, seeking sometimes one, sometimes another; which method is more useful than the former. Or, after considering what things excite to virtue, such as humility, by making acts of it, with great desire to advance in it. But that prayer may become more fervent, it is good to lay before God our own need of Him, our poverty, our want of grace, our perils, &c.: the love wherewith God has loved us from all eternity; the mercy wherewith He recalled us from our wanderings; the long-suffering and patience wherewith He bore with our rebellion; the labours, toils, insults, torments, and death of Christ, laying them in detail before our Saviour.

The Fourth, a constant Effort to advance.

The fourth means is a constant effort to advance in virtue; for so the estimation, desire, and habit (which is augmented by repeated acts) of virtue increases, and this effort is so necessary for progress, that not to go on in virtue is to go back, as the Fathers and spiritual teachers instruct us. The reason of this is that our heart can exist as little without love, as fire without heat; and love is either well-ordered and heavenly, or ill-ordered, as that which is earthly for the most part is: if it be earthly, we go back; if heavenly, we go on. And it will not be heavenly, unless we constantly battle against self-love, and corrupt nature, and endeavour to advance.

The Fifth, to walk in God's presence.

The fifth means is to labour with the recollection of God's presence, and His constant sight of all the secrets of our hearts. "Walk before me, and be thou perfect;" that is, "and thou shalt be, &c.," as it is interpreted to mean.

The Sixth, to propose to ourselves Christ as our Example.

The sixth general means is to propose to ourselves Christ, who is the Way, the Truth, and the Life, as the Teacher and Example of virtues, and to animate ourselves with this thought. Our life is a warfare on the earth, as Job testifies; Christ is our Leader and Commander; I have enrolled myself under Him, I follow His banner. He toiled, suffered thirst, hunger, cold, heat, insults, reproaches, humbled Himself even to the death upon the Cross to redeem me, and so entered into His glory. He invites me to the same, but wills not that I share it, unless I co-operate and sympathize with Him. The servant is not greater than his lord, nor the disciple than his master; the soldier ought to be ashamed, if he wishes for more comfortable and delicate treatment than was experienced by his Leader and Commander, and nevertheless desires to share His kingdom and glory.

VI.

Acts of Faith, Hope, and Charity frequently to be made.

The penitent should be instructed to make frequent acts of faith, hope, and charity. Of faith, with great humility and reverence, by the subjection of his intellect, and bringing it into captivity to the Supreme Truth in regard to the perfections of God, the mysteries of the Most Holy Trinity, the Incarnation, and the Holy Eucharist, and in regard to the rewards prepared for the righteous, and the punishments in store for sinners: of hope, with great desire of bliss, and great trust in the omnipotence, benevolence, mercy, and faithfulness of God, and in the merits of Christ, which He willed to be ours: lastly, of love, by rejoicing in the infinite perfections of God; by offering ourselves to Him, by desiring that all should love Him for Himself; by inviting all creatures to praise and bless Him; by exulting in the honour and worship paid to Him from every quarter; by lamenting that so many offend, neglect, and despise Him, and that we have offended Him; by deploring our blindness and that of others, and our lukewarmness in recognizing, esteeming, and obeying Him.

VII.

Also of Humility.

The penitent should be induced to exercise himself constantly in humility of heart, word, and work; and in order to attain to this virtue he should often consider over and over again; "What and how great God is!— and what am I?"—God, eternal, infinite, omniscient, most wise, omnipotent, altogether good! I a few years ago was nothing, soon nothing will remain of me; and what have I become through sin? After a few years what shall I be, and that for ever? Thus the penitent should humble himself under the Almighty hand of God, recur to Him in all things, acknowledging his own blindness, poverty, impotence for all good, and attribute all defects to himself, all good to God; so as to be benevolent and merciful to his neighbour, reckoning himself the last of all. For humility is the foundation of all virtues, without which no one attains any degree of perfection; since God resists the proud and gives grace to the humble; because the humble refer all gifts which they receive to

God, Who will not and cannot give His glory to another; but the proud are thieves in the House of God, and rob Him of His glory.

VIII.

We should learn to do all with a right Intention.

The penitent should in all things proceed with a right intention, looking solely how to please and glorify God, and with that view diligently watch over his affections, and the use of his senses by frequent self-examination; for else self-love will either uproot or weaken his intention, because "the imagination of man's heart is evil from his youth."

IX.

The Penitent should be instructed as to general and particular Self-examination.

In addition to instructing him as to general examination of the acts of the whole day at evening, he should accustom himself to a special examination of this nature: For a certain period a particular virtue should be practised during the day, or some vice or passion should be mortified. He should make his resolution in the morning, look forward for opportunities, and exercise himself through the day in acts of that virtue, or in mortification of this passion, striving to increase daily the number for good, and to diminish what remains of evil. At evening he should make up his accounts, and elicit grief for falls or negligences, after examining whether his progress has been greater or less. Resolutions should then be made for the next day, as to what virtue needs most to be exercised, or what predominant passion needs most to be subdued.

X.

Confession and Communion to be devout and frequent.

Exact, frequent, and devout confession and communion should be recommended. In order that the confession be devout, it should be prefaced by examination, and not only carried out with a humble and sincere opening of griefs, with true sorrow and efficacious resolution of amendment; but there should also be diligence in seeking means for that end, and in avoiding the occasions of sin. Absolution should be received with a lowly and grateful mind, as though from Christ Himself; thanksgivings should be made afterwards for having received it, and the resolution previously made should be offered to God, to be confirmed by His grace. "Stablish the thing which Thou hast wrought in us." In order that communion may be truly devout, a man should be in the first place (1), clean, not only from all deadly sin, but also from venial, and all inordinate affection; wherefore all the secret workings of the mind should be well examined. They may be known by the end to which they are directed. Secondly (2), an ardent desire of receiving

Christ should be excited, by considering our indigence, blindness, mental disease, impotence, and perils, and on the other hand Christ's riches, power, and love, whereby He desires to enrich us and be with us. "If any man thirst, let him come unto me" (John vii.). "To him that is athirst I will give of the fountain of the water of life" (Rev. iii.). "My delights were with the sons of men" (Prov. viii. 31). (3) He should deeply humble himself, considering on the one side his own nothingness and unworthiness, chiefly contracted by his own sins and ingratitude; on the other, Christ's worthiness. (4) He should receive Christ with lively faith, great trust, ardent love and desire, great humility, attention, and reverence. (5) Having received the Spouse of his soul, he should render humble thanks, which is done by subjecting the intellect by faith, adoring and loving Him, and desiring that He may be loved and glorified by all; making offerings of himself, addressing Him now as his King, now as his Spouse: by begging Him to give bounteous grace, undergoing some mortification during the day, reading a holy book, avoiding vain conversation, &c.

XI.

SUMMARY OF COUNSELS TO BE GIVEN BY PRIESTS IN ORDER TO LEAD A RELIGIOUS LIFE.

In general the penitent should be urged to direct all his efforts towards obtaining the end for which God made, redeemed, and sanctified him. Nothing should be valued but what tends to promote that end, nothing undervalued but what is useless for that object, nothing feared but what stands in its way. All things that he must do or suffer should be regarded as so many aids to it. All must be regulated or discontinued subject to that consideration. The Priest should instruct penitents how to pray, what prayers to use, and when and how often, according to their different needs and opportunities. They should be told to pray at least twice a day, at morning on rising, and at evening on going to bed. Besides this they should be urged, as often as it may be in their power, to be present at the celebration of Holy Communion, or at the saying of matins and evensong, and especially on Festivals; they should be instructed, if capable of being so, how to engage in mental prayer, to say the penitential psalms, or use like religious exercises, and be exhorted to make a daily examination of conscience, and be taught how to do it. They should be exhorted often to go to confession, and receive the Holy Eucharist, if possible, every Sunday, as S. Augustine advises. They should specially be urged to confess and communicate at the greater festivals, such as Easter, Pentecost, and Christmas, and the First Sunday in Lent. By and by it may be easy to persuade them to communicate oftener, and at length monthly, after which it will not be difficult to bring them to a weekly reception. The Priest should endeavour to win them to a religious observance of festivals and other solemnities by holy reading, meditations, and prayers. He should direct them to the purchase of suitable books of devotion for reading during special seasons. The wife should be urged to use her endeavours to gain over to a religious life her husband, and the husband in like manner his wife, and both to win the hearts of their children to the service of God. And it should not be forgotten to instruct them in the necessity of almsgiving, and giving the tithes at least of all that they possess.

CHAPTER VII.

WHETHER, WHEN, AND HOW ERRORS AND FAILURES INTO WHICH THE PRIEST FALLS IN ADMINISTERING HIS OFFICE MAY BE AMENDED?

I.

What should be done if he has not Absolved a Penitent rightly disposed, who has committed Mortal Sin?

IF the Priest, through forgetfulness, distraction, or mistake, has omitted to absolve a rightly disposed penitent, who has committed mortal sin, he is bound to absolve him as soon as he has the opportunity, even though after the expiration of a day or two days' time, because since the Sacrament of Penance partakes of the character of a court of judgment, the moral union between its different parts lasts longer than in most of the other Sacraments. But should much time have intervened, if it can conveniently be done, the penitent should first be admonished, and his sorrow should be renewed; but if he cannot be admonished, he should be absolved conditionally, especially if there is a reasonable fear that his sorrow has passed away. The reason of this is that he has a right to the Absolution, and is still desirous to obtain it. But if, after the opportunity of meeting has been too long delayed, the penitent should come again to confess to the same Priest, it may be said to him, Dost thou accuse thyself of any thing, and grieve over all the sins of thy whole life? and Absolution may be given to him on his assent, provided the Priest still bears in mind the former position of matters; but if he neither returns, nor can be met with, nor brought back, nor admonished when he comes after a long interval, without signal offence and scandal to the penitent, or signal confusion or loss of respect and character to the Priest, the Priest should commend the matter to God, and offer the Holy Sacrifice for his forgiveness, whatever his fault may have been. For the Priest is not bound to provide for the material entirety of the Confession, to the risk of scandal or grievous injury to himself, since the penitent may on account of any grave cause be excused from it. With this understanding, however, that there is a reasonable ground for believing that the penitent is likely to go to confession again before his death, and so to be absolved, at least indirectly, from his former sin; for if he should be thought likely to be in danger of dying before he would make his confession, the Priest should prefer his salvation to the injury of his own character. But the shame and loss of reputation which he is likely to encounter when with the penitent, may excuse the Priest, so long as he has a reasonable belief that he will go again to confession. I said in the outset, *a penitent who has committed mortal sin;* for if he has only confessed venial sins, though he ought to be absolved immediately, while he is morally present; yet if he has departed, no notice need be taken, unless there be a reasonable cause of alarm that he is in a state of mortal sin, and is unlikely for a long while to go to confession.

II.

What if he has omitted to inquire the Number and Class of Sins?

If the Priest before giving Absolution has omitted to question the penitent concerning the number and kind of his grievous sins, he may and ought to question him while still kneeling beside him, even though now absolved, and admonish him as to those duties, concerning which he has not been warned. Nor is it necessary to ask permission to do so, because the judicial inquiry is still going on. But if the penitent has already gone away, the Priest is, according to rule, under no obligation except as to penance, if the omission has been through his own fault; because no admonition can take place out of confession without grave confusion of the penitent and of the Priest. But if the same penitent should come back to Confession to the same Priest, he should be reminded of the defect on the last occasion, for else there would not be the full confession of all which the penitent is bound to make. I said, *if the Priest has omitted to question;* for if he had positively erred by saying that there was no need to reveal the kind or number of sins, the penitent should be reminded of them, if it can be done without grave scandal and loss to the penitent and to the Priest; for else the Priest would be the cause of violating a grave precept respecting what ought to be confessed in regard to kind and number. But since the confusion of the priest is ordinarily great, if he disclose his fault or ignorance to the penitent, since men that are liable to make slips with their tongues are prone to reveal such things to others, the Priest seems often to be delivered from this obligation if the penitent does not return to him. Some writers teach that he is not bound, generally speaking, to admonish the Penitent, in order to correct a mistake which has been even culpably made, if there is reason to fear scandal or grave loss to himself or to others, or grave offence to the penitent. But if the penitent should be admonished, some think that he might be shown his mistake out of confession, without even asking permission, by saying, "If such and such a sin were committed, it ought to be confessed in this or that way." It is better, however, to ask permission if the penitent needs to be set right out of Confession.

III.

What if he has neglected to Admonish him in regard to Restitution?

If the Priest should have neglected to admonish the penitent, in regard to making restitution, and he on that account omits to do so, the Priest is not bound on that account to make recompense for the injury, though he may have acted in vincible ignorance and with grave fault; because he is not obliged out of justice to a third party to admonish the penitent or hinder his loss—but at most out of charity; and hence he ought to amend his error if he conveniently can; but if not, he should commend the matter to God. The case, in which the Priest is purposely silent not desiring to enforce restitution on the penitent, is different, because the third party has a right to demand that no hindrance should be unfairly put in the way of obtaining what is justly due to him. The silence of the Priest either is, or is not, a cause of loss; if it is, he is bound to make it up, even though no fraud was intended; if not, the inward intention does not superinduce an obligation to make compensation, unless an external act became an efficacious cause of loss. It would be otherwise if that intention had imparted such weight to his silence as to incite the penitent to avoid restitution, whence others say that the Priest is bound, if the penitent's failure to restore were caused by the silence of the Priest. But others deny that the silence of the Priest is ordinarily a tacit sanction of withholding what is justly due, when the penitent is ignorant whether he is silent through forgetfulness or any just reason.

IV.

What if he has Obliged or Released from Obligation to Restore through some Innocent Mistake?

Should the Priest acting in good faith oblige the penitent to restore, when he is not bound to do so, or release him from his obligation when he is bound, the Priest is not bound thereby absolutely to make compensation for injurious results; yet if he find out the mistake he is bound out of charity, and probably even in equity, to admonish the penitent. The reason of the first part is, because where there is no intentional fault, nor any clearly necessary obligation to others, one is not in conscience bound to make restitution, unless, perchance any special contract has intervened, such as is not supposed in this case; but as those who undertake the office of advocate, physician, and counsellor, do not intend to bind themselves to more than common diligence, and ought to beware of being deceived or incurring blame,— liabilities akin to grave theological fault,—and are not, except to this extent, held to be blameable in the inner court of conscience, so the Priest does not lay himself open to a more grave charge; nor is he justly held to be liable for loss which has accrued without his own fault. The reason of the second part is that, according to the law of charity, I ought, whenever it is possible, to hinder my neighbour's suffering loss. The reason of the third part is, because one is bound to counteract the consequences of an action involving the aggravation of the loss; as, for example, if I had without any fault of mine grievously defamed another, or set fire to his house, I should be bound out of a sense of justice to repair the injury done to his character, or extinguish, if I could, the fire. I said *probably*, because some teach also that there is only an obligation arising from charity, when we can admonish without great inconvenience: because there is no obligation either out of the antecedent fault, nor from the debt incurred, nor from the duty itself, when the duty ceases:

as, for instance, if I had received from a thief a precious vessel, and, supposing it honestly got, had given it to another, should I afterwards become aware that it was stolen, I should not be bound in justice to tell the owner. The first opinion is more probable, nor are examples wanting; for if my being given the vessel was the reason why the owner did not receive it, I should be bound in justice either to make restitution, or to tell the owner. But the Priest is not bound himself to make restitution, when he has, so far as he could, admonished the penitent.

V.

What if through Culpable Error or Malice?

But if the Priest, out of very culpable ignorance or malice, has positively released the penitent from obligation, he is bound out of justice to take care that the losses are made good, or else himself to make them good, since he was the unjust cause of them. This applies even to a Priest who has taken the vows of poverty, and therefore has not and cannot have any means of making restitution without great detriment to his character or inconvenience, for though he would not be bound himself by the failure of the penitent or of any one else, because it would be unreasonable to exact it of him; yet if he could easily obtain it from his superior, or from any one else by asking for it for some pious purpose, he would be bound, as being to blame, to procure it, and in case of the penitent's failure, to make restitution for the reasons already given.

VI.

What if he has ordered the thing which ought to be restored to be given to the Poor?

If he has inconsiderately, or before the penitent has used sufficient diligence to find the owner, told the penitent to give the money to the poor, the obligation to find the owner and to restore it to him when found, remains; the penitent is bound in the first place, and, failing him, the Priest. Hence it is clear how cautiously the Priest should proceed in the matter of restitution; so that when he is not certain as to the obligation, or as to the immunity from it, he should not immediately settle the question, but take time to consider or to consult others, and should say to the penitent, "Are you not ready to perform all that you feel you are bound to do?" If he assent, he should say, "I will consider the matter; return after a while to me:" or, if he cannot, "Go to another learned man, and lay the case before him."

VII.

Whether it is necessary, before Correcting a Mistake, to Ask the Penitent's Leave?

If the Priest err in judgment, saying, e.g., that a contract of matrimony is valid when it is invalid, or that a certain vow is invalid when it is valid, he is bound to admonish the penitent if possible, and this may be done through another person, if the matters in question do not fall under the seal of Confession, except, indeed, it is clear that the penitent does not wish them to be revealed to another. But they do not fall under the seal, if they are not made known in order to explain the sin. But whether, before correcting such mistakes, the Priest is bound first to obtain legitimate permission from the penitent to speak of what has passed in Confession, as to the special points concerned, or whether he may admonish him without asking his permission, is not agreed. The more common opinion is, that if the penitent has been absolved, it is necessary that leave should be legitimately obtained from him in order to speak with him out of Confession respecting those things which fall under the seal.

VIII.

What the Priest should do when he reflects upon the Confessions which have been made to him.

In order that the defects which sometimes occur in hearing Confessions may be the more readily and perfectly corrected, it is expedient that the Priest, after his duties in this respect are over, should consider how he has discharged his functions, how he has dealt with such and such and each penitent, how he has instructed, examined, excited to sorrow, resolved doubts; how he might have done better, and may do better for the future : if he doubt of his solution of difficulties, or of his judgment in regard to sin, he should consult books or other learned or experienced men. So he may hope to discharge his office more readily, and perfectly, and fruitfully.

IX.

General Directions in concluding this part of the Manual.

The Priest should ordinarily receive Confessions in the Church or *open* vestry, particularly in the case of females. He should wear his cassock, surplice, and violet or black stole. All appearance of mystery should be carefully avoided, as being as much out of place as it would be in remitting the sins of an adult in baptism. It is a good plan to have the fifty-first Psalm and a special prayer to be said before and after receiving Confessions, written out and placed where the Priest usually sits to give Absolution. Lastly, the Priest should ever be careful never to suggest to the mind of the penitent any evil conception of which it is hitherto ignorant.

GILBERT AND RIVINGTON, PRINTERS, ST. JOHN'S SQUARE, LONDON.

THE PRIEST IN ABSOLUTION:

A MANUAL FOR SUCH AS ARE CALLED UNTO THE HIGHER MINISTRIES IN THE ENGLISH CHURCH.

PART II.

"Mortuo Lazaro, qui mole magna premebatur, nequaquam dicitur, revivisce, sed veni foras, ut nimirum homo in peccato suo mortuus, qui intra conscientiam suam abscónsus jacet per nequitiam, a seipso foras exeat per confessionem. Mortuo enim veni foras dicitur, ut ab excusatione et occultatione peccati ad accusationem suam ore proprio exire provocetur."—S. GREG. M. MORAL. XXII. 14.

PRIVATELY PRINTED FOR THE USE OF THE CLERGY.

TO

THE MASTERS, VICARS, AND BRETHREN,

OF

The Society of the Holy Cross,

THIS VOLUME

BEGUN AT THEIR REQUEST

AND CONTINUED AMONGST MANY LABOURS AND INFIRMITIES

WITH THE HOPE THAT IT MAY SERVE TO INCREASE PIETY AND DEVOTION

IS HUMBLY AND AFFECTIONATELY

DEDICATED

BY AN UNWORTHY BROTHER PRIEST.

ADVERTISEMENT TO THE READER.

THE reproach of the celebrated Portuguese preacher, Vieyra, in his day, that never were there so many confessions, but never less fruit of confessions, is one which the Priest needs to guard against at a time when the doctrine of Absolution is so widely disseminated amongst ourselves. For whereas contrition may save without confession, confession cannot save without contrition. And the difficulty in which the Priest is often placed is to feel so sure that contrition is experienced by the penitent as to be justified in giving Absolution. If English Priests are lax in requiring contrition it will be found that the same evils will appear in the English Church which Vieyra allows to have prevailed in the Portuguese.

Now contrition can sometimes only be excited by the interrogations of the Priest. Yet the Acatholic mind is set very much against questioning the penitent. Strange it is that not content with lowering the office of Priest under the Gospel to the office of Priest under the Law by denying to the former his power of cleansing from sin, it would even deprive the Priest under the Gospel of that authority to question and examine which was the special duty of the Priest under the Law. This objection to examination of conscience by the Priest is built upon the danger of its leading to ill results. Such an apprehension is easily met by the fact that medical men and their patients run equal risks, to say the least, with the view of healing bodily diseases. Why then do people object to the Priest's scrutiny while they tolerate that of the medical man? The writer will answer this question by a passage in the experience of a very dear friend. A. B. had been by God's grace free from such sins of the flesh as lead to contagious disease. Wishing to insure his life, he applied to a Clerical Insurance Company who required the production of a certificate from his medical man, who was not a Catholic. Accordingly questions were put to him by the medical man of a nature which made A. B. exclaim somewhat ironically, "Why Dr. ——, this is a Confessional." "Ah, sir!" said the Doctor, "but consider the difference of the object." Thus it is that spiritual health is counted for nothing in comparison of bodily cure and secular advantages. Any amount of shame and of what is repugnant to modesty is to be borne by sick folk at the hands of a surgeon or physician in the hope of recovery, but sick souls must pass through no such ordeal for a better deliverance.

More however depends on the examination of the patient by the Priest under the Gospel than was required of the Priest under the Law. The latter had only to search and examine whether the leper was cleansed with a view to pronounce him released from his isolation and exile: the former has to try and scrutinize the soul to see if it be fit to be cleansed, and warrant the exercise of Sacramental Absolution. The Priest must be minute without being curious, and not more minute than is absolutely necessary. He must gain all needful knowledge of the case of the penitent without imparting to the penitent any knowledge of evil with which he is not already acquainted.

It is obvious again that the Priest needs to be as cautious in ministering the remedy for sin which CHRIST has bequeathed to His Church, as a medical man ought to be in prescribing medicines for his patient, lest he become guilty of homicide. It is very often only by inquiry that the Priest can learn whether the penitent be a relapsing or habitual sinner, liable to occasions of sin, or has an explicit acquaintance with necessary truths; whether he should be absolved there and then, or have the absolution deferred. Cardinal Bona warns against that "false charity and damnable condescension which encourages most Christians to pass their lives in a disorderly manner, between sins and sacraments, confessions and relapses:" and Bellarmine against those bad confessors whose "evil facility of absolving causes so much evil facility of sinning."

The truth is, that very few religious persons have any conception of the amount of moral evil which seethes and ferments around them. Fathers and mothers do not suspect what goes on in their family, among their children and servants. As it is the medical man in full practice who alone knows to what extent physical evil prevails, so it is with the Priest who exercises his office of Absolver in the Name of CHRIST. To preach upon the subject of gross sins is all but prohibited to the clergy, though thousands fall victims to them.

And as it is with gross sins so it is with such sins as that of Pride. It is often only by very careful spiritual diagnosis that this is found to be the root from which so many luxuriant buds proceed. Many persons have gone to various confessors without ever having been warned that this was the fatal source of all their failures and relapses.

There is no resource for the spiritually sick save private Confession and Absolution, and to make that effectual it is often necessary that the penitent be examined with discretion and with expertness. To this object the Second Part of this book is dedicated.

*** To prevent scandal arising from the curious or prurient misuse of a book which treats of spiritual diseases, it has been thought best that the sale should be confined to the clergy who desire to have at hand a sort of Vade-mecum for easy reference in the discharge of their duties as Confessors.

CONTENTS.

INTRODUCTION.

	PAGE
Of Sin. What the Priest ought to bear in mind concerning sin	1
Of sin unto death and sin not unto death	2
Of distinctions between sins	3

CHAPTER I.

What must be observed by the Priest in general in regard to the more obvious sins, as well as in particular in regard to persons varying in age, sex, estate, or condition of life.

SECTION I.

What must be observed concerning Pride and its principal divisions, and the remedies thereof	6
Remedies for Pride	11
Spiritual Pride	14

SECTION II.

What the Priest should observe in regard to Covetousness and its offspring	15
Spiritual Covetousness	18
Remedies for Covetousness	19

SECTION III.

	PAGE
What the Priest should principally notice in regard to Impurity	21
Spiritual Impurity	30
Remedies against Impurity	31

SECTION IV.

Of Envy and its offspring	33
Spiritual Envy	38
Remedies against Envy	39

SECTION V.

Of Gluttony and Drunkenness	40
Spiritual Gluttony	49
Remedies against Gluttony and Drunkenness	51

SECTION VI.

Of Anger, and of the cursing and blasphemy thereupon	53
Spiritual Anger	60
Remedies against Anger, Cursing, Blaspheming, &c.	61

SECTION VII.

Of Sloth	64
Spiritual Sloth	65
Remedies against Sloth	66

CHAPTER II.

Further precautions which the Priest should take in the discharge of his functions as Confessor 68

CHAPTER III.

Concerning the mode of questioning penitents 80

CHAPTER IV.

How to question the ill or non-instructed 84

CHAPTER V.

HOW TO DEAL WITH DIFFERENT CLASSES OF PENITENTS.

	PAGE
How to deal with children	140
How to deal with adults	148
As to Vocation	149
Duties of married persons	159
Property of married persons	161
Obligations of parents	162
Of temptations likely to befall the above	164
Advice to parents	166
Duties of children in regard to parents	167
Of children's goods and rights	168
Of the duties of superiors	170
Of the duties of servants	171
Duties of Parish Priests	172
Sins of Priests	175
Sins of Parish Priests	176
Sins of Confessors	177
Sins of Bishops	178
Duties of Schoolmasters and Pupils	178
Duties of Guardians and Wards	179
Duties of Merchants	179
Duties of Buyers	181
Duties of Workmen	182
Duties of Officers and Soldiers	183
Duties of Soldiers	184
Duties of Judges	185
Duties of Advocates	186
Duties of Suitors	186
Restitutions	186
How to deal with accused persons	188
How to deal with the tempted	189
How to deal with Shamefaced Penitents	189
How to deal with those who despair of amendment	190
How to deal with the feebleminded	191
How to deal with Penitents whose Language is unknown to the Priest	191

CONTENTS.

	PAGE
How to Absolve Adults	192
Penances to be enjoined	201
How to deal with cases of a more difficult nature—Scrupulous	202
General Remedies for Scrupulousness	207
How to deal with persons who are tormented with scruples that they have yielded to inward temptations	208
Fearful Persons	209
Annual Confessions	210
Annual Review of Confession	211
Forgotten Faults	212
What must be mentioned in Annual Reviews	212
Distinctness in Confession	215
Sorrowfulness necessary in Confession	216
Deaf and Dumb	217
Condemned to Death	218
The Dying	222
Persons tormented by an Unclean Spirit	223
Difficult Cases	224
Those who are subject to Occasions of Sin	225
Two Kinds of Occasions of Sin	227
Marks of Near Occasions of Sin	228
How to deal with Occasions	228
Important Distinctions	229
Necessary Occasions	230
Interior and Exterior Marks of Occasions of Sin	232
Frequency of Relapse	233
Those who are in the habit of Sin or who Relapse	235
When the Relapsing should be Absolved	237
Precautions to be observed with the Relapsing	238
How to deal with Young People in regard to Absolution and Communion	239
Of General Confessions in the case of the Relapsing	239
How to deal with Sacrilegious Confession	240
General Confessions	241
Remedies for the Relapsed	244
How to deal with cases where extraordinary Contrition is exhibited	246
Use of Spiritual Retreats and Missions	248
Distinction between Habitual and Relapsing Sinners	248
Relapsing Ordinands	250

	PAGE
How to Absolve Habitual and Relapsing	250
How to deal with the Sick and Dying	252
Caution to the Priest	254
Remedies against Temptations	256
The Viaticum	258
Last Agony	260
Signs of Death	262
How to deal with Penitents who are liable to various Temptations	264
Remedies against Temptation	265
How to deal with persons of higher degrees of Perfection and Devotion	267
How to deal with the Secret Temptations of such persons	270
Of several Temptations to turn back	274
Of Secret Temptations to turn back	276
How to deal with persons who have Illuminations, Visions, &c.	276
How to distinguish the Motions, Visions, Suggestions, and Illuminations of the Good Spirit from those of the Evil	277
How to act in time of Spiritual Consolations	281
How to deal with Sensible Devotion	283
How to deal with Desolations	283
Rules to be observed in Desolations	284
How to deal with Communicants	286
Dispensations, Festivals, Fasts, Marriage	289
Of Penances	290
Example of Satisfactions ordained by Ancient Penitential Canons in the most common cases	292
Directions as to the Assignment of Penances	294
Different kinds of Penances	298
Secresy of Confession	301
Restitution	303
Order to be observed in regard to those who are bound to make restitution	305
What must be done to make the restitution equivalent to the loss	307
Causes of exemption	308
To aid pious persons in their desire for perfection	310
Mental Prayer	312
Contemplation	315
Vocation of Nuns and Sisters of Mercy	320

THE PRIEST IN ABSOLUTION,

ETC.

PART II.

INTRODUCTION.

OF SIN.

What the Priest ought to bear in mind regarding sin.

SIN is something committed or omitted voluntarily contrary to the law of GOD. To constitute an act of sin it is requisite (1) that there should be disobedience to GOD by violating one of His commands, and (2) that this disobedience should be a voluntary act.

It must be observed (1) that GOD's Law is violated when those persons are disobeyed whom GOD has commanded to be obeyed: this is why disobedience to the Law of the Church is disobedience to GOD, as well as disobedience to the law of the state; (2) that ignorance is no excuse for disobedience, if it proceed from our own fault, whether from disinclination to learn our duty, or from impediments to grace caused by our sins; (3) that inability to resist temptations is no apology if our inability arise from our putting ourselves into such situations as render sin a necessity. Sin may be divided into three divisions, sins of ignorance, of infirmity and of malice. Vincible ignorance, such as that of the Jews in crucifying JESUS CHRIST, may be allowed in extenuation of sin, as also weakness caused by the sudden emotion of some passion, by the remains of some evil habit, and by the violence of some temptation. But sin committed with full knowledge, and recklessness without being carried away by passion, or ignorance, or habit is without excuse: and so also if a man do not endeavour to control his passion and check his evil habit.

Of sin unto death and sin not unto death.

All sin is either unto death or not unto death. The one by breaking off friendship with GOD causes loss of habitual charity, which is the spiritual life of our souls, and the principle of all good works bearing fruit unto life eternal. It is otherwise with sin not unto death.

Sin unto death consists in breaking GOD's Law in matters of great moment; sin not unto death in matters of little importance. The difficulty lies in distinguishing what is and what is not of importance. Four things may aid us in this investigation—the Word of GOD, the judgment of the Church, the agreement of Fathers and theologians, and natural reason enlightened by faith. Hence the great need of study for priests in order to be qualified for becoming confessors. Sins unto death either in regard to the gravity of their nature, or of their subject may lose their deadly character through the want of knowledge, or of attention on the part of those who commit them. Sin not unto death may become deadly—(1) Because of the actual disposition to sin on the part of the sinner, which would have led him equally to commit a great sin if he had had opportunity; (2) because of the bad intention with which the sin may have been committed; (3) because of the scandal which results; (4) because of the peril with which a person gives way to venial sin; (5) because of the contempt to which it exposed the Lawgiver; (6) because of the consciousness at the time entertained that sin was being yielded to; (7) because of the collection of a number of venial sins, which together constitute mortal sin.

Of distinctions between sins.

The Priest must notice that commands relating to faith are different from those which relate to hope, and that hence commands may be said to be different according as they relate to different virtues. And so again when they relate to different acts of the same virtue, as for example, to be present at divine service on festivals is one, and to abstain from all servile work another, though both belong to the obligation of religion. Hence sins committed against faith, hope and charity are of different kinds, as are also perjury, blasphemy, and sacrilege different offences against religion. Many different kinds of sins may thus be found in a single bad action, since the action may be opposed to several different commands. To steal a chalice is an offence against religion as well as against honesty. The priest must also distinguish between several sins of the same kind, in order to learn the number of sins of which his penitent is guilty. Three things constitute a distinction between sins of the same kind: acts of the will leading to the commission of sin; acts of other faculties by which the evil will is carried into execution: and the number of things which form the subject of the sins. When an act of sin meets with a moral interruption and is afterwards renewed, two sins are thereby committed: this must not be confounded with a sin which lies in abeyance because of a mere physical interruption. A person might in this way give over his sinful purpose and renew it twenty times, and so commit twenty sins. Simple interior acts of the evil will virtually cease and are morally interrupted by voluntarily turning aside the thoughts to some other subject. To revive the will thus turned aside is to commit a fresh act of sin, which is not the case when the will has pursued its way unchecked. Exterior acts of sin are not interrupted by mere cessation of mental recollection, but by an actual laying aside of the means which the sinner takes to accomplish his object. Nevertheless the exterior act of sin which takes some time in accomplishment may contain a great many criminal interior acts, such as rejecting remorse, fresh plans, and the like.

The acts of other faculties by which the evil will is carried into execution, as they are multiplied render man capable of several sins; (1) when they are opposed to different commands—thus to strike, slander and insult are three sins, but to strike twice, thrice, or more is but one sin; (2) when each act of the same kind springs from separate acts of the will, as if I intend to strike but once and strike twice and so on: and when I determine not to keep the Lent fast, and break it every day. Again, though several objects make up the subject sinful, we do not commit several sins so long as there is but one act of the will in regard to them all, all are opposed but to one command, and all relate to one person. Some, however, think that the number of persons injured does not increase the number but only the gravity of sin.

CHAPTER I.

WHAT MUST BE OBSERVED BY THE PRIEST IN GENERAL IN REGARD TO THE MORE OBVIOUS SINS AS WELL AS IN PARTICULAR IN REGARD TO PERSONS VARYING IN AGE, SEX, ESTATE, OR CONDITION OF LIFE?

THE more obvious sins are those called capital, and such as more ordinarily follow from them. The capital sins are seven in number, namely, Pride,[1] Covetousness, Sloth, Gluttony, Anger, Lust, and Envy. They are called capital because all other sins spring from them as from heads.

SECTION I.

What must be observed concerning Pride and its principal divisions, and the remedies thereof?

Pride in its sinful aspect, is the inordinate love of one's own superiority, and of self. I say, inordinate,

---

[1] Against these we pray in the seven petitions of the LORD's Prayer: Pride, being the desire of having *our* names exalted; Covetousness, the being enslaved to the king of this world; Sloth, the reluctance to do the will of GOD; Gluttony and drunkenness, the misuse of food; Anger, unforgivingness; Temptation, the special thorn in the flesh, impurity; Evil, envy, which is the special sin of the evil one. These have their counterparts in the Beatitudes, or at least in some of them.

because to aim at superiority itself in a well ordered manner is not evil, but may be an honourable act, so it be done in a right way and with a right object. But the inordinateness of pride consists in a person's aiming at his own superiority, or at a greater dignity than belongs to him, and when he entertains these aims by valuing himself beyond his real deserts, and by thus thinking or feeling himself to be more than he is. Hence the proud is said to inflate or puff up himself because he somehow aggrandises himself by greater aims and sentiments than befits him.

One sort of pride is *complete* and *perfect:* the other is *incomplete* and *imperfect.* *Complete pride* is that whereby a man is so elated as to refuse subjection to GOD and his superiors, wishing to live as he himself wills: or so behaves himself as if he did not possess all he has by the gift of GOD, or as if they proceeded from his own nature. I say, so behaves himself, because it is not necessary for him to hold this formal opinion (for this would be heretical), but it is enough for him to lay claim to the gifts of GOD as being his own property, and by not considering whence he has them to behave himself, as if he had them from himself—a thing very possible, just as a poor person who enjoys the property of others may be as elated as if he enjoyed his own. This pride, especially when entertained in the first manner, is devilish, and a most heinous sin, because it is a formal turning away from GOD. *Incomplete Pride* is that whereby any one without refusing subjection to GOD and his superiors, and apart from that kind of insubordination aims at, esteems and loves his own importance beyond what is suitable for him or belongs to him. It is called *incomplete*, not because it is not properly speaking pride, but because it does not reach to the highest pitch of pride, and is the first act of pride, which in itself is only venial sin: since according to a received rule, when the object is indifferent in itself, and so lawfully to be aimed at, as superiority, dignity, praise, riches, meat and drink, the inordinate longing for the same is not in itself more than venial sin. I say in itself, because accidentally it may become mortal sin, just like other venial sins, by reason of scandal or of the end proposed.[1]

The first-begotten daughters, as it were, of pride are *ambition, presumption, and vain glory*. *Ambition* is the inordinate desire of dignity or honour, as in the case where honour unsuitable to the person who desires it, or beyond his deserts, is the subject of his aim. As for example, when a person wishes to be honoured on account of learning or of riches, which he does not possess, or to be raised to an office for which he is ill qualified. *Presumption*, under this head, is the aiming at some undertaking beyond one's powers and abilities. *Vain glory*, so called, because it lacks a proper foundation, is the inordinate aiming at human esteem and praises, as when a person aims at winning a better character or opinion than he deserves, either through things indifferent, such as riches, beauty, and the like, which do not in themselves merit praise, or through pretended virtue and learning. Should such esteem and praise be sought by words, it is termed *Boasting*;

---

[1] It must be remembered that mortal sin is involved in all *thoughts* of evil, which are consciously accompanied by the will, when no necessity impels, and when inclination is strongly engaged to indulge in them.

if by real acts, it is evidenced by inventing new fashions and strange costumes for the *love of notoriety;* if by feigned acts, it is called *hypocrisy,* as when one does anything to appear good, when he is not. These are ordinarily only venial sins; but they become sometimes mortal through the circumstances of the case, or in their effect, as when one solicits an office for which he lacks the knowledge or fitness, and so might foresee the grievous injury likely to result therefrom to others. In like manner, should a woman seek to dress luxuriously to the great detriment of her family, or by running into debt which she could not pay; should a girl attire herself with the view of making herself attractive and seductive; should she not to appear prudish, attend nightly assemblies, though she foresees a likelihood of some grave fall; should she boast of committing a grievous sin, or should she communicate unworthily, not to seem to others less religious, and so on.

Other offsprings of pride there are, such as *pertinacity, discord, rash judgments,* yea all sins. *Pertinacity* is an inordinate sticking to one's own opinion. *Discord,* in this sense, consists in a conflict of wills respecting what is good to do for GOD or one's neighbour, or respecting the good which one is bound to will. *Dissension* is an inordinate contrariety of opinions, as when one dissents from another in something about which he ought to consent, or exceeds in the way in which he manifests dissent. *Contention* is an inordinate contest of words respecting some truth, as when one opposes himself to an acknowledged verity in a mere spirit of contradiction. *Quarrel* is an inordinate attack upon one private person by another, out of vehement passion after the manner of an animal. *Contumely* is the wrong unjustly done to a person's honour, as when one casts anything in the teeth of another with the view of inflicting dishonour, or unjust disgrace upon him. *Detraction* is the wrong unjustly offered to a person's character, often in secret. *Rash judgment* is a firm opinion of discredit attaching to one's neighbour without sufficient foundation. These are weighty or light sins according to the difference of the matter or of the manner. To these may be added *self-assertion, self-complacency, self-satisfaction, self-contemplation, self-consciousness. Low spirits* and *despondency* often rack the mind when the soul is suddenly forced to see its own weakness and sinfulness, and surprised to find itself so much further from GOD than it had supposed to be possible.

The origin of this most sad turmoil in the soul is, first, because one feels his own superiority by not having his attention aroused to his own imperfections, indigence, poverty, and dependence upon GOD, whence his own superiority appears to him to be greater than it really is; because good when taken simply by itself appears to be superior to what it is when it is taken with a mixture of imperfections. From this feeling there arises the love and value of his own superiority beyond what is just. And hence it at length happens that he thinks himself equal to great matters and to such as go beyond his tether. Hence he aims at dignity and other things, to which excellency recommends men, as though suitable to himself, and he covets esteem, honour, and praise at the hands of others; and if he fails to obtain them he is pained and gets angry; if he compares himself with others, he deems himself worthier, fitter, abler, and so reckons little of them, and despises them; depreciates the doings of others, exaggerates his own; shutting his eyes to his own defects he keeps them open to behold those of others; is envious when he sees others preferred to himself. And hence it is evident how a person who accuses himself of any act of pride should be examined; he should be asked, for example, with what object, and in whose presence he boasted himself, dissented, contended and solicited a particular office; and what he has cast in another's teeth, or said about his neighbour. He should be asked also as to the extent to which he has given way in thought, whether it has been a life-long habit of thought and the like.

Remedies for Pride.

(1) Persons liable to this sin should exercise themselves continually in acts of humility. They should call to mind such thoughts as these—" Why is earth and ashes proud?" "What hast thou which thou didst not receive?" "My glory I will not give to another."

(2) They should meditate upon their own origin. "Thou wast born amidst corruptions, thou livest amidst corruptions, thou wilt die amidst corruption. Who then art thou, and what wilt thou be? Thy body will be the food of worms, and thy soul, where will it be in eternity? What art thou? Of thyself nothing. What canst thou do? Of thyself nothing, nothing in natural or still less in supernatural things. Thou canst fall, rush into destruction, resist God, abandon thy only good; but without the supernatural aid of God thou

canst not rise again, nor love nor seek thy good. Like an infant who would become loathsome in the cradle but for the care of his mother; so it is with thee: of thyself thou canst neither think nor aim at what is needful for thee. At every moment thou needest the hand of GOD to sustain thee, else thou wouldest fall back into nothing: thou needest His aid in all things, nor can GOD by His omnipotence deliver thee from this neediness. What dost thou contribute towards the performance of good works? Nought beyond thy consent to the aid with which grace furnishes thee, and even that still mainly proceeds from GOD.

(3) They should consider what it is of which they are proud? Is it knowledge? This idea is often mistaken: thou knowest nothing beyond what faith teaches, or right reason, which is a light from GOD, dictates. Of almost all else thou art ignorant. Lucifer knew far more than thou, and who is so miserable as he? Or are riches the cause of thy pride? What are they but clay, a portion of earth, or the offspring of earth? They render thee neither greater, nor happier, but rather lure thee to ruin. Or is it praise, and the great esteem in which thou art held by men? Praise is but a breath: the esteem of man but a shadow, or phantom of another's brain, often false, capricious, and scarce ephemeral, whereby thou tendest to be none the greater; but thou art only what thou art in the sight of GOD and nothing more. Or is it noble birth? Thou as well as the peasant art of clay. Nobility is exemption from the laborious burden of the commons, combined often with authority over others. This thy forefathers purchased or won, but thou hast contributed

nothing to obtain it. Death will take it away, and then thou wilt equal be, or perchance beneath the peasant. Or is it personal beauty? This depends on the fugitive complexion, and well proportioned combination of flesh and bones. Thy body, however beautiful it may be, is but a whitened sepulchre, full of all loathsomeness and abominations.

(4) They should ponder the perils and losses incurred by pride. "Pride," says the Preacher (Ecclus. x. 13), "is the beginning of sin, and he that hath it shall pour out abomination; and therefore the LORD brought upon them strange calamities, and overthrew them utterly." CHRIST saith, "I saw Satan, as lightning, fall from heaven."

(5) They should account themselves vile, unworthy of every gift of GOD, and unprofitable servants, and deal with themselves as such: seek for mean things, as being more suitable to their own character: avoid praises, love, and rejoice at being despised, embrace rebuffs, slights, and the like.

(6) They should contrast themselves with the Angels and Saints of GOD. What art thou in comparison of them? What are they in comparison of GOD? What then art thou?

(7) They should weigh well the wickedness of pride; they should say to themselves, it makes thee a robber: therefore when the motions of pride arise regard thine own unworthiness, beseech GOD not to suffer you to be overcome. "Not unto us, O LORD, not unto us, but unto Thy Name be the praise." When fallen through pride, they should be as much confounded as a robber caught in the very act.

(8) They should pay attention to the notes of pride, which are, to trumpet their own praise, fish out the opinions of others about them, to be vexed at being neglected, and at ill success in their undertakings; to be jealous or envious when others are praised or act in a praiseworthy manner, and they should mortify themselves in such things, and by accepting such occurrences. They should say every now and then in the day, "My GOD I was nothing, I am nothing, I shall be nothing. Because man would be as GODS, GOD became man, and so became nothing." JESUS on the Cross is the continual reproach of the proud.

Spiritual Pride.

All prosperity tends to excite pride, and thus spiritual prosperity excites in beginners spiritual pride: as they conceive a certain satisfaction in the contemplation of their works and of themselves, so they display an empty eagerness in speaking before others of the spiritual life, and in teaching instead of learning it. They condemn others in their own minds, when they see that they are not devout in their way. Sometimes, like the Pharisee, they avow in words their thankfulness that they are not as other men are and despise them. All this is fed and encouraged by the devil, knowing that all which people do in this state is not only worthless but tending to sin. They think none good but themselves, and condemn and disparage others. If their spiritual masters check them, they rebel against them, and undervalue their spirituality, and seek for other masters who may think more highly of them and accommodate themselves to their fancy. They avoid and even hate those who would restrain them and lead them aright. They make many resolutions and accomplish little. Wishing that others may esteem their spirituality and devotion, they vent sighs, and groans, and outward observances and gestures, and are more rapturous in public than in private. Sometimes they are disquieted lest their confessor should think less of them: excuse instead of accusing themselves: go to other confessors at times lest their regular confessor should think worse of them; try that their confessor may think more highly of them, suggesting ideas of their being better than they are. Impatience with self is another sign of spiritual pride, either men become angry with themselves on account of their imperfections when they had thought themselves to be already saints, or wish to be delivered from their sins for the comfort of living in peace and not for GOD. Great enemies of other men's praise they are great lovers of their own. They know not that were GOD to relieve them of imperfections they would become more haughty than ever.

SECTION II.

What the Priest should observe in regard to Covetousness and its offspring.

Covetousness specifically taken is the inordinate desire of riches. As we have said of pride in its inchoate state, so covetousness may be said to be in itself venial. But it passes into a mortal sin, if it causes a grave violation of charity, justice, religion and the like. From it there springs a *hardness of heart towards the poor,* or an inordinate *anxiety about increasing or preserving riches, knavery, perfidy or treachery,* and the like. *Knavery* is a vicious cunningness of mind which, if it be expressed in words is termed *falsehood,* if in acts, *fraud. Treachery* or *perfidy,* is to deceive one's neighbour to his loss contrary to the trust placed by him in us, such as the *revealing of secrets, opening of letters* and the like. I say, *specifically taken,* because taken generally covetousness is the inordinate desire of any sensible thing, whether it be an object of utility or of pleasure.

Hence first, (1) if the penitent accuse himself of *hardness to the poor,* he should be asked if he have addressed them in harsh or abusive words? if he have refused them alms, when bound by charity to give them aid, as in the case of his neighbour's extreme or grievous necessity? if he have exacted what is due to him from them too severely?

(2) If he accuse himself of *fraud* or *falsehood,* whether it was accompanied with peril or loss to his neighbour?

(3) If he accuse himself of *violating secrecy;* whether the secret was entrusted to his keeping, or whether he only promised to keep it? The first involves not only a breach of trust but also of justice, being a violation of a contract, and its gravity depends upon the matter of the secret and upon the loss ensuing. The second depends upon the intention of the person who promises whether his obligation rests upon trust or promise only, and ordinarily is a breach of confidence only, and when no grievous loss or injury to charity follows is venial, and even no sin at all, if the revelation be made upon

good and sufficient reasons, as for example, when a person is interrogated by a superior or judge to whom he must reply, or when on being unjustly wronged by the party to whom he made the promise, he could not otherwise preserve his own character. And this applies in cases where silence might lead to some great loss being inflicted upon the community or upon innocent individuals by the person, who entrusted the secret, which could not be averted but by violating confidence. Nay, even though he might not have any intention of the kind, yet if danger were apprehended from another quarter, or some soul's hurt, this still holds, because no one can bind himself for such emergencies. Besides these cases attention ought to be paid to the point how far the promiser bound himself to endure any grave ill rather than reveal the secret, whether to suffer death and the like, or as usually happens, whether only to moral and human, or not to too difficult a keeping of one's word.

(4) If he confesses to have *opened or read letters*, he should be asked about the nature of such letters, for though, speaking strictly, it is mortal sin to open and read letters,[1] since it is not usually clear that they do not contain a matter of importance, or that the writer would not be annoyed at their being seen by another, yet it may accidentally be venial only, as for instance, if the letters were opened out of curiosity, and it was thought quite certain that they contained nothing of moment, and that the writer would not be much annoyed: or it may be no sin at all, as when there

---

[1] I.e. as an act of injustice to the writer and receiver, and as tending to destroy general confidence in human society.

is the express consent of the writer, or at least his silent and presumed consent, and when the opening takes place on reasonable grounds: as when legitimate authority prescribes it, or you feared great loss would ensure to yourself, or that harm was likely to accrue from the letters to another, which else you could not avert; for you may consult for your own advantage against injurious letters, though you ought not then to read more than serves that end. Care must be taken, moreover, not to come to a rash conclusion on the matter. So it should be said in regard to opened letters, which a person has lost by some mischance, or left in a public place unintentionally. Some casuists have thought that letters torn into fragments and thrown into a public place by the owner may be read, as being derelict, and having thereby ceased to be his property. But others hold that the owner by tearing them up showed his intention to preserve their secrecy, and therefore that strictly speaking it is wrong to unite torn letters and read them. And this rule applies to all writings which the holder wishes to keep secret; hence if any loss accrues to him by a person reading papers or letters in his possession, the reader is bound to make compensation.

Spiritual Covetousness.

Persons are sometimes not content with that measure of the Spirit which God gives; are disconsolate and querulous because they do not find the comfort they expected in spiritual things; are never satisfied with listening to spiritual counsels and precepts, with reading books which treat of their state, and spend more time in this than in doing their duty, having no regard to that mortification and perfection of inward spiritual poverty, to which they ought to apply themselves : load themselves with pictures, rosaries, and crucifixes, curious and costly; now taking up one, then another, now changing and then resuming them. At one time they will have them of a certain fashion, at another time of another, prizing one more than another, because more curious or costly. Some may be seen with an Agnus Dei, relics, and medals like children with coral. Attachment to these things in form, number, or curiosity is in direct opposition to poverty of spirit, which looks only to the substance of devotion, which makes use indeed of these things, but only sufficiently for the end, and disdains that variety and curiosity in them, for real devotion must spring from the heart, and consider only the truth and substance which the objects in question represent. All this is attachment and imperfection, and the soul which would go on unto perfection must root out that feeling utterly.

Remedies for Covetousness.

(1) Consider how unstable are all the riches of this world. " They all pass away as a shadow ;" (Wisdom v.) " they have slept their sleep, and all the men whose hands were mighty have found nothing." (Psalm lxxvi.) " Just as," says S. Augustine, " he that sees riches in his sleep, is rich while sleeping, but he will awake and find himself poor."

(2) What will become of the riches which I amass with so much anxiety, perhaps with the loss of my soul? Others at last will carry off the fruits of my labour. My heirs, or their sons will be prodigal, and then what benefit have I caused by my riches? Rather let me use diligence to obtain the necessaries of life for me and mine and trust to Divine Providence. GOD knows what is most conducive to every one's salvation.

(3) How poor all the goods of this world! They are external and cannot make their owner better or happy: but restless, forgetful of heaven, proud, lustful, a despiser of Divine things, cruel to the miserable. "There is not a more wicked thing than a covetous man, for such a one setteth his own soul to sale," says the Preacher. If riches could make a man happy, GOD would not bestow them on His enemies, on Heathen, Turks, Infidels, heretics and wicked people in general.

(4) The Only-begotten SON of GOD, "though He was rich, yet for our sakes became poor;" if there had been a better way to Eternal Life than the contempt of riches, He would have chosen it, and showed us how to enter upon it.

(5) Be merciful to the poor, and beneficent to thy neighbours. Contraries are cured by contraries. "He that giveth to the poor shall not lack; but he that hideth his eyes shall have many a curse." (Prov. xxviii.) "He that hath pity on the poor lendeth unto the LORD." (Prov. xix.) "Inasmuch as ye have done it unto the least of these My brethren, ye have done it unto Me." (S. Matth. xxv.) "To do good and to communicate forget not, for with such sacrifices GOD is well pleased." (Heb. xiii.)

Section III.

What the Priest should principally notice in regard to Impurity.[1]

Impurity is what may be termed disorder and irregular pleasure of the senses, such as produces vehement perturbation of bodily functions in any one contrary to what the Apostle terms "keeping his vessel in sanctification and honour," and leaves behind a feeling of degradation and shame. The pleasure which is simply sensitive is derived from some sensible object, which has no intrinsic tendency to excite evil passions, such as scent of flowers, hearing of music, taste of food, sight of modest pictures, touch of muslin, &c. That which is carnal is derived from some carnal object, directly (1) or remotely (2) connected with irregular pleasure. The first is due to impure touch, or look, and creates disordered emotions in the human system, such as arise out of contemplation of impure objects, or out of physical causes. The second is derived from a carnal object, which in itself is not impure though it may tend to excite pollution: such as the touch of a hand, or the sight of a beautiful face and the like, which may cause throbbing of the heart and slight perturbation of the animal spirits.

[1] It is scarcely needful to observe that the main object of entering into this subject of spiritual pathology, is to aid the priest to avoid needless and dangerous inquiries, and at the same time not to omit probing the wounds of sin when necessary for the patient's entire cure, often not only in soul but also in body and mind.

(3) Contemplation of an impure object may be practical or only speculative. Practical, when it represents the object in a delectable manner, that is to say, either by presenting it simply before us, or as being delectable to the sense, and so adapts it to the mind of the person who contemplates it. But the speculative, is that which represents the object as it is in itself without any delectation or making it present to the mind, as we may say superficially, such as happens to those who make a study of cases of conscience and distinction of sins with a view to confession, which is not intrinsically sin, any more than the delectation arising out of any newly acquired knowledge.

(4) Delectation connected with direct carnal impurity enjoyed with full deliberation and allowed of by oneself, or indirectly caused by oneself, is in unmarried persons mortal sin in every degree of it, because all such delectation is naturally directed to disorder in the human system, and is the beginning thereof: and this in unmarried persons, if voluntary or caused by oneself is mortal sin. This is so, because man's nature being corrupt through original sin he has no power, if he allows a lesser delectation, to hinder a greater, and so there is danger in his consenting to the lesser. Wherefore the right government of the human race requires that it be strictly prohibited, lest any corruption and confusion of the whole human race result, and prejudice be done to the end of marriage, which is the propagation of the human race, in order that the number of the servants and sons of GOD be increased.

(5) But sensitive delectations unconnected with

grossly carnal pleasure, and allowed out of no impure object, and originating from some virtuous cause, are not essentially sinful, so long as there is no danger of consent to impure delectation, such as from embraces, contact of hands, kisses out of ceremony or kindness, because these are not intrinsically immodest, nor closely allied to grossly carnal pleasure, and take place from some reasonable cause.

But persons should be warned that it is highly dangerous to indulge in such sensible delectations, since in corrupt human nature there is always reason to fear consent to impure feelings. When these delectations are owing to vanity or levity they are not blameless: and if the parties are conscious that they have thereby exposed themselves to the peril of consenting to impure feelings they grievously err, unless they take very great precautions to avoid the risk which they incur.

II. If the penitent accuse himself of impure thoughts he should be asked whether he has indulged in them voluntarily and with voluntary delectation? If he says "no," there is no need of further inquiry on this point. If he says, "I was sensible of delectation," he should explain whether he indulged in it voluntarily and with pleasure, or whether he instantly checked it? There is no harm in the being sensible of delectation provided there is no consent, but there is merit in strenuous resistance. If he say "yes," he should explain as to the subject, whether it be unchaste or obscene. For though every impure thought and delectation, specifically taken, is connected with grossly carnal pleasure, yet taken generically it is all which is unbecoming to an ingenuous and modest man, and is often confounded as being one and the same by inexperienced persons. If he confess consent to delectation in what concerns grossly carnal pleasure, he ought, unless it be otherwise clear, first, to explain whether he be a celibate or free from vows: next he should be inquired of as to (2) number and (3) kind. As to kind, because the sin of taking pleasure in impure thoughts is greater or less according as the subject is more or less gross. (4) Should he confess voluntary delectation of this character he should explain if he has committed any impure action, or willed to do so, if the opportunity were afforded him. And if so, what he has committed or willed, and with what persons; since the sin of thought becomes more or less heinous according as the act itself would be more or less sinful: as for example, to sin with a married person is more wicked than to sin with an unmarried.

III. If he accuse himself of sins of look, he should explain whether he voluntarily looked at an object intrinsically impure without any reasonable cause, or whether any delectation connected with gross carnal pleasure was voluntarily allowed. If so, it will be needful (as always in this matter) to know his quality, whether single, or married, or vowed to celibacy; yet probably if no desire has been indulged in he need not explain whether he be married, since it is doubtful whether a married person is under the same obligation as a person vowed to chastity. If nothing more has been committed than simple delectation, it would be unnecessary to explain the quality of the person looked at. If the object of his regards was not impure, inquiry should be made, as to what was his intention in looking for example upon women? whether it was out of curiosity only and with steadfast gaze. If it were out of curiosity only, and not with steadfast gaze and without any likely danger of consent to carnal delectation, venial sin only has been committed; for curiosity is a mere wish for closer inspection, which formed without reference to a special end, is venial sin. But if the look has been accompanied with carnal desire, it is evident that grave sin has been committed, when there has been full deliberation, or corrupt inclination. But if his looking have been free from such intent and been for the sake of politeness or of courtesy, so to say, he has committed no sin.

IV. If the penitent has caused in himself impure sensations or pollution, we must observe that the cause may be one of three kinds, self-efficacious, self-inefficacious, and accidental. The first is indulgence in impure thoughts or touch or sights, such as is naturally causative of evil: the second is light and playful touch of one of the other sex, or curious though not steadfast gaze upon the form of the person, amatory conversation, embraces, kisses, pressure of hands, and intertwining of the fingers—all which are not necessarily productive of evil. The last is riding, luxurious ways of resting or sitting, conversation with persons of the other sex, heating food and exciting drinks: all which have a remote influence in producing an evil effect.

And hence a decision must be formed how the penitent has sinned: for (1) he who aims at bringing on sexual excitement or pollution even by means of a lawful and in itself indifferent action, commits a grave sin, because he desires something in itself gravely opposed to chastity. (2) He who does anything likely in itself to cause impurity, is guilty of mortal sin, if he does it without a reasonable cause; since he who does anything which is likely to bring about a certain effect must have the effect laid at his door. I say *without reasonable cause;* for if there be reasonable cause, and there be no likely danger of consenting to impurity, such a thing may be done without blame. Thus a surgeon may do many things, else indecent, for the sake of curing disease : a confessor may study cases of conscience : a theological professor for the purpose of instructing others may show when and how sin is incurred in this or that matter, and how sins should be confessed, although it may be foreseen that irregular excitement may arise in consequence. Hence all things, which, if indulged in without any reasonable cause, such as thoughts, touch, looks and the like, are certain of themselves to lead to an impure conclusion, involve mortal sin. While on the other hand things not necessarily causative of ill results, such as jests, which though of questionable tendency are not positively obscene, touch, and kisses out of sportiveness, though accompanied with delectation yet without any consent unto it —these bring slight blame. Unless indeed experience teaches that there is likelihood of the person consenting to delectation in them, in which case it would be different. And so, if a person knew that by some casual act, though there were no impure intention nor consent, he was likely to incur irregular excitement or pollution, he sins gravely though not against chastity : yet no sin is incurred if the act be good or at least not bad—at any rate, if it be called for by necessity or any just reason of doing or persevering in it. This is explained (1) because an accidental cause is not truly the cause of all that results from it: (2) because an effect which is produced contrary to intention is not put down to one's account, unless he were bound to avoid the cause. But there is no such obligation whenever the cause arises out of necessity, or out of something which may be classed as good or useful: for then we have right on our side, and the effects which follow are rather suffered than produced by us. Otherwise we should be forced to leave very many acts undone, though useful, good and necessary, and this would tend to the injury of the human race and would be intolerable. I say, he does not commit grave sin, at least not against chastity: for if his act were of grave heinousness in opposition to another virtue, the mortal sin would be committed against it, as if for example a person should get drunk with the prospect of consequent impurity.

At the same time the law of purity is not infringed by many acts which being indifferent in themselves nevertheless often lead to inconvenience. Hence impure feelings may arise in the mind without inflicting any stain of sin, as when a person is called upon to study cases of conscience, or hear confession connected with this subject, or to examine or heal a wound, as in the case of a surgeon or nurse. They may arise also out of casual contact or conversation with one of the other sex or out of a particular posture. In all these cases care must be taken that there be no consent to sinful emotions, and that such acts as we have described as dangerous in their results be allowed only on reasonable and just grounds.

V. If a penitent accuse himself of impure words he should explain his intention or feeling at the time, the way in which he uttered them and before whom. It is possible that they might be due to coarse vulgarity, sportiveness and .levity, without any inordinate affection, in which case the sin is less. But if they be accompanied with impure feelings, and with an impure object, the sin becomes greater according to the condition of the person himself or of the person in view. If the words have been very serious violations of purity, much will depend upon the number and kind of persons before whom they were spoken, according to the scandal which is likely to result and the ill effects likely to be produced in his own mind or in those of his hearers. For he may thereby have excited in himself or in others a vicious inclination, of which the devil may take advantage hereafter for the purpose of temptation. "*Woe to that man,*" it should be said to such a penitent, "*by whom offences come.* Thou wilt have to give account for the souls whom thou in this way leadest to falls and perchance eternal misery. According to the number of persons whom thou hast set a bad example and to whom thou hast been a stumblingblock, so numerous are thy sins. Still worse if they had been innocent and as yet scarcely knew how to beware of evil, being still in the nursery of piety, and easily influenced for evil or good." Should the penitent say, that it was in the presence of married persons, he should be reminded that if any ill result followed, his responsibility would be increased so much the more. Should he say, "I did not give utterance to any impure words, but I laughed at them," he should be asked whether it was accompanied with sinful delectation, whether he laughed out of natural impulse, or voluntarily and deliberately continued to laugh and thoroughly entered into the meaning of the words. He should be warned that by laughing at impure words he urged others to prolong their indecent language with greater boldness : and that by giving them an opportunity of such prolongation to the danger of lapsing into sin on the part of himself or of others, or by giving them his countenance, he sins grievously by way of scandal, though there may be no inward approval on his part, since to give outward sanction to mortal sin is mortal sin. This is equally true of impure songs, gestures, sights, readings. It is a grievous fault to read such books when there is any likely danger of impure consent: though not so, if there be no peril of this sort and curiosity be the sole motive, though at the same time it is dangerous so to do, except when there is a good reason for reading them as well as a good intention in reading them.

If nocturnal pollutions during sleep be confessed the penitent should be questioned whether they were intended by him to take place, whether he did anything to excite or cause them proximately or remotely, and whether on waking he wholly consented to them. Any one of these contingencies would involve a grievous sin; otherwise as being involuntary there would be no fault incurred, except such as might arise out of partial consent. Pollutions of this kind are natural or unnatural—the former being like any other effort of nature by way of evacuation, and therefore in themselves sinless; but the latter being forced and voluntary, the result of evil imaginations, conversations, readings, and sensual excesses, and therefore sinful. The penitent is to be told that his efforts must be directed to be simply passive, and to avoid being active, when such assaults are imminent, and folding his hands calmly together, calling on JESUS to help him, to pray against indulgence in impure delectations.

Spiritual Impurity

May be so called not because it is so in fact, but because it is felt and experienced sometimes in the flesh owing to frailty when the soul is the recipient of spiritual communications. Impure motions of sensuality are felt very often by some in the midst of their spiritual exercises and when they cannot help themselves, even when they are deeply absorbed in prayer or engaged in receiving the Sacraments of Penance and the Holy Eucharist. These motions, not being in their power, proceed from one of three sources:

(1) *Sensible sweetness* in spiritual things in persons of delicate constitutions. As that which in man is spiritual, the higher part of his nature delights in GOD, so that which in him is sensual, the lower part, is moved towards sensible gratification, and while the spirit prays, the flesh makes itself felt by rebellious agitations.

(2) *The Evil Spirit*, who when the soul is engaged in prayer, or disposing itself thereto, disquiets it by the foul movements of man's lower nature, and so often dissuades him from prayer, as being the time when the

devil assails him by unholy images in close relation with certain spiritual things and persons. Sometimes nothing can be done to relieve this state of things until the bodily health is improved.

(3) *Fear* of these depraved motions which men have entertained before they are actually conceived by them.

(4) *Spiritual friendships*—when the remembrance of such affections does not increase recollection and love of GOD, but leaves behind remorse of conscience, in which case they spring out of sensuality, whereby earthly love increases and the love of GOD cools down.

Sometimes when spiritual persons are speaking of spiritual things, or doing good works, they are conscious of a certain energy and elasticity arising out of the recollection of persons whom they have seen or loved, and they go on with a certain measure of human joy.

Remedies against Impurity.

(1) To pray humbly for the gift of continence, confessing that it is only GOD Who can enable the penitent to keep himself pure.

(2) To submit with humility to the laws and order of GOD. It is the humble obedience of the spirit which obtains the subjection of the flesh.

(3) To abstain from excess in food or drink, since what is taken beyond what is required for bodily sustenance brings on temptations to sexual delectation, which are kept in check by fasting, abstinence, and moderation. Next to GOD's grace this is the principal remedy.

(4) To keep strict watch over the senses and never

to expose oneself rashly to danger of temptations, in looking, hearing, touching, reading, and the like.

(5) To avoid idleness and familiar conversations with those of the other sex; not to court them and pay them attention, but to observe the utmost rules of modesty and decorum, when thrown into company.

(6) To read pious books, meditate upon the Passion of the LORD and upon the four last things. To seek frequently for Absolution and often to receive the Holy Eucharist; to use discipline, or hairshirt, after the example of the Apostle who says, "I keep under (or render livid) my body and bring it into subjection."

(7) To walk in the presence of GOD and when the temptation knocks at the door to consider—"GOD sees me;" or to say, "LORD, I love Thee," and to turn the mind in a different direction. Against this sin the only preventative is flight, "if," as says S. Augustine, "thou wouldst be victorious." Or fortify the forehead or breast with the sign of the Cross with strong confidence in CHRIST.

(8) To treat the enemy with silent contempt, for he assails the timid with greater ferocity, but flees from the courageous and from him that relies upon GOD, not being able to bear being despised.

(9) To have recourse to CHRIST as Leader with all trust, as the lover of purity, saying, "LORD, I am Thine, save me, I beseech Thee; if Thou leavest me, I perish."

(10) To think of the ever Virgin Mary and her purity, and to beseech GOD to hear her intercessions in behalf of those who long for likeness to her immaculate example.

(11) To bring before his imagination a corpse in a state of corruption, as though it addressed him in these words: "Remember my judgment, for thine also shall be so, yesterday for me, to-day for thee."

(12) To meditate on the evil results of impurity—how it ruins the health, and debilitates the mind; how it blinds the understanding, and degrades the soul, and levels with the brutes, creates disgust of heavenly things, horror of the world to come, love of this world and hatred of GOD, &c.

SECTION IV.

Of Envy and its offspring.

Envy is grief or pain caused by the welfare of one's neighbour in proportion as it is felt to take from the excellence of the person who envies; whence envy is said to be derived from *in* and *video*, because the envier cannot behold another's welfare without pain, but is pained by another's merit or power, because he thinks his own excellence is thereby diminished. Envy is classified as mortal sin, as opposed to charity, and may be venial through the smallness of the subject matter of it—as when a boy is grieved on account of the praise bestowed on a fellow-scholar, because he thinks his own excellence to be lessened thereby.

The daughters of Envy are five: (1) Detraction or hasty judgments; (2) Joy at the ills which happen to our neighbour; (3) Desire that evil may befall him; (4) Backbiting, which is secret talking against him, naturally tending to break up friendships, and to generate discord, whence it is a weightier mortal sin, generally speaking, than detraction, since it destroys friendship which is more valuable than reputation; (5) Contemptuousness, which is an unjust attack upon the honour of another, and this, if defects or faults are cast up to another, whether present or absent, to undeserved disgrace, is termed reproach; if cast in his teeth is called insult; if he be exposed, either present or absent, by deeds or words, to ridicule, is termed derision; but if with some irony or disguised banter he be made the subject of laughter, it is called scoffing; if, lastly, by gestures or other unbecoming bodily motions, it is called mocking.

Sadness on account of the good fortune of our neighbour may occur in four ways: for (1) one may grieve on account of another's good fortune, not because it is good for him, but because it may be bad for others, as in the case when a person is elevated to such a position as may enable him to crush the innocent or injure the commonwealth, and this sadness is allowable, but not in the case where such fear or opinion is illfounded, or where the sadness is caused by a dread that delinquents may be righteously punished. (2) A person may grieve on account of another's good fortune, not because he is so fortunate, but because the grief arises from the thought of his own misfortune; this feeling is termed emulation, and is good if it relates to spiritual qualifications, as when any one on seeing the merits of another grieves that he himself does not possess them; for thus it is that men are excited to imitation; but when it relates to temporal blessings, it may be good, if they be suitable and with a due end in view; but it may be bad if they be unsuitable and aimed at with a bad end in view. (3) A person may grieve on account of another's good fortune, because he is unworthy of it. This feeling is called indignation and may be right, as in a case where a person grieves on account of the good fortune of another when he is incapable of making a good use of it; for example, of discharging the duties of an office, or because it has been conferred upon him unjustly. It may also be wrong, as in the case of spiritual or temporal goods, which GOD permits sinners to enjoy. (4) One may grieve on account of the good fortune of his neighbour, in so far as the latter equals or surpasses the former in such good fortune, and this is envy and a bad feeling, because he grieves over what should cause joy, namely, his neighbour's good. This is true of the case in which a shopkeeper grieves over the concourse of customers to a neighbouring merchant while they leave him; yet it is possible that there may be no grievous sin in this, because he may grieve on account of his own loss, and not solely on account of the profit of another. In this case there is only lawful emulation, and such grief often is caused when many flock together to obtain a benefice, or scholars undergo an examination for the headship. We may say in general that sin is incurred only when the grief is directed against the person who succeeds better than ourselves, and not when it is elicited solely by the consideration of our own loss of dignity or income.

Hence if the penitent accuse himself of envy, those feelings, which are often confounded together, must be distinguished, and he should be asked under which feeling he thinks his envy to range itself. And it is all one whether he accuse himself of hatred towards his neighbour, and of rejoicing at his misfortune, or of impotent desire that it should befall him. For hatred is two-fold—personal and not personal. Personal hatred is termed enmity, when a person wishes evil to befall another out of the dislike he bears him, accounting that to be good for himself which is evil for the other. And this is grievous or not according to the difference of the subject matter. Hatred differs from envy in that the tendency of the former is to ill as such, whereas the tendency of the latter is to good, as having regard to what derogates from one's own excellence. The second or hatred not personal is that which regards not the person but some quality in the person, and is called the hatred of disgust, which causes me to shun the person of my neighbour not because of my personal dislike, but because of some adscititious quality which may be injurious to the community or to myself or to another. Thus I may hate another or wish him harm because he is troublesome to me or opposes me, or is possessed of great power which is hurtful to me. This hatred, so long as it does not reach the person but only affects the quality of a person, may be allowed, if the order of charity be maintained, but if it be violated, such hatred becomes illicit. And the order of charity is infringed if we wish a greater evil to happen in order that a less may be avoided.

Whence (1) it is unlawful to desire a neighbour's death in order that we may avoid a special temporal evil.

(2) It is unlawful to wish one was dead in order to get rid of a cough or little headache.

(3) It is unlawful for a son to be glad of the death of his father, or to wish for it on account of the inheritance which would consequently descend to him.

(4) A father may lawfully desire the death of his son who is now in a state of grace, when he has a clear prognostication of his being likely to die a reprobate.

(5) I may lawfully desire the death of any tyrant, rather than that he should oppress the Church, because the consideration of spiritual good is to prevail over that of temporal, and that of public good over that of private.

(6) I may lawfully desire the death of a person by whom I have every reason to foresee that I shall be unjustly put to death.

(7) I may lawfully desire my own death when I foresee that by living I shall incur great spiritual damage.

(8) One may lawfully desire his own death rather than to live and offend God any more, or have the bliss of futurity too long delayed, or in order that he may avoid some misery which is worse than death, such as perpetual imprisonment, or the entire loss of his goods. And this is true, generally speaking, of cases when a greater ill is to be avoided, since this evil is not desired as evil, but as preventive of some greater evil. And this may occur when one is grieved at another's good fortune. For we may feel grief or joy lawfully about the same thing upon different grounds: thus—a son may grieve on account of his father's death because it is accompanied with evil results to himself, but rejoice on the same account, because he perceives that it has been ordered by God for the furtherance of his father's

salvation. So CHRIST also willed to be sorrowful on account of His approaching death because it was a natural evil, and yet He endured it joyfully, despising the shame, and willed it to take place, because it was ordained by the will of the FATHER for our redemption. We add, as pertaining to this subject, the case of one who has suffered some wrong from another person, and feels for a long time displeasure and aversion. This feeling must be purged away by prayer and charitable offices; and as long as it is involuntary is no sin, but if voluntary, inquiry must be made whether the person who entertains this feeling has wished evil to befall the wrong-doer or has willed to inflict evil upon him.

Spiritual Envy

Suggests emotions of displeasure at the contemplation of other men's goodness. People dislike to be outstripped by others on the spiritual road, and cannot bear to hear them praised. They are vexed with other men's virtues, and are sometimes unable to restrain themselves from contradicting the reports of their excellence: they depreciate them as much as they can, and feel acutely because they themselves are not thought so well of, for they wish to be preferred above all others. This is a failure in the charity which "rejoices in the truth." There is a holy envy at the virtues which others have, but this is only to grieve that we do not possess them, but to rejoice at the same time that they possess them, and that GOD is served at any rate perfectly by them, and so loses the less by our imperfections.

Remedies against Envy.

The penitent must

(1) Ask of GOD to bestow sincere love of his neighbour.

(2) Rejoice at his neighbour's good fortune, as he would over his own.

(3) Perform acts of kindness towards him of whom he is envious; pray for his good; thank GOD for benefits conferred on him as if on himself.

(4) Have little regard for worldly things, and account himself unworthy of GOD's gifts, but his neighbour worthier of them all.

(5) Think that his neighbour is not the worse off nor himself better off because he is envious.

(6) Nay, think that he is worse off himself, since whoso loves his neighbour shares thereby his good fortune, and obtains a reward in heaven which is forfeited by envy.

(7) Consider that envy makes us like to the devil, since we thereby grudge GOD the glory which accrues from our neighbour's good fortune: for from it is manifested GOD's goodness, wisdom, clemency and compassion.

(8) Consider that the envious man is a self-torturer to no purpose and with much loss.

(9) Consider that at last he must resolve to wish well to his neighbour or he will not be saved.

(10) Consider that CHRIST sought his salvation with so much love—how then shall he wish his fellow-creature to be deprived of good?

Section V.

Of Gluttony and Drunkenness.

I. Gluttony is the inordinate desire of and indulgence in meat and drink.

This inordinate desire is fulfilled in five ways:

(1) In quantity, by taking more than is convenient.

(2) In quality, by desiring food of too rich or sumptuous a kind.

(3) In mode, by eating too greedily or voraciously.

(4) In time, by eating too often or without reasonable cause.

(5) Contrary to the end, as when a person eats solely for the pleasure of it.

To understand this more clearly we must observe that to eat till we are satisfied, may mean that we eat only so much as is requisite for satisfying our hunger, and this is no sin. But it may also mean that we eat more than is required to sustain nature or is convenient. And in this consists the fulfilment of inordinate desire, because meat and drink were ordained solely for the sustenance or convenience of nature. The same quantity does not suit all nor the same person for a continuance, but it should be adapted to the necessity, infirmity, utility, person, time and place: and the same may be said of quality, which should be proportioned to the state, condition, powers, and person, so that no excess should take place.

(2) If one eat on account of the pleasure he receives from it, he sins, because he perverts the order of nature

by directing the end to the means, and not the means to the end. For GOD has annexed pleasure to the use of meat and drink, that we may be led on thereby to the use of them. If the pleasure which is felt in the use of meat and drink be referred to an honourable end, as for example to sustain nature, which is the real use of it, no sin is committed, for it is for this end that GOD has willed that pleasure should be attached to the use of meat and drink: whence we may say that such a one does not eat and drink for the mere sake of pleasure, but for the sake of sustenance only, to which he refers the pleasure. But he is said to rest on the pleasure, as the end to be aimed at, who eats on that account only, and takes enjoyment in it; and this is held to be done by him who eats and drinks to excess or to such an extent as is not necessary nor useful to sustain life. And this is true of other sensual delectations, because the rule of all delights in this life is that some necessity, utility or convenience of life is involved in them.

II. Excess in food (as opposed to abstinence, the virtue that according to the law of reason moderates the appetite, use and pleasure in food,) is to speak generally a venial sin; this is true of excess in drink (as opposed to soberness, a virtue which according to the law of reason moderates the appetite, use and pleasure in drink,) unless in both cases the result of such excess be to take away the reason. The reason of this is that they are acts relating to indifferent things which may be honourably desired. I say generally speaking, because accidentally mortal sin may be involved, e.g.

(1) If one seriously injure his health by immoderate

use thereof, as when he contracts gout or any grave defects,—since man is not lord of his own body, but only minister and guardian,—whence he would not only sin against self-charity, whereby he is bound as much to avoid doing himself harm as to avoid injuring another, but also against the law of GOD.

(2) If he render himself incapable of discharging important duties.

(3) If he eat and drink till he become sick, or take means to evacuate the stomach for the purpose of eating and drinking anew; for this is to sink below the brutes.

(4) If he thereby become unable to discharge his debts, or make due provision for his family.

(5) If he make pleasure in eating and drinking a main object, so as to be ready to offend GOD, provided that he may ever enjoy it, and so that "his god is his belly."

(6) If he cause grievous scandal by his excess, or expose himself to the probable danger of committing some grievous sin.

Finally, if he eat human flesh or blood for pleasure's sake, or without necessity, being a thing repugnant to the natural instinct even of barbarians.

III. The principal excesses which are most commonly indulged in, are gormandizing and intoxication. Gormandizing is the inordinate use of food, or eating at unseasonable times. It is called also surfeiting, and is taken to mean frequently repeated acts of drinking and voracity. Intoxication is excess in drinking, so as to produce violent perturbation or loss of reason. It is divided into entire or partial. Partial intoxication is excess in drink to the extent of some perturbation of reason, while still retaining such power of using it, as suffices for moral actions: this power may still remain, though the imagination may be more or less disturbed, the tongue stammer, the feet totter, the eyes see double, or the house seem to go round and round, and so entire intoxication may be thought as yet to be incomplete, provided the person be still able to distinguish between moral good and evil. Entire intoxication is excess in drink to the extent of violent deprivation of reason and of the direct power of using it. Many theologians divide entire intoxication into formal and quasi-material: formal being excess in drink for the sake of pleasure, even to loss of reason; material being excess in drink without just cause even to the loss of reason. The first is called formal, because as sobriety is a virtue which moderates pleasure in drink; so intoxication, which is opposed to it, must be excited by pleasure. Others hold that intoxication through drink is opposed to sobriety even though it is not indulged in for the sake of pleasure, as when one drinks for his friend's sake, though disliking to do so all the time, even to loss of reason: or if two persons unwillingly engage in a drinking match even to loss of reason, because it seems to belong to sobriety to moderate even such a use of drink. Finally, some call all excess in intoxicating drinks intoxication, though there be no perturbation of reason, and call all excess in food gormandizing; but this is inaccurate, for it would be as just to say this of a person who drank largely of water for the sake of cooling himself, as of a person who exceeded only so far.

IV. Partial intoxication is not in itself more than a venial sin, since it is not a grievous ill to disturb the reason slightly by excess in drink, provided the use of reason be retained in relation to moral good and evil. But formal and entire intoxication is deadly sin, at any rate if it cause the loss of reason for some time, say for an hour. The reason is (1) that it is a grievous disorganization and deformity, without just cause, and specially for pleasure's sake, to deprive oneself of the direct power of using his reason, by which man has been raised above the brute, and so to render him incapable of performing in a human manner the duties which pertain to virtue, business, and necessities of soul and body, and so to debase the image of GOD and degrade it to the condition of brutes. (2) That no one is master of his own reason, but that every one is only steward and tenant thereof: therefore as it is mortal sin to cut off one's hand without just cause, because no one is master of his own body, so it would be mortal sin to deprive oneself of the use of reason and of its direct power without just cause, inasmuch as reason is the greatest good which man possesses and distinguishes him from the brutes. (3) That it is mortal sin to deprive oneself against self-charity of great natural goods, so also it is the same if one deprive himself violently of the use of reason and of its direct exercise. Whence whoso intoxicates himself by drink for pleasure's sake, sins against charity and sobriety; against charity, by depriving himself of a great natural good without just cause; against sobriety, because he deprives himself of it in such a manner. It is no argument against this to say that one may deprive himself by sleep of the use of reason, both because this deprivation is not violent and repugnant to nature, but natural, instituted by the Author of nature for the restoration of animal forces and spirits; and also because the power of using reason is not so taken away by sleep, but that man may recover it as soon as he awakes, and so he may always be able to act in a human manner, which is impossible in the case of intoxication.

The signs of complete intoxication are—

(1) When one has so disturbed the use of reason that he can no longer distinguish between moral good and evil.

(2) When one cannot remember on the morrow what he did to-day, what he said, how he got home.

(3) When he does what he is not accustomed to do in full possession of his faculties, such as to use impure or absurd language, though he is otherwise modest and sensible; when he swears, blasphemes, or throws the family into confusion, though he is at other times moderate and gentle. Yet even with these two last provisos when one is able to retain the distinction of what is lawful and unlawful, though his limbs shake, intoxication is not complete.

(1) One is not excused from mortal sin if he deprives himself of reason through excess in drink for pleasure's sake, or without reasonable cause with full knowledge of what he is about: since that is essential evil.

(2) He sins grievously, who without intending to become intoxicated drinks as much as he can without any regard to whether drunkenness is the consequence or not.

(3) So too he who has every reason to think or suspect that drunkenness will be the result, yet goes on drinking, because he exposes himself to the danger of it, and so by interpretation wills it.

(4) Also when he can avert the danger and neglects to do so, though loss of reason succeed in an hour or two; and when he could be on his guard as having some well-grounded suspicion of its coming to pass, and yet makes no wise resolve against it. S. Thomas teaches that he who is often drunk may always be on his guard, or at least has it in his power and ought to be so, and so always sins mortally.

(5) So too he who knows that when he has drained one glass he is usually intoxicated if he goes out of doors, but not if he does not go out, may indeed drink a glass without grievous sin, provided he has a firm purpose not to go out, and be in the habit of keeping to it—else he may not.

(6) So too if he know by experience that by going to a certain house or company and drinking in this manner he is wont to get intoxicated ten out of twenty times, he sins as often as he does it without making due provision against it, even though he do not chance to be intoxicated; since he exposes himself to the formal danger or at least to the probable danger of drunkenness.

(7) It is mortal sin to become intoxicated by tobacco, opium, and the like, because reason and its direct power are thereby overthrown. This is a different kind of intoxication from that induced by drink, and hence ought to be explained in confession.

(8) It is allowable to drink for the purpose of making

merry, but not to become intoxicated in order to drive away grievous sorrow, nor in order to cause insensibility to pain, as in the case of a surgical operation, because drink is ordained solely for the sustenance of the vital powers. It is probable that a person may, when ordered by a medical man, become inebriated, if it be necessary for the cure of a grievous complaint, just as it is lawful to suffer amputation under the same circumstances, and the rule of temperance allows one to take what is essential to preserve life. Hence many infer that we may give way to intoxication when urged upon us with the alternative of a mortal blow, and when it is the only chance for escaping some deadly disease. Others, however, deny that there is any analogy between the loss of a limb and the loss of reason, and affirm that the loss of reason is not a means provided for the preservation of life—nay, that intoxication is very injurious to bodily health. Reason is not, they urge, to be subordinated to bodily life, and therefore to destroy reason for the benefit of the body is to invert the order of nature. Moreover, they do not concede that there is any value in the argument that the loss of life is a greater physical evil than the temporary loss of reason, if loss of reason be not a natural means for the preservation of life.

(9) If one invites another to drink out of friendship or politeness, though he foresees a great probability of his getting drunk, he sins grievously, since he invites him to essential evil, such as the other cannot indulge in without sin, and so leads him into intoxication, or at least to the very likely peril of it. The same may be said of those who challenge or compel others to drink

as much as they do themselves, since they involve themselves or others in a probable danger of intoxication, if not there and then, yet at any rate afterwards, which is grievous, even though sleep may supervene. In like manner they commit grievous sin who go on supplying those who are intoxicated or who are nearly so with wine, or who do not hinder others from becoming intoxicated when they can easily do so. But if one foresee that by refusing drink to another he may be the cause of some blasphemous language, the drunkenness must be given in to, inasmuch as it is a less sin than blasphemy. Nor must any one be kept from drunkenness by violence, unless some extreme evil be impending, since it is not the duty of a private individual to use force for that end.

(10) If any one by persuading another to drink be the cause of mischief which he must have foreseen, such as neglect of his proper duties and business, so as to be unable to pay his just debts, he is bound to make compensation to those whom he has injured. And if he leads another by his example to get drunk, he commits the sin of causing a brother to offend, unless indeed the offender was a person who would be likely to become intoxicated of his own accord.

(11) If one cause a fool or a child as yet incapable of reason to be once or twice intoxicated, his sin is not of a grievous character, because he does not deprive him of reason, but should he do this often, he would be the means of his acquiring a bad habit and of his injuring his health, and the sin incurred would be in proportion to the injury caused.

(12) It is sinful for an officer of justice to cause a

person to become intoxicated when charged with a crime, or when condemned to death.

(13) The question has been raised whether a person unjustly imprisoned may give his guard drink to enable him to escape; or whether a person may give traitors drink with the view of discovering their treachery in regard to the betrayal of a fortress: and upon these points authors are not agreed.

Spiritual Gluttony.

This consists in *exterior without interior mortification*, and in striving after spiritual sweetness rather than after pure and true devotion, and thereby men overstep the limits of moderation by killing themselves with penances and weakening themselves by fasting. They take upon themselves more than they can bear without rule or advice, conceal their austerities from those to whom they owe obedience and even practise them in defiance of express prohibitions. They dislike the *penance of reason and obedience* and undertake bodily penances merely for the sweetness which attends them. Not understanding that obedience is better than sacrifice they try to persuade their confessors to direct them according as they have set their hearts upon doing; and when contradicted become fretful, faint-hearted, and relapse. They think they are not serving GOD when they are thwarted in serving Him after the devices and desires of their own hearts. It is the same in regard to frequent communion. They try to communicate oftener than their confessor advises or would advise, if he knew all, being more anxious to communicate than to make good and profitable communion. In communicating they try to find some sensible sweetness in the act, instead of worshipping in humility and praising GOD within themselves. If they fail in obtaining this sweetness they think they have done nothing, and know not that the least benefit of the most Holy Sacrament is that which touches the senses; and that the invisible grace it confers is far greater, for GOD frequently withholds these sensible favours from men that they may fix the eyes of faith upon Himself. But these people will feel and taste GOD as if He were palpable and accessible to them, not only in Communion, but in all their other acts of devotion.

Hence even when praying they think the whole business of prayer consists in sensible devotion, and if they fail in obtaining it they are cast down, and under the idea that they have done nothing. This effort after sweetness and disappointment in missing it destroys true spirituality and devotion, which consist in perseverance in prayer with patience and humility, mistrusting self solely to please GOD. When such people miss this sweetness in prayer and in other religious acts they begin to shrink from them and sometimes give them up altogether, being led by their inclination and not by reason. They waste their efforts in seeking spiritual consolations, and taking up fresh good books and meditations in this pursuit. This spiritual gluttony enfeebles the will so that it becomes incapable of great acts of self-denial, and revolts from the rugged path of the Cross.

Remedies against Gluttony and Drunkenness.

(1) Avoid as much as possible whatever excites the appetite, such as pleasant, varied, and seasoned food. If you cannot do this, at least do not take enjoyment in food, but use it only for the natural end.

(2) At table always take less than you require, at least what is less pleasing to the palate, though you might lawfully take it; so you will learn to restrain your appetite and grow in grace.

(3) Always retain full control over your appetite; hence, when more inclined to take food, pause or eat slowly.

(4) Consider how degrading it is to descend to the level of the brutes by being the slave of pleasure; yet they cannot be compelled by violence to eat more than nature demands.

(5) Consider how many ills spring from this sin. Bodily disease, mental obscuration, extinction of holy desires, rebellion of the flesh against the spirit, and all by ministering the provocations of appetite! who would strengthen his enemy to his own loss?

(6) Consider the vileness of the things for which the appetite craves; and the goal to which all superfluities tend.

(7) Set before your eyes the pattern of our Blessed LORD and of the Blessed Virgin, and consider with what moderation and temperance their meals were conducted, and with what common food they were satisfied.

(8) And above all, weigh well at a time when you do not feel hungry or thirsty your past experience, the

advantages or disadvantages resulting from the quantity or quality of diet; then subtract what is superfluous and avoid what you have found to be hurtful, and do not allow yourself to be drawn away from your rule by pleasure. If appetite urge you, consider that if you yield to it, you will become too weak to conquer it; if you do not yield, you will offer to GOD a pleasing sacrifice, to Whom if you deny the little which He requires, He will as you deserve deny you grace to overcome greater difficulties. This slight mortification will not deprive you of life nor injure your health. If it chance that you are overcome, blush for having succumbed to so slender a delight, and punish yourself by a severer act of abstinence. In order to settle your dietary it is expedient from time to time to subtract even more, as experience teaches us what quantity is necessary and what is superfluous for ordinary purposes.

(9) If you wish to indulge a little more for the sake of innocent recreation or companionship, for the avoiding of excess and surfeiting, drink slowly at first so as not to upset the stomach, but to strengthen its tone and so turn the gifts of GOD to a good purpose : then look well to it that your blood does not get heated, that your head keeps cool, your appetite subservient to reason. If on the contrary your appetite gains the mastery, and you be less able to restrain it, in this case you must curb it. In short, when at any time you chance to become exhilarated, take heed not to exceed or to let appetite trip you up. Learn by experience not to abuse the gifts of GOD in so base a manner. So shall your appetite be subject to you, and you shall reign over it.

Section VI.

Of Anger, and of the cursing and blasphemy consequent thereupon.

I. Anger generically is desire of revenge. This may take place without sin and be justifiable: as when a father is moderately angry with the faults of his child, a superior with those of his inferior, a teacher with those of his pupil, so they respectively chide them or punish them on that account. But taken specifically, anger is an inordinate desire of revenge. This inordinateness may appear either in the manner, as when vengeance is sought for with too much heat, or in the object, as when vengeance is sought for or taken without just cause or legitimate authority, or if it be out of proportion to the offence, or be indulged in out of mere lust for revenge and gratification of malevolence. The first inordinateness is generally venial, but may become deadly if anger be allowed to assume the enormous dimensions of rage or madness: as in the case in which a person knowingly and wilfully so gives the rein to anger as to break forth into violent gestures and exclamations, and other outrageous manifestations of temper, or even to lose his reason. The second inordinateness is generically deadly sin in being repugnant to charity and sometimes to justice: to charity, in so far as out of hatred or mere lust of revenge evil is desired or procured to one's neighbour: but to justice, if revenge is taken without just cause or be disproportioned to the offence.

II. These are the daughters of Anger: (1) *Indigna-*

tion, which is shown by turning away from one's neighbour because the indignant person conceives that he is unjustly treated by the other; and this if done on just grounds and with due moderation, may be blameless. (2) *Mental agitation,* consisting of thoughts how to devise various modes of revenge, and thus adding fuel to the fire whereby the mind in some measure is agitated. (3) *Rancour,* which is the same as long-standing and enduring aversion. From anger and these daughters of anger proceed other outward sins, such as abuse, whereby one outrages another by throwing something in his teeth to his disgrace, or even by tearing up or burning his letters in his absence. Also calumny, whereby one lays at the door of another some false charge, or imputes some defect to him. So also derision, scoffing and mocking, of which mention has already been made under the head of Envy, after which follow cursing and blasphemy. Cursing is some direful imprecation by which one solemnly wishes another some evil. Blasphemy is some insult or outrage against GOD, as when one assigns anything falsely to GOD, or refuses Him what is His, or gives to creatures what belongs to the Creator, or even says what is true, when it tends to His dishonour or to His disesteem, by way of indignation against Him, or of contempt or of expostulation, or by the use of words which now and then contain or are considered to contain the idea of irreverence towards GOD, or of disesteem of the Divine excellence, though not intended directly to dishonour GOD.

III. If any one accuse himself of cursing, or of some dire imprecation of evil or of blasphemy, he should be asked (1) what words he used : for the uninstructed confound blasphemy with imprecations, (as they do fornication with adultery, &c.) and imprecations with swearing. Even if they make mention of the devil, or call a person by a bad name, they say they have been swearing. (2) If he has really uttered an imprecation he must explain, whether it was on inanimate things, or on cattle, or on man? With what intention? Whether it was with the will that the cursing should take effect? Whether to the person's face or in the presence of others, whether before many or one? If with full intention, what were the evils which he so imprecated? Whether he meant only evils in general, or if he could he would inflict such and such evils in particular? The reason of all this is that people do not sin alike in the different imprecations which they use. For (1) suppose a person out of anger or impatience wishes ill to some inanimate thing, such as a stone or piece of wood against which he stumbles, or to some labour or occupation in which he is engaged but does not succeed to his heart's desire,—such a sin is venial and only committed against gentleness. (2) Or if out of anger or impatience he say—Would I had never been born? Would I had been a brute? or, Curse the day on which I was born, or first set eyes on thee, or married thee? In such a case he sins grievously, if he deliberately wishes ill to himself or to others. And it would be blasphemy if said with any reference to GOD or with any indignation against Him. But if he only intended to curse the day of his birth, or of his marriage, which have caused him so many ills, sins, or chastisements, it might seem to be in itself only venial, since he is held only to mean that such a day was very unhappy for him : or it might be considered no sin at all, if the malediction were uttered without excess in demeanour. Thus Job cursed the day of his birth.

(3) If any one curse animals without any intention that what he imprecates should befall them, his sin is only venial in itself: but if with the intention that a great evil may thereby befall himself or another person, his sin is of a grave kind, unless he be so carried away by impetuosity as to be incapable of fully understanding what he is about, or of deliberation.

(4) To wish a human being a great ill intentionally, as to say, "Devil take thee," "GOD strike thee dead," is deadly sin, and often not only an offence against charity, but also against justice; as when a tremendous malediction is uttered in a person's presence to his great dishonour. But to wish some slight ill without any great dishonour resulting to the person so assailed is simply of a venial character.

(5) If a father curses a child, or a master a maid-servant, or manservant, without any intention that the malediction should take effect, so long as there be no grave dishonour inflicted or grave scandal incurred, there results no guilt beyond that of venial sin intrinsically, and this is true even if a stranger be the subject.

(6) If any one out of passion wish the devil had him even without any intention that the thing should come to pass, he is not cleared from deadly sin intrinsically—that is to say, having regard to the object: because there appears to be excessive baseness and perversity in such a thing, so that the nature of the hearer revolts at it.

(7) If a son curse a parent or grandparent to their

face, he sins grievously also against piety, though he do it without any intention of the curse taking effect. The same is true if he do it to those who stand in the place of parents, or being an inferior if he do it to a superior. It is the same, strictly speaking, in the case of married persons. But if the object be a brother or sister, it is often only venial, as against piety, though if accompanied with intention it may be deadly, as against charity.

(8) To utter the name of the devil in a passion without adding any imprecation is unbecoming a Christian, and might be a grave fault by reason of the scandal which would follow if it became a habit.

(9) Persons who use imprecations, though they often escape the charge of grievous sin, because they do so in unguarded moments, or because they lack decision of will, and though they employ terms of imprecation usually more as exclamations to signify that they are displeased or to frighten others, nevertheless should be exhorted against such practices on account of their being unbecoming. Moreover parents, who in their children's presence often and habitually wish them, so far as speech is concerned, grievous ills, yet without any intention that such results should follow, sin grievously if they do not amend their habit, because they teach their children by their example to wish them and others ill in return, and make them obstinate and disobedient, by forfeiting their reverence and esteem, which is a great evil; and hence it is in vain that parents plead the disobedience of their children to excuse their own language, since they themselves are the cause thereof.

(10) But if the imprecation have introduced into it sacred terms or things, it becomes blasphemous, and converts what should save souls into instruments of destroying them. Herein great irreverence in regard to GOD is perceptible, though such profane wishes may be uttered without any desire of their coming to pass: whence such persons as have fallen into the habit of using these expressions are bound under peril of deadly sin to amend, and are otherwise incapable of receiving absolution. But if any one in a passion, yet without any feeling against GOD, make simple mention of sacred terms without any scandal resulting therefrom, and without any derogation to the honour of GOD or of divine things arising out of the circumstances of the case, it is a taking of GOD's Name in vain and a grievous sin of a venial nature: but as scandal in such a case usually ensues, and the hearers consider that GOD and divine things are thereby dishonoured, deadly sin is often incurred. Hence ordinarily, if the speaker has an entire perception of the dishonour which he thereby inflicts upon GOD, he sins grievously: if he has only a glimmering idea of the effect of his words his sin will be of a venial kind, because of the want of entire freedom of will: but if he has no apprehension at all of the outrage which he commits against GOD, there will be no sin in that case incurred, but only a first movement thereunto for a single instant of time; nevertheless a grave obligation of correcting the habit remains in full force. Moreover, if any one in jest utters blasphemous words without any direct intention of dishonouring GOD, yet should dishonour to GOD be coupled with that jest in the mind of the hearers, the result is the same as if

it were intentional blasphemy. And if any one slightly changes the words to avoid blasphemy, he does not blaspheme indeed, because he does not make light of the Name of GOD or sacred things: yet he may sin by reason of scandal or impatience. While on this subject we should note that penitents should be asked whether they often use imprecations, though there may be every reason to think that they have had no evil inclination to desire that what they imprecate may take place, so as to learn whether such is their custom. Many go on confessing this sin for several years without endeavouring to amend, because they have haply only a feeble and languid purpose to reform.

IV. If the penitent accuse himself of using reproachful and insulting words, he should principally explain what persons he has so treated.

For (1) if women, boys, and men of the lowest class abuse each other by calling one another witches, harlots, knaves, and the like, they are not said commonly to commit sin, because the speakers do not mean what they say and the hearers do not believe what is said, as being the effect of passion. (2) If a father or a superior respectively utter an abusive expression to a son or an inferior with the intention of correcting or setting down, without exceeding the proper degree of correction or without inflicting any graver disgrace than the fault deserves, no sin is incurred. Thus CHRIST called the disciples, who went to Emmaus, fools, and the Apostle termed the Galatians foolish. (3) If the abuse be merely of a slight character, or devoid of any intention to inflict dishonour, or no great hurt ensue to the fame of one's neighbour, the sin is only venial: and thus many parents escape the charge of deadly sin when they call their sons asses, &c. (4) If small defects be cast in another's teeth out of jest or for the sake of innocent amusement, so long as another is not vexed or angered it is only banter. (5) But if one's neighbour is grievously dishonoured, it is a grievous sin. And in this way even parents sin when they call their children at random devils, &c., chiefly because they exasperate them and make them rebellious, and by their own example lead them to imitate their conduct, which is a grievous ill. Moreover, if any one by abuse injure the honour of another, he is bound to make reparation though his character be not injured. But that reparation may be effected by kind address and conversation, showing respect, asking pardon, &c.

Spiritual Anger.

This comes on when spiritual things cease to give sweetness and delight, and people become peevish and easily angered by trifles, like babes weaned from the breast: or when they are angry with the faults of others in a restless zeal for censure, sometimes blaming them and that with anger, as though they were constituted guardians of virtue: or when they are impatient with their own imperfections, as though they would become saints in a day: having no humility, the more they resolve they fall and become more angry with themselves, having no patience to wait for the help of GOD.

Remedies against Anger, Cursing, Blasphemies, &c.

(1) Put before you the example of GOD. He is provoked hourly by continual outrages, and yet how mercifully He deals with us, and even crowns with benefits the sinner His enemy. If He chastises us with adversity, it is because He desires that it should turn to our good. Should He smite us as often as we deserve, what would become of us?

(2) Next consider the example of CHRIST. How mild and humble was He from His Birth even to His Death! How kindly did He deal with the ignorant, with persecutors and slanderers! "Learn of Me, for I am meek and lowly of heart."

(3) Reflect that it cannot be but that annoyances, insults, and injuries should befall us. Where human beings are concerned there must be weaknesses and defects. Ask yourself if you have not yours, which others have to bear with? When you wait upon a sick person and are offended by his conduct when he is out of his mind or makes mistakes, you are not angry with him, but have compassion on him. Your neighbour, your children, the members of your household are weak, blind, ignorant, and cannot think of everything.

(4) Anger renders you unfit to discharge rightly the functions which belong to your condition, and disagreeable to your neighbour, alienates others from you, and obstructs the illuminations of Divine grace in yourself and the fruits thereof in your neighbour. Gentleness is the reverse of all this, and restrains anger. "The meek will He teach His way." (Ps. xxv.) "Go on

with thy business in meekness, so shalt thou be beloved of Him that is approved." (Ecclus. iii.)

(5) While you feel anger rise, say, "Most gentle JESU, I love Thee!" and sweetly restrain your anger, or if you cannot do this leave the place where you are, turn your attention to something else, begin to talk of another subject, &c.

(6) Be lowly in heart, gentle in speech, do your work tranquilly and without haste, and obstinate persistency to obtain your aims, for else you will be moved to anger if your schemes fail.

(7) When you are going to act with others remember that you must expect contradiction in many things and to be slighted, and so prepare your mind to endure with patience through the love of CHRIST.

(8) Reflect what you wish your neighbour to be towards yourself, and be such to him; when he is angry answer him gently, "A soft answer turneth away wrath."

(9) Never stir up and foment anger in your mind, not even against yourself when you have failed in any particular, because when the mind has got into that state you may easily vent your anger upon others. Mourn over your lapses into anger, make amends for your failures, and get rid of all irritations by putting your whole trust in GOD. This will help you against blasphemies, imprecations, and bad language; for when anger is subdued such consequences will be avoided.

(10) Besides this, when people are in the habit of uttering maledictions they should be shown the wickedness of it, and the temporal harm and scandal which is likely to arise from it. "With what measure soever

you mete unto others, it shall be meted to you again." God has nothing else but benediction in view for us, and yet do we curse one another? God gave us tongues to bless His Holy Name; how can we bless Him with our tongues if we surrender them to the power of the devil? how shall we dare to dye them with the Blood of Christ? Upon such persons as are given to this habit penance at any rate should be enjoined by way of counsel, that they should resolve every morning until their next confession not to curse, and whenever they fall into their old habit to smite the breast on the day of their fall and to lament.

(11) Such as blaspheme should be shown the very great enormity of blasphemy, whereby the despicable creature viper-like attacks its Creator, though rarely with impunity even in this life. They should be enjoined to avoid places, and companies, and amusements, wherein they are likely to be excited to such language; and if it be habitual, they should every evening examine their conscience in this respect, and every morning and throughout the day beseech the help of God, and resolve firmly not to blaspheme, and to say often, "Glory be to the Father," &c. But if a person from any cause blaspheme two or three times in a month without being under the influence of habit, a very heavy penance should be enjoined him, such as frequent confession, fasting on certain days with only bread and water: humble kissing the ground night and morning for the space of eight days; frequent acts of faith and contrition, &c. according as the confessor judges it to be best and possible for the penitent. And if the penitent after his last confession has seriously endeavoured

to break through his habit, he should be urged to persevere though he relapse once or twice. But if he has manifested no endeavour or only a very slight effort to amend, or very little intention of adopting the means prescribed, his absolution must be deferred.

Section VII.

Of Sloth.

I. Sloth, taken in its largest acceptation is an act of disinclination or mental relaxation in the exercise of virtues on account of the labour, vexation, and difficulty which is experienced in their cultivation, without however setting any less store by virtue intrinsically; as when a person is vexed at having to attend church on a cold day, or observe Lent strictly, or any other positive precept, and so performs his duty negligently, whether on account of the difficulty which he finds in fulfilling such acts, or on account of the love of the advantage or gain which is to be derived from the opposite course. Sloth taken thus is a universal vice opposed to all virtue, since it is the cause of virtuous actions being ill performed. Intrinsically it is only of a venial character, but it assumes a deadly hue if a duty of grave obligation is thereby omitted—such as the being at church on Sunday, &c.

II. Sloth taken specifically is grief and disgust which is conceived in regard to the friendship of GOD as being hurtful, because it must be sought for and preserved by means of the toilful exercise of virtues and of the avoidance of worldly pleasures, so that the slothful person grieves that he is bound under pain of damnation to give glory to GOD by observing His Commandments, as his ultimate object; or because he was created for GOD as his end and ought to cleave to Him by avoiding pleasures in order to attain felicity. This is in every way deadly sin as being directly opposed to the desire of loving and pleasing GOD.

III. The daughters of Sloth are: (1) Hatred of spiritual things whereby a person by wishing that such things had no existence, despises the goodness of GOD —as when he wishes that he had not professed to belong to CHRIST, Who requires self-abnegation in order to attain to bliss; or that he had never been called to enter the religious life on account of the difficulties to be overcome in it. (2) Want of courage in carrying out what belongs to the service of GOD. (3) Despair of surmounting difficulties and of obtaining salvation. (4) Illwill or anger towards those who urge them on to virtue and to fervour. (5) Torpidity or languor of mind in fulfilling what is commanded. (6) Wanderings in prayer and other spiritual exercises. We must estimate the gravity of all these both from the object and from the effect which is the consequence of them.

Spiritual Sloth.

People are wont to find their most spiritual occupations irksome and avoid them as repugnant to their desire for sensible sweetness, and loathe them when this sweetness fails. Under the influence of this desire or of the disgust which its non-attainment begets they give up or return to prayer with a bad grace, and so turn away from the way of perfection, which is the abnegation of self-will for the Will of GOD. They think GOD should will what they will, and are sorry when they must will what He wills and reluctantly yield their will to His. They imagine that what is not according to their will is not according to the Will of GOD, and that what pleases them, pleases GOD. They also find it wearisome to obey when they are commanded to do what they like not. The more spiritual the work, and so the less full of sweetness, the more irksome do they feel it to be, and so walk on at their ease, gratifying their own wills and miss of the strait way that leadeth unto life.

Remedies against Sloth.

(1) Consider how much CHRIST, your SAVIOUR and King, did for the glory of His FATHER and your soul's salvation, though He had no need of you, and how little you value His labours.

(2) Whatever external operations GOD exhibits He exhibits for the salvation of our souls; all His desires, all the care of His Providence, all the effects of His mercy aim only at making us love and worship Him that so we may be saved—does not this paternal care and affection deserve our love and devotion?

(3) How little and brief toil is demanded of you in exchange for an infinite and eternal reward? Are you not worthy of all confusion, if you be unwilling to expend it for your salvation? The least action done for GOD avails a thousand times more than all the deeds

of Heroes for vain-glory; you weary yourself for vain things, what ought you not to do for eternal good?

(4) What would you think of your servant, if he served you negligently with ample pay in prospect? And would you serve GOD, who proposes such good things for you, more negligently than worldlings serve the devil when he offers them lies?

(5) The lukewarm is injurious to GOD by defaming His Service as if He did not deserve to be served, or had not proposed a fair reward; he disgraces CHRIST by serving Him less fervently than the world.

(6) You are between two horns of a dilemma. You will be either eternally happy or unhappy; if you be lukewarm, you are in the highest danger of damnation, for "cursed is he who doeth the work of GOD negligently," (Jer. xlviii.) and "because thou art lukewarm I will spue thee out of My mouth." (Rev. iii.) Finally, recall your sins to mind, the shortness of life, the strictness of the Judgment, the torments of hell, and you will recognize the necessity of shaking off lukewarmness.

Lukewarmness too is worse than coldness, just as to have felt the fire of the HOLY SPIRIT and to have lost His influence is worse than never to have experienced it.

CHAPTER II.

FURTHER PRECAUTIONS WHICH THE PRIEST SHOULD TAKE IN THE DISCHARGE OF HIS FUNCTIONS AS CONFESSOR.

(1) To be actually in a state of grace is not sufficient for a profitable discharge of this priestly function, however sufficient it may be for its lawful performance. The Priest should be in an habitual state of grace, so as never to forfeit it by an act of deadly sin. He should strive to avoid slight faults, at least such as are observable and frequent, and to practise Christian virtues as becomes one who is a teacher and minister of sanctity. How shall he, who is familiar with vice, inspire in his penitents an extreme horror thereof? How shall he who exhibits by his conduct contempt of virtue rouse them to love and practise it? How shall he whose pride is excited by the least word direct others to forget injuries? How shall he preach continual patience to members of a family, who cannot repress or disguise his feelings of vexation at having to hear a confession, and who contradicts his own preaching by the outward signs of his own weakness? How shall he inflame others with divine love, if his heart is void of it, and so full of the love of the world and

its dissipations, that the sentiments he strives to impart to others are foreign to his own soul? May not the cause of the penitent remaining almost insensible to his arguments be that such a Priest is at a loss what to say, or that he says it with coldness? On the contrary, if he be a man piously established in the grace of GOD, and seriously engaged in doing what he ought to recommend to others, how fruitful will he become in ideas, in warm and penetrating expressions, capable of affecting the mind and touching the heart? Thus, depending on the special aid which the LORD grants to all His faithful ministers, the Priest will realise that with a life removed from the perils of the world and consecrated to the practice of virtue, his penitents will see nothing in his conduct out of the confessional which contradicts his teaching therein. And thus edified by his good example, they will resort to him more willingly and with better dispositions, for they will be full of esteem and veneration for him. But this he will in vain hope for if his manner of life causes scandal by lowering the dignity of the minister and of the ministry.

(2) Moreover it is often necessary to be in an habitual state of grace even to discharge sacerdotal functions legitimately. A Priest cannot tell when he may be called upon to hear a confession. If by any fall into deadly sin he be obliged to send away the penitent, it may be with enormous loss to the latter: or if he succeed in making an act of perfect contrition on the spur of the moment, it is a risk he could not recommend his penitent to run; the only alternative he has is to hear the confession in a state of deadly sin; that is to say, an enemy of GOD ventures to dispense unworthily His

Grace and Blood: the absolver goes away condemned, while the sinner departs absolved. If this ministry has its dangers even for a virtuous Priest, how shall one in so miserable a state escape them? Perchance he will only load himself with fresh faults, by an excess of gentleness in passing over sins in others which he cannot correct in himself, and so becoming not a father, but a ravening wolf; not a minister of GOD, but a rebel and a minister of the devil; not a physician, but an assassin of souls. Thus a Priest is bound to keep in a state of grace not only for his own sake, but also in order to be able to aid others in ministering Absolution. More than this,—this ministry demands above all others a positive fervour; the difference between the language adopted after the heart is inflamed by fervent prayer and that which results from negligence and coldness does not admit of any comparison.

(3) We would not maintain that a Priest who was not always in this state of holiness ought to abandon this part of his ministry. The grace of Sacraments does not depend on the worthiness of the minister, nor is the blessing of Absolution proportioned to the holiness of the Priest, and the good advice which he gives to penitents may often bear fruit. The exercise of this ministry may be a good means of repairing time lost through sin, and of obtaining the grace of a lasting conversion. In fact, while labouring with zeal and charity for the good of others, the Priest may not lose sight of his own, but should rather seek to benefit himself by the good which he does to his neighbour, in applying to his own case secretly and mainly the good advice, the holy affections, the expedients, and the

means which he suggests to penitents in this school of sanctity.

(4) All the more that the Priest lacks of being in an habitual state of grace and fervour does he need to have rectitude of intention. No human motive ought to influence him in entering upon or in persevering in his duties as an absolver: it should be the sole desire of pleasing GOD and of aiding souls. This is most suitable for the ministry in which he occupies the place of GOD, and before angels and men represents JESUS CHRIST. It is also most necessary in order to draw down upon him that aid of the HOLY SPIRIT which he requires in order to avoid being deceived to his own detriment and to that of others, and in order to save his own soul and those of his penitents. For what hope can he entertain in these respects, should any other but a divine motive lead him to examine the cases of conscience, in which man needs to be reconciled to GOD the Judge of all, and in which the important affair of everlasting life is concerned?

(5) It is in vain that the Priest flatters himself that he has this rectitude of intention if he acts contrary to it, and extinguishes it. This he does, if he be not indifferent to all sorts of persons, if he love better to hear the confessions of persons in a high estate than those of persons in a low condition,—of those who are learned than of those who are ignorant, of women than of men. In fact, he must ever recognize the fact that all souls are equal in the sight of GOD, redeemed by the same Blood, destined to the same glory, and equally capable of glorifying GOD. But he gainsays this if he with some is all attention, patience, and gentleness, but

with others inattention, severity, and impatience; if he would rather be besieged by a great number of penitents than have only a few who are in the sight of GOD well attended to and thoroughly cured; if he seek some temporal benefit by means of his penitents; if he be jealous of his brother-clergy because more penitents frequent their confessionals; if he be much put out because one of his penitents betakes himself to another confessor; finally, if he seek by any means to draw away penitents to himself. Thus before hearing confessions he must ever be careful to have a right intention, and pray GOD to enable him to retain it while exercising his ministry. An excellent means of securing it is to turn especial attention to the confession of the poorer classes, inasmuch as there is less temptation to fail with them through vanity, respect of persons, or through too tender affections; the Priest will labour amongst them with more merit, often with more fruit; and they will be more inclined than the rich to pray for him out of gratitude.

(6) Prayer should be offered not only for a right intention but also for other helps. Say unto GOD, "Grant me wisdom that sitteth on Thy throne:" "Make me a clean heart, O GOD," &c. The Priest needs a twofold grace so as not to be injurious to himself and others, but on the contrary to be really useful to himself and others in a matter of a supernatural character which is beyond all human cleverness—the justification of the sinner. Not only should he pray at the outset, but he should resort to GOD again and again for aid whenever he finds himself in any difficulty, whether in framing his decision as a doctor, or

in exciting compunction and prescribing remedies as a physician, or in pronouncing sentence and imposing penance as a judge. His supplications will not be in vain. GOD not infrequently gives His faithful ministers a sensible proof of His willingness to aid them in this great ministry of charity.

(7) Girt about with all these precautions, the Priest may proceed with confidence to the exercise of these functions: but he must keep an habitual watch over his heart in order to exclude every bad feeling, and preserve a holy fervour. For how much danger is there that he may be assailed by disordered feelings, impatience, vanity, and perverse inclinations which may lead him to too great lenity or severity: absolve or unadvisedly send away the penitent: neglect to understand and explain his case and the mode of healing his wounds; or pervert a sacrament ordained for exciting a powerful horror of sin in others into a subtle and secret means of fomenting passions and sin in himself! The Priest then must keep strict watch over his own heart. And further, in order to enshrine in his soul the flame of holy fervour which he should kindle in others, he should have a lively recollection of the Presence of GOD. As he dispenses the Divine Blood for cleansing souls, it would be very useful for him to unite every confession with the five Most Blessed Wounds, often forming tender affections, and beseeching the SAVIOUR or His Divine FATHER for the sake of these sacred wounds to grant that his labours may be for the glory of GOD, for increase of grace to himself, and for the profit of the penitent. In addition to this, if he combines a union of his own heart with the acts of

contrition and prayers which he suggests to penitents, he will have discovered the secret of making the confessor's work a sort of continual meditation and prayer, which will preserve him from many faults and produce fervour and sense of GOD's Presence, whereby he will draw much blessing on himself and on his penitents.

(8) Vain however will be his efforts to watch over his heart, if he do not watch over his senses. For instance, his eyes should not be fixed upon women whose confessions he is actually hearing nor upon those who are in waiting; nor should he gaze through curiosity about the church, else he runs the risk of becoming inattentive to what he hears, of getting a bad reputation for curiosity and inattention, or of exposing himself to very dangerous temptations, such as the enemy of souls is on the watch to suggest in a ministration so fatal to his influence. Besides the eyes the tongue must be watched. Not that through any fear as to temptations from this source the Priest should neglect to fulfil his duty by making proper inquiries as to the nature, number, and circumstances of grievous sins, especially such as tinge them with a deeper or lighter dye. For inquiries of this sort, which are absolutely essential, GOD vouchsafes His special protection both to the penitent who is bound to satisfy them, and to the Priest who must sit in judgment in matters of the most foul kind. But in that case the Priest has need of a twofold reserve, both to choose fit expressions for treating such subjects, and to restrain him within moderate limits of investigation. Thus he should not exceed the bounds of strict necessity, and of the evident.needs or manifest and obvious advantage of the penitent: especially in

such cases where by endeavouring to secure a full and entire confession greater good is risked. Never must the Priest obtain a less good at the expense of a greater. And if reserve is necessary in this case, much more so when women have to be instructed or reproved in these matters. It is here, above all, that brevity is required. And indeed the Priest should on every subject be brief and reserved with women and girls. Not that he should curtail anything necessary for their good, but he should avoid with the greatest care long addresses even of a spiritual character. It is only too easy during long interviews, for which there is no real necessity, to be exposed to the incursion of impure affections, and to lose more than is gained.

(9) It is therefore expedient from time to time to implore the divine illumination so as not to be overtaken by the secret intrigues of sympathy, which makes the Priest consider too long and superfluous discursiveness to be short, reserved, and necessary. Those who are waiting to take their turn think otherwise, and give way to inward murmurs, often, it is true, wrongly, because they condemn without knowledge of the case. In fact it often happens that in spite of all his wishes, the Priest cannot be short nor curtail useless dilatations. Some people, even such as are accustomed to Confession, are sometimes tempted in so many ways, sometimes so particularising, so worried, so troubled, so easily disturbed if they do not say all they have to say, (and they cannot describe it all by giving an instance,) that it takes a long time to devise a remedy for their real needs. In such a case the Priest must not through fear of what may be said come short of what his

duty before GOD requires as judge, father, and physician. Nevertheless this observation, combined with what has gone before, ought to urge him more and more to be curt and severe in his interviews with women, by confining himself to saying what is necessary. I say, severe, not that he should frighten them by harsh words and repress that full confidence which they ought to have in him, but that his converse with them should never degenerate into familiarity, and be always tempered by the respect due to their spiritual father; a father, who by affording his children a ready access to him through a sincere desire for their salvation, inspires in them still greater veneration for his authority as judge, representative of GOD and physician. Thereby he should eliminate all low and human affection which he might feel for them, or which they might feel for him. This circumspection is the more necessary when the youth or appearance of people, or the subjects of confession, or their great piety or wickedness might cause more easily bad impressions on his or their hearts. Piety, I say, for it has been more than once a rock upon which imprudent confessors have been wrecked, who by commencing with a simply spiritual esteem, have ended insensibly with a sensual and carnal love. To preserve himself from so great a misfortune, the Priest should abstain from every word which springs from tenderness. Thus though he may say "my dear son" to a young man, prudence forbids him to say "my dear child" to one of the other sex. And the more they have to reveal great weakness or sins of impurity, the more concise should he be in his interviews with them. His curtness in speaking of these sins will assist in inspiring in them more horror of them, and save him from such evil thoughts as the devil might suggest in regard to their proneness to this class of sins. Nothing more shows the fearfulness of Satanic devices than that it is possible that a Sacrament which was instituted to drive forth from souls sin and the devil, and make them living temples of the HOLY GHOST, may be profaned by abusers of its ministrations to the grossest iniquity.

(10) Thus no care can be too great in dealing with young females in particular. The Priest should be rather severe than affable: should not allow them to speak face to face nor to kiss his hand. He should not appear to recognize those who come to confession, still less inquire their names. Even pious persons shrink from making a full confession when they perceive that they are recognized. Prudence suggests that the Priest should not look at his penitents nor follow them with his eyes, as they leave his presence. All kinds of familiarity must be avoided; he should not stop to talk with them in the church after confession, nor receive little presents from them. If it be needful to speak to them in regard to their spiritual life, he must be more particular than he is required to be in hearing their confession. The conference should not be private, but public and in the sight of every one: moreover it should not be long continued, and not repeated except when absolutely needful for spiritual direction. In visiting sick women care should be taken to use as much prudence as possible, not closing the door of the apartment unless absolutely necessary, and not to look towards the sick person: especially where

there is danger of affectionate feeling, as in the case of known piety. The Evil one directs his efforts continually towards the conversion of feelings of admiration for the devotion of others into carnal attachment to them. (2) The Priest should beware of allowing any preference for hearing the confessions of women to make him put off or send away men who come for the same purpose. Nor is it following the example of the most holy confessors to prefer to give up his time to those who are more advanced rather than to those who are less perfect and stand more in need of priestly assistance.

What is most needed in a Priest is that he should be a model of holiness to his penitents. In this ministration he co-operates with GOD, and hence it is not enough that he live in a state of grace, he must also be addicted to the practice of all virtues. Else he may be lukewarm and distracted, and for want of prayer and mortification he may go through his work in a bare perfunctory manner. Love will not inflame his words; when he corrects he will lack zeal, when he counsels he will have little faith in his own prescriptions. He will be in danger of absolving unworthy penitents, or of not warning those who are in fault, or of giving way to their obstinacy. In short, he will lack courage to check the faults to which he himself is conscious of being prone. What scandal may arise when such a Priest gains the character of being silent upon the gravest faults one need not portray. Good had it been for him, if he had never been ordained. Hence the Priest should be very strict with himself in his own confessions. Good is it for him to make an extraordinary general confession over and above that which we may suppose him to have made once for all. This should embrace the mode in which he says the Divine offices, and how he celebrates the Holy Eucharist. His house is his church: his book the Sacred Scriptures; his business to succour the poor, instruct the ignorant, and minister the Sacraments. His time should be occupied in study, specially of moral theology, in reading religious books, in prayer and self-examination: in a word he must live by rule, and not by haphazard. But the two pivots upon which the whole life of a Priest should turn, are prayer and mortification. Mental prayer should, as a serious meditation upon the great mysteries of salvation, occupy daily half an hour. But prayer will not suffice unless it be intermingled with mortification. He who grants to his body all that is lawful, will end in conceding what is unlawful. We must "keep under the body and bring it into subjection."

Finally, the Priest should be reserved in speech, diligent in searching out not only sins, but the roots of them also, the causes and the occasions, in order to apply the suitable remedies. Gravity and modesty, proper demeanour, and dress, these should distinguish him. Any gesture likely to be injurious, such as taking snuff, which is undignified, should be avoided. The confessions of women should not be heard when there is too little light, and they should always be received in church, except in some extraordinary necessity. Nor should persons be allowed to come within earshot of the confessional.

CHAPTER III.

CONCERNING THE MODE OF QUESTIONING PENITENTS.

(1) WE have said already that the Priest cannot be too careful in questions about sin to avoid giving the penitent thereby any further acquaintance with evil. Yet at the same time he must often supply the want of knowledge on the part of the penitent, lest through ignorance a part of the confession be kept back, which is the most necessary to be unfolded. Not to be impatient, and not to travel too fast, is the great secret of avoiding great indiscretions. Meanwhile the Priest must be careful also not to be too reserved in questions, lest he risk thereby the loss of a great good for the sake of a less. It is easy for an adroit Priest to ask questions, especially upon the subject of purity, so as not to be understood by any one except such as is guilty of what is supposed. If a child confess "bad thoughts," it may be asked "what sort of thoughts?" for in children they are often confined to anger and revenge. Children should be always exhorted to remember that they are always in the presence of GOD, and that they should never do what they would be ashamed of their parents' seeing.

(2) In the case of foul sins it suffices to learn the

nature thereof, and not to inquire the mode of its commission: and should the penitent wish to explain, he should be told it is unnecessary. The Priest should beware of being thought to ask out of needless curiosity, especially in the relations of married persons. In such cases the questions should be suggested by the parties themselves, and if it seem needful to pursue the subject the Priest should content himself with generalities, such as " Have you lived together in a Christian manner, so that your conscience does not reproach you for anything?" In some cases the penitent needs instruction upon the duties of the married life. His replies will indicate the extent to which questions may and ought to be put.

(3) As reserve is needful upon the subject of purity, so is it no less necessary upon other points. Questions should only be put where the Priest has some reasonable ground for thinking that the penitent has failed in any duty, or that he conceals his fault through shame or ignorance.

(4) The Priest is bound to do all he can to heal the ignorance of penitents, especially as regards the principal mysteries of the Faith. Upon these points the Priest should question them so as not to disconcert them, and should make the simplest inquiries, " How many Gods are there? How many Persons in One GOD? Which Person became Man for us?" and the like. Their answers to these will show what their amount of knowledge or ignorance is. Very often the Priest will discover that their faith is sound though their replies are indifferent; and that enlightened by the secret grace of GOD they are moved to believe on the authority of

GOD, and not merely on that of their pastors. So far as concerns acts of the theological virtues, he should inquire if they can say the Creed of the Apostles and the LORD's Prayer, and make an act of Contrition. If they understand what these mean, they are competent to receive absolution, so far as knowledge of them is concerned: for the Creed is an excellent act of faith, the LORD's Prayer of hope, and the act of Contrition of love. In the case of ignorant persons we must bear with habitual, virtual, implicit or feeble motive of belief as the basis of their worship, as for instance, in the celebration of the Holy Eucharist. If penitents know the Creed, the LORD's Prayer, and can make an act of Contrition, it must not be required as essential for absolution that they understand them explicitly as being acts of the three theological virtues.

(5) Two means there are of meeting the case of such ignorance as renders the penitent incompetent to receive sanctifying grace. One is to make him sensible of the necessity under which he lies to be instructed, and to recommend him or to impose on him by way of penance the being present at catechisings and sermons, and the reading or hearing read books which treat of Christian doctrine. The other is a more prompt method, not waiting till he learn by heart these subjects, to instruct him concisely and make him recite after the priest the above forms, so as to be sure that he believes, hopes and loves as he ought. After this he may receive absolution, if there is no other obstacle. This second mode may be employed in respect of adults of a more common class, who are ashamed and troubled at being asked if they know the great truths, and yet by their confession give cause for doubt as to their know-

ledge. Such should receive gentle and energetic assistance in making these acts. After this the Priest may be free to question them if they are in the habit of reciting these and like forms, and according to their answers proceed to urge them to make use of other remedies. We may add to this fatal ignorance, which debars many from absolution, the very common deficiency of that true contrition, which is required for the same. Many who are very scrupulous in self-examination scarcely think of true penitence. Some seem to satisfy themselves with exciting in themselves contrition after they leave the priest: some wait for him to do it for them: some only try to do so while they repeat the short forms which precede the act of absolution. Hence one of the things most necessary to be urged upon penitents is sorrow for sin and a pious resolution for the future. The Priest should make them feel the extreme importance of this, and suggest means to attain to it,—such as to ask GOD for it, to dwell upon the motives to it, and carefully to excite themselves to it. They should be advised to make frequent acts of perfect contrition, and after this they may be advised to lay aside all doubts, and to feel duly disposed to receive the Sacraments.

(6) Another kind of ignorance deserves notice. It is that which may be an occasion of sin for the penitent or for those under him, or of scandal. This consists in dangerous intimacies or friendships: negligent or ignorant ways of bringing up children, or of managing servants or employed: and in bad examples to others. Not only must the inward life, but the outward demeanour also, come under review, especially in the case of such as are more liable to remarks and censures from the world.

CHAPTER IV.

HOW TO QUESTION THE ILL OR NON-INSTRUCTED.

(1) He should be asked if he know the principal mysteries of the Faith, for if he know not the four great mysteries of God, the Rewarder and the Avenger, of the Holy Trinity, of the Incarnation, and of the Death and Passion of Jesus Christ, he is incapable of receiving Absolution. In addition to this, he should be asked if he know the Creed, the Ten Commandments, the Sacraments, &c., at least in substance. The Priest should at least instruct him in the four great truths, and show him how to make acts of faith, hope, love of God, and contrition, with an injunction to gain further instruction upon other necessary truths. Persons in a higher class of life, but equally ignorant, though ashamed to confess their ignorance, should be invited to join the Priest in making the above acts. The Priest should say, "If you like, we will say them together,— 'I believe, O my God, that Thou, Truth itself, hast revealed Thyself to Thy Church as One God in Three Equal Persons, Father, Son, and Holy Spirit; I believe that the Son was made man, died for us on the Cross, rose again and ascended into heaven, whence He will come to judge the quick and the dead, and send

the good to heaven and the bad to hell.' You believe this with all your heart, do you not? Let us now make an act of hope,"—and let him inquire similarly of this,—" and of an act of love and contrition." One celebrated confessor used always to make his penitents say an act of contrition before assigning them a penance and before giving them Absolution.

(2) He should be asked if he has given in to superstitious practices, fortune-telling, and the like.

(3) The penitent should be asked if anything preying on the conscience has been concealed. The Priest should say, " Does anything in your past life trouble you? tell all your trouble, and hide nothing." The penitent should be instructed that if he hide anything out of shame, his confession will be more injurious than beneficial. He may need to be told that he may confess something heretofore hidden without repeating his entire confessions in the past.

(4) He should be asked if he has fulfilled his penance, and if not, whether through ignorance, procrastination, or wilfulness.

(5) He should be asked if he have caused others to sin, if he have combined with or availed himself of the aid of others in this matter, if he have been partaker of other men's sins. If a publichouse keeper, whether he have given drink to drunkards : if a woman, whether by want of modesty in speech, jokes, laughter, looks, indecent attire, she have excited bad thoughts in men : whether there have been formal co-operation in sin with others, as in fornication, or as in protecting a thief or an assassin from discovery, whereby one co-operates in their bad intentions, by giving them encouragement : whether

there have been material co-operation, as when one gives drink to another who gets intoxicated.

It may aid the Priest to question and explain on the Ten Commandments in some such way as the following:

I. This Commandment binds to the practice of Faith.

Do you know what this means? Have you not outraged it in many ways?

Faith.

Faith is a supernatural and theological virtue which is infused into man, which makes him cleave firmly to all that GOD has revealed and to all that the undivided Catholic Church has handed down to us for our belief, both because GOD Who is Truth Itself cannot deceive us, and because the Universal Church cannot wholly and with one accord fall into essential and important error.

Sins of Omission.

1. Ignorance of the truths in the Creed: of the Divine Commandments and ecclesiastical ordinances: of the Sacraments which have already been imparted, and of those which ought still to be received: of things without the knowledge of which the duties of our condition cannot be fulfilled.

2. Negligence in making use of the means of instruction.

3. Omitting acts of faith.

4. Being ashamed of appearing to be a Christian.

5. Not resisting or preventing persons sinning against the faith when we can.

6. Neglecting to instruct those who have been committed to our charge.

Sins of Commission.

In thoughts and feelings:

1. Inward opposition to speculative truths or practices of the Faith.

2. Voluntary speculations and doubts.

3. Inward heresy, or obstinate error on some matter of faith.
4. Apostasy or renunciation of the faith.
5. Reading books likely to imperil faith.
6. Keeping such books in our possession.

In words :
1. Impious language.
2. Jests about religion.
3. Unnecessary and dangerous disputations.
4. Uttering maxims opposed to those of the Gospel.

In acts :
1. Dissembling one's faith.
2. Entering frequently into company with unbelievers and heretics.
3. Attending the conventicles of heretics, and incurring the danger of being led astray, or setting a bad example.
4. Leading a heathen life, and neglecting all religious acts and exercises.

By co-operation :
1. Encouraging those who speak against religion.
2. Suggesting error.
3. Lending, disseminating irreligious books and tracts.
4. Ridiculing those who practise religion.

Motives for Reflection and Sorrow.

Alas! what sins against Faith! In spite of the clearness of prophecies as to the Founder and His disciples, and the success of their work, preserved in the Old Testament by the Jews, the greatest enemies of Christianity. In spite of all that accompanied the establishment of Christianity, and its Divine scheme: the knowledge of GOD which it supplies: the purity of its morality: the happiness which it promises: miracles wrought by JESUS CHRIST in proof of His Godhead: miracles of the Apostles for the same end: the courage and gladness with which they laid down their lives to establish the truth of what they had seen with their eyes: the trials to which those who embraced Christianity were exposed, and the rapidity with which it was propagated by means most alien from those of men, and notwithstanding infinite obstacles: the tortures and death endured by the Martyrs.

The blood of the Martyrs did not abate the fervour and zeal of Christians, but rather added to their numbers. This faith, in spite of persecutions most horrible and widely spread, has flourished and abounded. The Mysteries prove the Divine Author, since a religion from GOD ought to be less comprehensible than if it had come from men: being above reason they are not opposed to it. And the way in which these mysteries so humbling to human reason have been accepted, proves GOD to be the Author of Christianity.

This Faith has been received though preached by unlettered men of no influence or authority in all parts of the world: by men of talent and genius, in spite of all prejudice of education, and all resistance on the part of earth and hell.

The penitent should be told to make an act of Faith in such verities as those upon which he has doubts.

II. This Commandment binds to the practice of Hope, Charity, and Religion.

HOPE.

Hope is a supernatural infused theological virtue, which leads us to desire the possession of GOD our Sovereign happiness: and to wait for it as well as for the means of obtaining it with a firm confidence founded in the inviolable faithfulness of GOD in His promises, and in His mercy by the merits of JESUS CHRIST in keeping His Commandments with exactness.

Sins of Omission.

1. Of acts of hope for a fixed time.
2. Indifference in regard to heaven.
3. Neglect in flying to GOD often to obtain His grace.
4. Neglect to confess when mortal sin has been committed.
5. Neglect to excite in oneself contrition when he is in danger of hell.

Sins of Commission.

I. *Want of Hope.*

In thoughts and feelings:

1. Distrust of GOD's mercy.
2. Despondency and design of giving up altogether when dwelling on the difficulties to be surmounted.
3. Despair, as to evil habits, that GOD has forsaken us, and that salvation is impossible.
4. Consequent neglect of acts of hope, prayer and confession.

In words:

1. Expressions evidencing distrust and despair.
2. Murmuring against Providence.

In acts:

Sins committed in despair.

By co-operation:

Suggesting thoughts of distrust and despair in others by words or acts.

II. *Excess of Hope.*

1. Heretical presumption.

α. Belief that one can be saved without grace.

β. Belief that grace is all-sufficient, and that co-operation with grace is unnecessary.

2. Rash presumption.

α. Exposing oneself to occasions of sin.

β. Not having recourse to GOD in time of temptation.

3. Arrogant presumption.

α. Self-reliance, and trusting to one's own good works.

β. Delay of conversion till death or some other period.

γ. Thinking, speaking, acting presumptuously.

CHARITY.

Charity is a supernatural infused theological virtue, which leads us to love GOD, because He is infinitely loveable in Himself on account of His perfections; and to love ourselves and our neighbours for the sake of love to GOD, i.e. because we belong to GOD, were created in His image and represent Him.

Love of God.

Sins of Omission.

1. Culpable ignorance in what regards the love of GOD.
2. Want of meditation upon His perfections.
3. Want of affectionateness towards GOD.
4. Omitting acts of love to GOD.
5. Omitting to refer all actions to Him.
6. Neglecting to hinder His being offended.

Sins of Commission.

In thoughts and feelings:
1. Wrong notions about GOD.
2. Wishes that GOD was not as powerful as He is to punish sin, or so holy as to be unable to bear the wickedness of men, &c.
3. Hatred of GOD.

In words:
Complaints and murmurs against Him.

In acts:
1. Every mortal sin, since every one causes us to lose the friendship of GOD.
2. Indolence in His service.

By co-operation:
1. Direct or indirect approval of those who offend GOD.
2. Causing them so to offend.

Love of one's Neighbour.

Sins of Omission.

1. Ignorance of the necessity and of the practice of loving one's neighbour.
2. Neglect of corporal or spiritual works of mercy.

3. Not turning aside from him corporal or spiritual ill when able to do so.

4. Not promising him corporal or spiritual good in such cases as we should have wished him to promise it for us.

5. Refusing to render easy services.

6. Loving our neighbour only after a human fashion, or through interested motives.

Sins of Commission.

In thoughts and feelings:
1. Thoughts not to his advantage.
2. Suspicions, doubts, hasty judgments.
3. Hatred: when? against whom? how long cherished?
4. Consequent wishes for vengeance, rejoicing in the evil which happens to those who are hated.

In words:
1. Harsh and injurious words.
2. Spiteful jests.
3. Imprecations.
4. Injurious reports.
5. Slanders.
6. Flattery.
7. Bad advice, sinful orders.

In acts:
1. Scandal by outward signs, words, and actions; in action and silence.
2. When? with what results?
3. Unjust lawsuits; and refusal of reasonable accommodation.

By co-operation:
1. Sanctioning the sins of others by commendation.
2. Sharing in their sin.

Self-charity.

Sins of Omission.
1. Forgetfulness of one's last end.
2. Neglecting to be instructed in or to reflect upon the truths

of salvation, to frequent the Sacraments, and to be diligent in performing pious devotions.

3. Ruin of one's health by excess or want of care.

4. Idleness in doing nothing, or anything but what one ought, or what one ought without sanctifying it.

Sins of Commission.

In thoughts and feelings :

1. Self-esteem.
2. Desire of being esteemed, applauded and praised.
3. Being self-opinionated.
4. Self-will.
5. Ill-regulated attachment to this life, and its consequences.

In words :

Language which breathes self-love, vanity, propension to honours, riches, and false pleasures.

In acts :

1. Dislike to mortification of the body.
2. Gluttony and intemperance.
3. Excess in sleep.
4. Excess in innocent diversions.
5. Unlawful pleasures.

The penitent should be asked if he has loved GOD, loved his neighbour for GOD's sake, and loved himself without excess. He should be reminded that GOD, as an infinitely perfect Being, ought to be the object of the affections of a heart which He has created solely for Himself: that he should see in his neighbour GOD who made him : and that by loving himself in a disorderly and irregular manner he really hates himself: and to say, "O my GOD, too late have I loved Thee, I will delay no longer."

RELIGION.

Religion taken as a virtue, is a moral virtue which causes us to render to GOD the worship which is due to Him, by offering to Him all the homage which the Supreme Being deserves, and by honouring in respect of Him all that is holy.

Sins of Omission.

In regard to God:

1. Not to frequently adore GOD, i.e. bear witness to His infinite Majesty, and submit exteriorly and interiorly to His sovereign power.

2. Not to offer oneself often to GOD by making to Him with all the heart a sacrifice of the mind, of love, of will, of body and goods.

3. Not to feel continual and lively gratitude for so many and great benefits in the order of nature and of grace.

4. Not to praise and bless GOD always by one's acts and often by one's words, through having too little zeal for making Him known and loved.

5. In lack of devotion,—that is to say of that holy ardour which leads us to do all for GOD with fervour.

6. Not to pray often,—at least morning and evening, before actions of importance, in temptations and other dangers, or to pray without inward and outward reverence, without attention, devotion, and desire of obtaining one's requests, without humility and confidence, and without asking in the Name of JESUS CHRIST.

7. Not to meditate on one's last end, the recollection of which is so useful, and the forgetfulness of which is so injurious.

8. Not to frequent the Sacraments as often as is necessary for one's sanctification.

9. Not to take the necessary means for learning one's vocation, such as continual prayer, advice of enlightened persons, and fulfilment of the will of GOD by a truly Christian life.

In regard to what is holy:

1. Such as speaking disrespectfully of the Saints, of the clergy, and of magistrates, of holy places and things.

Sins of Commission.

In want of religion or in irreligion:

1. Blasphemy, or language derogatory to GOD directly or indirectly; accusing GOD of injustice or cruelty; blasphemy

against holy people, holy places, or holy things. Blasphemy may be interior or exterior; in the latter case it is aggravated by the consideration of the persons who witnessed or were scandalised by it.

2. Tempting GOD, by some word, act, of omission or commission, in expectation of some extraordinary result where there is no reason to look for it. The act is explicit if a miracle is expected; implicit, if ordinary means are neglected for converting a soul, healing the sick, or gaining knowledge.

3. Sacrilege in profaning a consecrated person, place, or thing.

In excess of religion or in superstition:
Superstition is either Divine worship given to a creature, or disordered worship offered to GOD.

Divine worship given to a creature: by idolatry, divination, magic, and the like.

In disordered worship of GOD: by Jewish ceremonies, false relics, certain number of prayers, genuflexions, candles, and abstinence from indifferent acts of labour.

The penitent should be exhorted to worship sincerely the true GOD, and to treat with reverence all that pertains to GOD.

(6) On the Third Commandment.

The penitent should be asked concerning perjury, broken vows, and imprecations: if he have sinned by perjury, whether in a court of justice, in which case, he sins both against religion and justice, and must unsay it, or make reparation. If by violation of a vow, he should be asked if it was really a vow and not merely a wish or resolution; whether in making the vow he were aware that he would incur the guilt of deadly sin by not keeping it. Vows may be changed or dispensed with. In commuting them, it is enough that the alternative be less liable to be broken. To frequent the Sacraments is the safest kind of commutation. Perpetual vows may be exchanged for temporal: real for personal. For dispensation, it is required that the vow should be very liable to infraction, very difficult of execution, and that regard be had to the levity or imperfect deliberation with which the vow was made. It is good to add some commutation to such dispensations. As to imprecation, the penitent should be asked if he have cursed the Saints, holy days, &c., which is a greater sin than to curse the world: whether he have done it in particular places: and he should be told to avoid such scenes of temptation to imprecation. Moreover, he should be asked in whose presence he have cursed, as scandal may be added to imprecation accordingly. And he must not be excused because he has cursed through habit or violence of temper, for though he may know less than others what he says, yet he does know more or less the extent of his fault.

Oaths.

An oath is an act of religion whereby we call GOD to witness the truth of what is said or promised.

Sins of Omission.

1. Not to honour GOD's holy Name.
2. Refusing to take an oath when the interests of the Church or State require it.
3. Not to take sufficient care beforehand that oaths are not false, unjust, or imprudent.
4. Not to repair the wrong done by false oaths in stating what is false, or suppressing what is true.
5. Taking an oath with the lips only when obliged to swear.
6. Not checking others who take oaths without necessity, or who use profane expletives which are commonly regarded as swearing.

7. Not to take means to correct a habit of swearing—such as resolving daily to break oneself of it, signing one's lips with the sign of the cross, preserving silence when excited, making acts of mortification and giving alms after yielding to it.

Sins of Commission.

1. Want of devotion in uttering the Name of GOD or of JESUS, without attention and religion, on every occasion and in a temper.

2. Perjury or false oaths, in attesting as true what one knows is false, and in attesting as true what is true, while believing it false; in attesting as certain what one has doubts upon: in using equivocal language, and suppressing what is true.

3. Rash and imprudent oaths: calling GOD to witness without strong grounds for doing so. Oaths should only be taken for the six following reasons:

α. To remove unjust suspicions.
β. To defend an innocent person.
γ. To show loyalty to the State.
δ. To profess one's belief.
ε. To confirm treaties and contracts.
ζ. To affirm a truth which else would not be believed.

4. Unjust oaths, to secure a bad object: to promise to do evil: to promise a lawful thing without any intention of keeping one's word. It makes a further difference whether such oaths have been accompanied with blaspheming the Name of GOD, with execrations and imprecations and cursings: what ill may have been wished—how many may have been scandalised by it.

5. Breaking one's promissory oath. One's promissory oath should not be kept in the case of anything bad. And one is exempted from the necessity of keeping it, if it was made under the influence of a substantial mistake: or if considerable change has taken place in the circumstances of the case, so as to render keeping it impossible: if the person to whom the promise was made releases the promiser: or if any one who has a right to do so, releases him: if a lawful dispensation be granted: and if the commutation of the promise into something better be not in effect a totally different promise.

6. As to many expressions which savour of swearing, it depends whether the user of them meant to swear in adopting them, and how many were scandalised by it.

The penitent should be reminded that GOD'S Name in itself is holy; and that every knee should bow at it; and that he has dishonoured it in the above ways. He should be urged to ask for pardon on account of the many outrages committed by his mouth; and to resolve to strive to pronounce GOD'S Name with reverence, and avoid every word which can offend his neighbour's sense of what is due to GOD.

Vows.

Vows are acts of religion, and their violation is ordinarily speaking sacrilege, being a promise made to GOD, so long as the vower has the power of reason, and can distinguish between a simple promise of intention and the obligation of a vow.

Sins in regard to vows:

1. Making a vow of celibacy, when not sure of being able to keep it.

2. Not fulfilling vows when made; not fulfilling them at the given time; not fulfilling them entirely.

3. Exposing oneself to the risk of not fulfilling one's vow by doing that which will prove a hindrance to it.

4. Not fulfilling the vows of those from whom we inherit property.

The penitent should be reminded that what he has vowed, he has vowed to GOD, and not to man. Above all, there are the vows of baptism, which he is bound to fulfil with the utmost exactness.

(7) On the Fourth Commandment.

He should be asked if he have neglected to go to church on Sundays and on the festivals of higher obligation, and whether it have been through any necessity, —as when shepherds cannot leave their flocks; mothers their children; relations their sick: when travellers cannot stop on their journey for good reasons; or when suitable clothing is wanting. Penitents should be questioned if they have done servile work on days of obligation, and if so, (1) what kind of work, and how long. Some theologians excuse from mortal sin those who work for two hours only: others allow a longer time, according to the lightness of the work and the reasons for working. The penitent should be asked how many times he has worked with the impression that he was committing mortal sin thereby: and it should be explained to him that to work for a long time even secretly for pleasure's sake and without recompense is sinful. (2) Inquiry should be made why he worked, whether out of necessity or the custom of the place. Poverty may be an excuse to those who cannot else provide for their own wants and for those of their families, as it may also those who mend their clothes on these days for lack of time on other days. But persons who work on festivals for their own house and without pay must be admonished that their conduct incurs the guilt of sin. There are cases when people may be allowed to work on such days in order to avoid temptations to idleness which are accompanied with the danger of particular sins, but these are exceptions to the general rule, justified only by peculiar circumstances. Workmen and domestics are bound to quit employers who insist upon their working on all days alike, and hinder their getting to church, unless their quitting them be attended with great mischief. This applies to the case of children whose parents oblige them to work on holy days. Penitents should be asked if they have kept the Friday, Lent fasts and vigils.

Observation of Sunday.

Sundays and festivals are to be sanctified—

1. By abstaining from sin and from all servile and unnecessary work.

2. By being present at the Holy Eucharist with devotion, as well at other Divine Offices.

3. By performing acts of charity and piety.

Sins against the Commandment which forbids certain works.

1. We must abstain from sin, such as excess of eating and drinking, theatres, and all places likely to tend to thoughts and acts of impurity.

2. We must abstain from work—specially from what causes others to work—from buying and selling, and making bargains.

3. We must not indulge in hunting, fishing, gaming, in unnecessary travelling, in drinking in public houses.

4. In giving too much time to visits and promenading.

Sins against being present at Divine Service.

1. Why not at Divine Service? How often not?
2. How often too late?
3. How often without religiousness?

α. Outwardly by unbecoming dress or attitudes, talking; signs and gestures to the discomposure of others; curious looking about, even with want of purity, to the scandal of others.

β. Inwardly, by voluntary distractions, how long continued? at what part of the service? without taking means beforehand to prevent them? or at the time to put them away?

γ. Neglecting to take to church children and domestics: to instruct them how to attend: to watch over and rebuke if needful their behaviour.

Sins against the duty of performing other good works.

α. Neglecting to meditate on the Gospel of the day and the great truths of salvation.

β. Neglecting to attend the Divine Service and instructions at church.

γ. Neglecting to make frequent acts of faith, hope, and charity.

δ. Neglecting to renew our baptismal vows.

ε. Neglecting Confession.

ζ. Neglecting holy readings.

η. Neglecting devotion to the Holy Trinity and the Passion of JESUS CHRIST.

θ. Neglecting the practice of corporal and spiritual works of mercy.

ι. Neglecting to prepare for death.

κ. Neglecting to have children and domestics properly instructed in Christian doctrine.

The penitent should be bidden call to mind how many Sundays and festivals he has profaned instead of sanctifying them, and to make acts of contrition for his past neglects. He should resolve to make up for past omissions and commissions, and try to live a life of prayer to GOD.

(8) On the Fifth Commandment.

Children should be asked (1) if they have hated their parents, which is a sin at once against religion and charity: (2) if they have disobeyed their parents in any grave matters, done what they were expressly and justly forbidden to do, stayed out late in the evening and gone with bad companions of either sex. Children however are at liberty to choose their own condition of life, marry or not marry, become or not become clergy or religious. (3) They should be asked if they have failed in showing respect to their parents in their presence or otherwise, by actions or words, by contradiction or vexing them. Children who fail thus should make amends by asking pardon of their parents, especially in the presence of those before whom they behaved ill. Whether this should be made a condition of absolution or a simple counsel depends on circumstances.

Parents, who confess, should be asked if they have neglected to cause their children to be instructed in the doctrines of the Church, to attend Divine service, and to avoid bad companions, or persons of the other sex: if they have blasphemed in their presence: if they have failed to correct them for their faults, such as lying or stealing: if they have allowed their daughters' beaux to come and stay at their houses: and above all, if they have put children of different sexes in the same bed: if they have denied them necessary food: and if they have forced their children by unjust means to marry, or become priests or religious contrary to their wishes.

Masters should be asked if they have duly checked their servants for blaspheming, or for neglecting their duty at the three great Festivals: for not going to church, or for tendering dishonourable proposals. Masters are bound to prevent such scandals as arise out of fairs, theatres, and the like. Husbands should be asked if they have supplied their families with necessaries; wives, if they have caused their husbands to blaspheme, by extravagance, contradiction and disobedience, and by not rendering due benevolence. Wives often by refusing this latter particular are damned, and cause the damnation of their husbands, by driving them to thousands of iniquities. But the questions should be veiled in discreet language, and then only where a well-founded suspicion exists—"Do you obey your husband in what belongs to the married state?" Or, "Is your conscience disquieted as to the duties of your married state?" Such questions however should never be put to women who lead a truly Christian life so far as is believed and known about them.

Duties of Fathers and Mothers towards their Children.

They ought to love and care for their children. This love should not be disordered, they must not love their children more than GOD, or in a way injurious to them. They must sanctify this love.

Their care for them must be of a temporal and spiritual kind. Temporal—so as to keep off all evil that can happen to them: feed and clothe them suitably to their position in life, and provide for them in like manner. Spiritual—they must labour for their salvation by setting a good example, and instructing them, by watchfulness, correction and prayer. They ought not to oppose their children, if they wish to enter into convents, when GOD calls them.

Sins in regard to children yet unborn.

1. When the mother has not offered them often to GOD, and prayed that they might receive Baptism.
2. When she has not avoided everything likely to hurt the foetus.
3. When the husband has grievously vexed and annoyed his wife, to say nothing of bodily violence.

In regard to children just born.

1. By not selecting a skilful midwife.
2. By not providing for the child's baptism.
3. By putting it off.
4. By not obtaining a good and virtuous nurse for the child.
5. By refusing it needful comforts.
6. By illtreating it through impatience.
7. By putting brothers and sisters into the same bed.

Neglect of instruction.

1. Neglecting to instruct them in necessary truths.
2. Neglecting to make them learn by heart prayers for morning and evening, before and after meat, acts of faith, hope,

charity, and contrition, to sanctify their actions, and go to church and confession.

3. Neglecting to send them to be catechised, and to inspire in them great horror of sin.

4. Neglecting to make them renew often their baptismal vows.

Sins through want of watchfulness.

1. Neglecting to put out of the reach of children whatever may be an occasion of sin, such as bad books, bad pictures, company of immoral or lax persons.

2. Not giving them good teachers, nor taking proper means to spur them on to make progress.

3. Putting them under the care of servants likely to injure them by their talk and example.

4. Not giving them rules for rising and going to bed, and for purity and modesty in bed.

5. Not making them work in a way suitable to their age and condition.

Sins through neglect to correct them.

1. Neglecting to correct them for their faults.

2. Correcting them unadvisedly, imprudently, excessively, passionately, with bad language.

3. Partiality to one, so as to pass over lightly his faults, while the faults of others are heavily visited.

4. Direct or indirect approval of misconduct.

Sins through want of setting a good example.

1. Not setting them a good example.

2. Showing a bad example by untruthfulness, uncharitableness, impurity, criminal acts, want of outward modesty.

3. Leading them intentionally to bad actions.

Sins in regard to their vocation.

1. Not advising them to pray, meditate, and consult GOD as to what state of life He calls them to.

2. To be guided only by human motives in advising them concerning their vocation.

3. Opposing their vocation.

4. Forcing them to embrace any state of life by coldness, threatenings, and bad treatment.

5. Hindering their fulfilling the duties of their state.

Reflections and Lamentations.

The penitent should be reminded that his children are GOD's more than his own, and be moved to contrition by the thought how by his negligence and bad example he has turned them aside from the service of Him to Whom they belong; he should be exhorted to pray for them that his example may not have caused them loss.

Duties of Children to Parents.

Children owe their parents love, respect, obedience, and service.

Sins of Omission.

1. Want of love, by not taking interest in that which concerns their parents: by not rejoicing in their happiness, and not grieving over their misfortunes: by not wishing for their salvation and praying for them: and by not giving outward marks of attachment.

2. Want of respect: by not having an inward esteem for them, and not honouring them outwardly in words, actions, and behaviour.

3. Want of obedience: by refusing to obey them when their commands are in unison with the law of GOD: or by obeying only with difficulty and murmuring.

4. Want of service: by not comforting them according to their power in spiritual and temporal needs: by not obtaining for them the Sacraments when death is at hand: by not burying them according to their condition: and by not paying their debts, and carrying out their last wishes.

Sins of Commission.

1. Hating them: rejoicing at any ill which befalls them, or wishing it to befall them.

2. Speaking unkindly or disdainfully to them: provoking them to anger: using wrong words to them: offending them by jesting upon them: spreading reports and slanders against them: daring to use violence towards them—by threats or blows.

3. Paying no respect to their expressed wishes: disobeying their clear commands: distressing them by leading a licentious life: launching into useless expenses, taking money or selling goods to meet them: forcing them to consent to an ill-assorted marriage.

Reflections and Lamentations.

Thou hast sinned by not honouring, loving, listening to those by whom GOD has given you birth and who occupy His place. What punishment dost thou not deserve for having failed in the essential duties imposed on thee by nature and religion? Pray for a filial piety which may lead thee to render them what is due to them, and to pray continually for them.

Duties of Masters towards Servants

Are the same in degree as those of parents towards children.

Sins of Omission.

1. Not loving them as brothers in CHRIST.
2. Not finding out whether they understand their religion, and not instructing them wherein they are ignorant.
3. Not encouraging them to confess and to use the means of making good confessions.
4. Having no zeal for correcting their faults, nor taking means to render their corrections useful.
5. Not giving proper and sufficient food.
6. Not providing for their temporal and corporal needs when they are sick.
7. Not sending them to the parish Priest for instruction.
8. Not watching over their behaviour.

Sins of Commission.

1. Having more servants than is necessary.
2. Taking such as are not virtuous and well conducted.

3. Setting them bad examples.

4. Leading them to sin by words and acts; making them accomplices in acts of injustice, impurity, intemperance, and revenge.

5. Speaking to them in a proud and disdainful manner, and rating them soundly for the least faults.

6. Breaking through engagements with them: withholding wages or delaying their payment.

7. Irritating them to passion and oaths.

8. Neglecting them when they fall sick.

9. Taking advantage of their distress to lower their wages.

10. Dismissing them without sufficient cause.

11. Taking away or refusing to give characters, prejudicing people against them.

12. Giving them too much or too little freedom.

13. Ridiculing them on account of their being religious.

Reflections and Lamentations.

Reflect, that he who neglects his own family is worse than an infidel. Remember, that GOD has intrusted thy household as to thy stewardship, for which He will call thee to strict account. Bewail the faults which thou hast committed in this matter, and resolve henceforth to make their sanctification one of the great objects of thy solicitude.

Duties of Servants towards their Masters.

Sins in choosing a Situation.

1. Taking a place without endeavouring to learn something about it, and to consult the advice of others.

2. Taking a place which is likely to be dangerous to salvation on account of masters, occupation, or fellow-servants.

3. Taking a place with a disposition to sacrifice one's soul to interest or other objects.

Sins against contentment with one's condition in life.

Instead of loving the work which GOD assigns, not submitting in the spirit of penitence: not offering to GOD one's sufferings:

murmuring against GOD, Who has placed us there, and suggesting to others like unchristian sentiments.

Sins against the respect and love which are due to masters.

By Omission.

1. Not honouring and respecting masters, be they what they may.
2. Not loving them with the supernatural love which leads one to rejoice at their happiness and to pray for them.
3. Not to bear with their defects.
4. Not to give them outward marks of honour and respect in meeting them, speaking to and waiting on them.

By Commission.

1. Entertaining feelings of contempt and aversion for them.
2. Wishing them, and that habitually, harm.
3. Speaking to them insolently, and abusively.
4. Turning them and their ways into ridicule.
5. Publishing their secrets: injuring their reputation, or their goods. Not instantly repairing the loss which has been caused.

Sins against Obedience.

1. Not obeying strictly, without murmuring, and instantly,—causing them loss by delay on this head.
2. Leading others to disobey by words or example.
3. Obeying them in things essentially wrong or forbidden.
4. Becoming partners in their misdeeds often and in special ways: and not repairing the loss which has been caused thereby.

Sins against Fidelity.

I. In words: by lies, false or indiscreet reports.
II. In work—
1. By loss of time.
2. By spoiled work.
3. By causing linen, clothes, furniture to be destroyed or injured, without restoring the loss or obtaining forgiveness.
4. Causing others to do one's work at the expense of his employer.

III. Betraying the confidence of masters in important matters with serious results.

IV. In regard to money matters.

1. By stealing or making masters pay dearer for things than they cost.
2. By not hindering others from stealing, such as children, fellow-servants and strangers, and by not giving warning against them.
3. By not giving up the full proceeds of sales.
4. By causing or alleging unnecessary or pretended expenses.
5. By making people pay to see the master.
6. By obtaining favours for unworthy people.
7. By selling favours which cost nothing.
8. Expending too much on food.
9. Taking, giving, allowing beer, wine, &c.
10. Taking perquisites which are forbidden by the employer.
11. Becoming a partner in the injustice of others.

Sins in regard to children.

1. Not watching over children intrusted to one's care.
2. Not training them in piety.
3. Not warning their parents when they commit grave faults.
4. Setting bad examples by word or deed.
. Giving them a taste for pride and vanity.
6. Not observing the rules of modesty in dressing them.

Sins in regard to leaving.

1. Leaving a situation where one can easily be saved without satisfactory reasons.
2. Not leaving a situation where salvation is imperilled either on account of proximate occasion of sin, or of being required to do what GOD's law forbids.

Reflections and Lamentations.

Consider that you have neglected opportunities for obtaining a good reward from GOD by serving your master with fidelity. You should behold CHRIST in the person of your employer and serve him as JESUS CHRIST. Lament the loss of merit you have sustained, and resolve to repair the same by dutiful obedience, patience, and humility.

(9) On the Sixth Commandment.

The penitent should be asked (1) if he have wished his neighbour ill, or have rejoiced at any ill which befell him, and he should be required to specify the kind of ill, whether death, disgrace, poverty and the like. The main point to be ascertained is whether in wishing any specified ill, he desired only that ruin in general might ensue, or that some special loss might befall his neighbour. One thing to be elicited is whether at the moment of wishing ill he had a deliberate will to see its accomplishment. He should be asked whether he have wished ill to strangers or relatives: especially to parents, wife, or children. He should be asked why he gave in to such wishes,—if he had a weighty reason for them, and were in a great passion,—in which case it is likely that he indulged in a formal wish for the accomplishment of the ill. And it is no excuse to urge that he did not mean anything by his wishes. Hence the number of times of committing this fault should be investigated, and any relapse should render delay of Absolution necessary, unless clear signs of contrition be evidenced. (2) He should be asked if he have abused his neighbour in the presence of another. In this case he is bound to make amends in the presence of the same, either by apologising or by tendering marks of esteem, provided that the injured party does not dispense therewith in order that his feelings of annoyance may not be renewed, or that others may forget the injury done to him, or through fear that the act of satisfaction might awaken afresh the sentiment of hatred. If the wrong has been done secretly, the injurer must ask for pardon secretly. We may observe that the words of abuse bandied about in the lower classes do not always convey the same amount of outrage which they literally contain, are not intended as such by the speakers nor understood in that light by the hearers. Penitents should be asked if they have caused and fomented strife by carrying tales from one to another.

Lastly, they should be asked if they have indulged in any enmity, and have refused the customary tokens of good feeling to their enemies. And it is not safe to absolve persons who profess to have forgiven those who have offended or wronged them, while they pretend that they are bound for the sake of society to let justice take its course. At the same time such persons may be absolved though while condoning the offence they claim a fair equivalent for the injury which they have sustained (provided that the offender be not too poor to give satisfaction,) or require that the offender go away to some distance for fear that his presence may revive old quarrels and render it impossible for the injured person to endure his insolence.

The Sixth Commandment forbids Corporal and Spiritual Murder.

Corporal Murder.

Persons are guilty of this if they do anything to harm their own health or life, or the health and life of others.

Sins against the care men ought to have of their own health or life.

1. Wishing for death through impatience or despair.
2. Doing anything with the view of bringing about one's own death.

3. Exposing oneself unnecessarily to the evident danger of loss of life.

4. Curtailing one's life by ruining health in excesses, labours, amusements, and even by mortifications.

5. Not doing what is reasonable and necessary for the preservation of life of ourselves and others.

Sins against the prohibition to attempt the life of one's neighbour and to injure his health.

1. Being glad at the death of another, or desiring it.

2. Striking, wounding, mutilating, and killing on one's own account, through malice or revenge.

3. Injuring a person's health by overtaxing his powers or causing him vexation.

A person may be guilty of murder—

1. In fact—by really killing a person by sword, poison, &c.

2. By commandment.

3. By advice.

4. By allowing it—when one is in duty bound to defend the person whose life is taken away.

5. By co-operation in aiding the crime.

6. By abuse of power, as is exhibited by judges who condemn contrary to law.

7. By ignorance,—such as physicians, surgeons, apothecaries, midwives, drivers, and all who by not being sufficiently educated or trained cause any one's death.

8. By indiscretion,—such as mothers, nurses, who overlie children; give them bad milk; neglect them in the cradle, or leave them within reach of danger. Those who being in the family-way do not take precautions to avoid premature births, or cause abortion. Nurses of the sick, and others who cause people to be buried alive.

Spiritual Murder or Scandal.

Scandal is an outward act, or permission of an outward act, which being bad or having the appearance of badness causes another to sin or hinders his doing something good.

Sins of direct Scandal.

Leading any one to evil, or from good—
1. By orders.
2. By advice.
3. By request.
4. By flatteries.
5. By ridicule.

Sins of Scandal by co-operation.

Aiding or encouraging a person in something bad, carrying or writing letters of intrigue. Taking in lodgers of bad habit and repute when they have no intention to amend. Lending one's house for balls, criminal intercourse, unlawful gaming, and smuggling. Concealing stolen goods. Sanctioning by one's presence places of improper amusement.

Sins of Scandal by causing others to sin.

1. Introducing indelicate modes of dress.
2. By wearing the same.
3. Exposing indecent pictures.
4. By going often into company with a person, using familiarities, taking liberties.
5. By making questionable proposals.
6. By obscene or dangerous songs, dissolute gait or manner.

Principles of co-operation to and in a bad purpose.

1. It is wrong on any pretext whatever to co-operate in anything essentially bad, such as blasphemy or perjury.

2. It is wrong to suggest to another a proximate or remote occasion of sin.

3. It is wrong to give or sell any one what is good or indifferent in itself, when it is certain or probable that he will put it to a bad use, and has no stronger reason for acting otherwise. This applies to publicans, milliners, apothecaries, printers, booksellers, and servants.

No one can lawfully co-operate in what has outwardly a bad end, unless—

1. The thing itself be essentially good or indifferent.
2. The same mischief or greater result from refusing.
3. One has no intention of doing wrong.
4. One is obliged by the State or those in authority over us to prevent the mischief.

No one can co-operate lawfully in what has outwardly a bad end, and is bad intrinsically, unless there is a good reason or at least more powerful reasons according to the degree of evil which is foreseen to result. Thus the stronger the reasons ought to be, the more closely one is called upon to co-operate, or that our refusal renders the evil less likely to result at all: or the more likely another is to suffer thereby: or the greater the evil likely to result: or the less right any one has to exact our co-operation: or the greater the obligation to hinder such evil result.

Reflections and Lamentations.

How often hast thou sinned through want of love to thy neighbour, and injured him in these ways? in treating thy friends as thy enemies? in scandalising instead of edifying? in leading them to sin for whom CHRIST shed His Blood? Repair the injuries thou hast done by praying for the repentance of those whom thou hast seduced into sin.

(10) On the Seventh Commandment.

Penitents should be questioned as to *thoughts,* whether they have had corrupt desires, or taken " morose delectation" in impurity, and whether they have clearly turned their attention to them and consented to them: whether girls, widows, or married women have been the subject of their thoughts, and what evil they thought to do with them. Many of the lower class, commonly speaking, specially in the country, deem whoredom a greater sin than simple fornication; while on the contrary they are not familiar with the sin of adultery, hence it is inexpedient to suggest such a sin to their mind. It is well to inquire in regard to these thoughts, to which they have assented, how often they have occurred and how long they have been indulged. Inquiry may be made how often in the day, in the week, or in the month, and during what time, minutes, hours, days, &c., they have consented to such thoughts. If however they cannot answer satisfactorily, they should be asked whether they have lusted after persons whom they have met or who have come into their minds, or whether they have been in the habit of dwelling impurely upon the thought of one person in particular through their never resisting bad acts of consent thereto; and whether they have always lusted after such a person or only as often as they looked upon them. Lastly, they should be asked if they have taken means to follow up evil thoughts, for then such means, however indifferent in themselves, become endued with interior wickedness, and therefore are to be explained as being exterior sins or deeds in their commencement.

As to obscene *words*, Penitents should be asked (1) in whose presence and how often they have uttered them, in regard to the scandal which is caused thereby,— whether before men or women, married or unmarried, young persons or adults. For young persons are more easily scandalised than adults, particularly such as are addicted to this vice. (2) What terms they used— such as to make mention of the organs of generation, which is close upon deadly sin. (3) Whether they have spoken out of anger, or joke, for in the case of anger there is less danger of any pleasure or scandal resulting from the use of impure language. The Priest should take heed not to absolve people who fall back into such ways of conversation, however much they may plead jesting as an excuse, unless they give signs of amendment or of extraordinary grief on account of their offence. (4) Whether they have boasted of committing any sin of this sort, for then there is often a concurrence of three sins, scandal to the hearers, boasting of the commission of sin, and pleasure taken in speaking of the sin; and therefore penitents must be asked what special sin formed the subject of their boast. Also they should be asked whether they have felt pleasure in hearing others talk indecently, and whether they tried to stop them when their interference was likely to be attended with good results.

As to *acts*—they should be asked with whom they had to do: whether more than once with the same person: when it took place, with the view of learning what occasions of sin might be avoided: how often the sin was consummated, and how often it was interrupted before consummated. And then the Priest may form his judgment as to the number of sins committed, by discovering how often the sin was broken off and renewed again before consummation: since it is possible that the sinner may have determined to sin two or three days, and never retracted his determination during that period. Persons guilty of self-pollution should be asked about immodest touch apart from pollution, and warned that it is deadly sin: also whether at the time of pollution they had in their mind the desire of carnal intercourse with one or more persons, for in that case distinct acts are committed accordingly. In regard to married persons, the Priest is bound ordinarily only to inquire, *when he finds it necessary,* of wives, if they have rendered due benevolence, and that only in the most modest way he can, and not to inquire further, unless he be asked questions himself.

The Seventh Commandment forbids different sins of impurity, and sins of intemperance come also under this head.

Sins contrary to Purity.

Sins by exposing oneself to the occasions of sin.
By looks:
1. Looking at dangerous pictures, nude figures, indecent acts.
2. Indecent dress, specially if on purpose.
3. Reading books of a dissolute or exciting character.

By words:
1. Talking licentiously or obscenely.
2. Suggesting to others evil of which they are ignorant.
3. Using words of double meaning with a bad intent: singing lewd songs.

By dangerous company:
1. Frequenting licentious company, disorderly houses, indecent amusements, and, under some circumstances, even public promenades, balls, and theatres.
2. Being on too familiar or tender terms with persons of the other sex, and intensifying them by letters, meetings, presents, &c.

By familiarities:
Too free and easy ways, indelicate conversation, kisses with improper feelings.

Interior Sins.

1. *Desires* to commit impurity—if long indulged? with unmarried or married persons?
2. *Thoughts* on obscene subjects indulged in with pleasure and willingness: not rejecting such thoughts at the time: neglecting means to prevent consenting to them when they continue: being more or less to blame even when they were not voluntary.

3. In *memory*, by taking pleasure in recollecting past impurities: in *understanding*, by voluntarily applying the mind to dwell upon them: in *will*, in consenting to irregular emotions of love, desire, vexation, &c., which inclination to such sins causes to grow in the heart.

Incomplete Exterior Sins.

1. *Improper emotions*—whether caused by the penitent? if so, whether voluntarily checked? whether prayer, acts of contrition, renewal of baptismal vows, thoughts of hell, or other efficacious means, together with prayer, have been adopted? whether any bad result came of them?

2. *Liberties* taken with oneself or others—whether in the last case the proposal came from oneself or another?

Complete Sins.

1. *Last excess of impurity*—with what condition? with unmarried or married? relations or consecrated to GOD? according to which kind of sin, fornication or adultery, incest or sacrilege is concluded.

2. *Unnatural acts*—which are the most detestable.

Sins against Conjugal Chastity.

1. Criminal indulgences.
2. Counteracting the chief end of marriage through the fear of having children.
3. Following passion only as the rule in the use of marriage.
4. Excess in the same.

Origin of Sins against Impurity.

1. Neglecting to take means to be chaste.
   α. Flying occasions.
   β. Labour.
   γ. Mortification of senses.
   δ. Distrust of ourselves.
   ε. Humble and persevering prayer.
   ζ. Constant meditation on the last ends.

2. An idle life.
3. Wine and good cheer.
4. Pride, vanity, desire to please.
5. Unmortified life.

Reflections and Lamentations.

Reflect that by Baptism thou hast become a temple of the HOLY GHOST. In Holy Communion thou hast become a living tabernacle: no more thine own, but JESUS CHRIST'S: thy members His members. How hast thou profaned them? Wilt thou allow them to be enslaved to an abominable passion which Christians ought not even to mention? No: renounce for ever so fatal a vice. Suffer a thousand deaths than once defile thy soul. Prepare for temptation by self-distrust, watchfulness over thy heart and senses: continuance in prayer and in labour and mortification. Resist temptation with readiness and with courage, taking the shield of faith.

Intemperance.

Excess in eating and drinking.

Sins of Omission.

1. Neglecting to beseech GOD's blessing before meals: and to thank Him afterwards, and this through human respect.
2. Not sanctifying one's repast by saying one's grace without devotion and by way of routine.
3. Not resisting inwardly an inclination to sensuality.

Sins of Commission.

In eating:
1. Choosing delicacies.
2. Only eating what one likes best.
3. Grumbling when food is not prepared to one's taste.
4. Eating more than is necessary, and even to disable one from his duties, and to cause discomfort.

In drinking:
1. Being passionately fond of wine or strong drink.

2. Being proud of being able to drink much without being affected.

3. Drinking often during the day without needing it.

4. Frequenting public-houses and passing much time there.

5. Being intoxicated—to lose one's reason: to be much affected: to incur considerable bodily disturbance. Habitually, or to the ruin of health.

6. Urging others to drink, designedly causing them to be intoxicated.

Reflections and Lamentations.

Reflect that you have made a God of your belly: sought in most of your meals to satisfy sensuality. How unworthy of a Christian nourished by the bread of Angels. Loathe the outrages you have committed by excesses. Never drink or eat without necessity. At the sight of drink fear to offend GOD, and beware of incurring His displeasure.

(11) On the Eighth Commandment.

The penitent should be asked if he has taken the goods of others, and describe who they be: whether one or several persons, whether once or many times; for every time that anything of importance has been stolen, deadly sin has been committed, and in that case restitution is imperative. This is true when a number of small thefts amount to something considerable.

Restitution must be made, if possible, immediately, though it be with some difficulty. It is seldom safe to give absolution first, and let restitution follow, for it is as easy to get people to be let blood as to relinquish money. Where the penitent is known to be timorous and scrupulous, or where immediate restitution is next to impossible, absolution may be given, provided that the person to whom satisfaction is due be not in extreme want, and that caused by the dishonesty of the penitent. It will be well to advise restitution to be made, in case of its being deferred, little by little, or to do some work by way of payment.

The following rules about restitution are recommended by one casuist.

1. If a person have stolen in company with others, the amount of his liability will be determined by the fact whether he was drawn into the theft, and so the theft would have been committed without him, or whether he concerted with and instigated others to commit it. In the latter case he would be bound to restore the whole, in the former only his quota. Often however it is necessary in the case of ignorant persons to enjoin restitution generally, and leave the amount to their conscience.

2. Where no gain has been derived by the theft, unless such a result were foreseen from the first, restitution is not required.

3. If the person robbed is unknown, restitution must be performed by almsgiving. This is a convenient mode of restitution whenever there is a difficulty of restoring even to a known individual. Shopkeepers who cheat by giving less weight or measure, must restore to the persons they have cheated by giving more weight or measure.

The Eighth Commandment forbids injustice: justice being a moral virtue requiring us at all hazard to render to all their dues.

Sins against Legal Justice.

Legal justice leads individuals and members of society to render what is due to society and its head.

1. Not to obey the laws of the Church, such as attendance at Divine Service, fasting, prohibition of marriage during certain seasons, and payment of tithes and other devotions.
2. Not to obey the laws of princes, magistrates, and police.
 α. Hunting on prohibited ground.
 β. Fishing in prohibited rivers.
 γ. Smuggling.
 δ. Not paying rates and taxes, customs, registrations, and other dues.
 ε. Selling above the price allowed by law.

Sins against Distributive Justice,

Or against that principle which leads the commonwealth or its head to distribute favours or imposts to the subjects according to their ability, merit or demerit.
1. Enacting unjust laws.
2. Not imposing burdens in proportion to the means and substance of those who are taxed.
3. Not proportioning the rewards and alms which one bestows according to the merit and poverty of individual cases.
4. Not punishing evildoers according to the laws.
5. Nominating unworthy persons to office. Persons who do so are held liable for the consequences and losses incurred, and for making amends.

Sins against Commutative Justice.

This binds individuals to render to others what is strictly due, and is violated in four ways. I. Receiving unjustly. II. Detaining unjustly. III. Causing loss unjustly; and IV. Breaking a formal or implied contract.

I. *Receiving unjustly.*

This is theft or larceny, and consists in taking unjustly another's goods against the will of him who owns them.
1. Is he who takes them poor? Only extreme necessity can be any plea. Is he a member of a family? He has no right to any money except what he gains independently and not on

account of his parent. If he appropriates any, it is theft. The same is to be said of expenses incurred by him, which his parent is forced to meet, or of presents made by him. Is she a wife? She has no right except to what has been assigned her by dowry or covenant. If she incur useless expenses for vanity's sake, gaming, or presents, she robs her husband. Is it a servant, who robs his master? The sin is worse. It is aggravated if the money stolen is public or religious. Its gravity may depend on the amount, whence it was taken? (as from a church,) how it was taken? (as by violence,) and for what purpose? (as for debauchery.)

2. Whether repeatedly? how often? and whether with the intention of repetition?

3. Whether in concert with others? commanding, advising, and urging by way of positive co-operation? or by way of negative co-operation in not hindering the loss to one's neighbour. Some lie under the chief obligation, as detainers of the stolen property, and when they restore, the others are set free. If the others restore, the detainer is bound to reimburse them.

4. The gravity is increased if the person robbed be poor, and by the consequences, such as its being the cause of violent temper, oaths, hatred, and of false accusation of innocent people. Persons are bound to repair whatever loss may result from the theft.

5. The time elapsed since the theft must be considered as well as how often the robber has contemplated restitution.

6. So too how many communions and confessions have been made without restitution having been made, which causes all to have been sacrilegious.

Other persons guilty of injustice by receiving Stolen Goods.

1. Those who fraudulently do not give what they ought.

2. Officers of justice, judges, pleaders, gaolers, solicitors, physicians, surgeons, &c., who exact what is not due or more than is due.

3. Shopkeepers who pass off bad articles for good: who sell

blemished animals for sound: who take advantage of people's necessities or ignorance to sell at too dear a rate, or buy at too low a price: who by falsehood persuade people that articles cost them more than they do.

4. Artisans who cheat in their work by performing it ill: day-labourers who waste time or cause others to waste it.

5. They who receive presents, gain at play, or buy of them who cannot give, ought not to play, or sell.

6. They who lend on usury, when they could lend without inconvenience gratis.

7. Those who join usurious societies without taking pains to ascertain the fact.

8. Those who take payment for what they are bound to do, or for doing what is injurious to another.

9. Those who usurp rights which do not appertain to them, or do other vexatious things.

10. Beneficed Clergy who indulge in useless expenditure, or give to relations who are in no need.

11. Those who appropriate treasure contrary to the laws of the country.

12. Those who take no sufficient pains to discover the owner of lost property which they have found, and failing the owner do not bestow it on the poor.

13. Those who make compensation contrary to rule.

14. Those who commence and prosecute unjust suits.

15. Those who make donations upon false titles: accept a void will: forge obligations or receipts.

II. *Sins by Unjust Detention.*

1. Keeping things lent, found, or gained by usury.

2. Neglecting to fulfil the duties of an heir in regard to legacies, debts, and acts of restitution.

3. Borrowing without being sure of being able to repay.

4. Putting off paying debts, especially to work-people and servants.

5. Being rendered unable by one's own bad conduct to discharge obligations.

6. Not taking the proper means to learn whether one was bound to restore property the possession of which was dubious.

III. *Sins by causing Loss Directly.*

1. By injuring animals, trees, crops, by design or negligence.
2. Obstructing one's neighbour's advantage, or causing him loss by lying, slander, violence, fraud, and unjust suits.
3. Excusing one person to the prejudice of another, in imposing taxes, &c.

Loss caused by Co-operation.

1. By command.
2. By assisting to carry out a command.
3. By advice.
4. By urging, approving, using flattery, or insult.
5. Concealing or selling what was stolen, or sheltering the thief.
6. Putting him on his guard.
7. By not hindering, as one's position required, being a father, servant, or magistrate.

Loss caused by Ill-discharge of Duties.

1. Undertaking what one is unequal to in knowledge and necessary qualifications.
2. Not discharging faithfully one's duties through negligence, human respect, or interest.

IV. *Sins in regard to Contracts.*

1. Not keeping to agreements while they were in force and the person could do so, and had no just reason for not doing so.
2. Breaking a promise seriously made with the intention of binding oneself, if it were accepted, when he to whom it was made has not relieved him of the obligation, or though no change of so considerable a kind has occurred to make it likely that any exemption would be made.
3. Appropriating what has been given otherwise than by will, when the gift would have been valid between living persons,

except for ingratitude on the part of the receiver and injustice on the part of the giver.

4. Receiving what has been given into one's trust, when he could not have been made heir or legatee.

5. Exacting something of appreciable value on the ground of loans. Not restoring what has been received by such usurious contracts, nor the loss suffered by payment of interest.

6. Co-operating in usurious contracts.

7. Cheating in exchanging money on the plea that money is due to the exchanger.

8. Creating private monopolies by a number of merchants combining together either to sell at an exorbitant price, or to get sole hold of a particular article of commerce, and preventing others from getting hold of it.

9. Buying at the current price with the covenant that the vendor shall at his own risk reserve the articles bought till the price has risen.

10. Selling with a covenant of redemption, which binds the buyer to resell at a lower price though no deterioration in value has taken place.

Reflections and Lamentations.

Reflect on the injustice of which you have been guilty, and resolve to make restitution; for without a willingness to do this you must be damned. You must render to Cæsar that which is Cæsar's, to every one what is due to him. Beseech GOD to reveal to you all the injustice you have committed, with a resolution to make reparation without delay and at any sacrifice.

(12) On the Ninth Commandment.

The penitent should be asked if he has taken away any one's character, whether he laid to his charge truly or falsely: if truly, whether the fault was public or private, where committed, whether by rumour or by a judge's sentence: whether he took away his character in the presence of one or of more, and of how many;

and if he have told the story as it was related to him, or as he knew the facts to be. If the charge be false, the defamer is bound to unsay what he said: if it be true, he ought to do all he can compatible with truth in order to lessen or do away with the ill impression he has created; to say all he can in the person's favour; and he should be required, as in the case of restitution of money, to do this before receiving absolution. To make one's neighbour's sins known is to slander him, and a sin, if the intention were to tarnish his character. This does not apply to cases when it is desirable that faults should be corrected, or injury to others prevented. Under the same head are included rash judgments: judgments are not to be considered rash where there are just grounds for conclusions, or where persons are right to harbour suspicions in order to prevent likely misfortunes, such as theft by their domestics, or bad associations for their daughters, so long as they keep their suspicions to themselves.

The Ninth Commandment forbids falsehood and revealing secrets.

Sins against Truth.

False witness:

1. Asserting on oath in a court of justice that to be true which one believes to be false.
2. Asserting as being a certainty that whereof one doubts.
3. Suppression of truths which one is bound to declare.

Slanders:

1. Imputing to one's neighbour what one knows to be false and injurious to his reputation, by words, writing, or before a number of others.
2. Laying to his account as though certain what is not so.

One is obliged to repair such injuries by unsaying them.

Other falsehoods are either injurious or agreeable or beneficial to one's neighbour, but are intrinsically bad and forbidden.

Sins in violating secresy.

Slanders:

1. Exposing without great necessity the sins of one's neighbour or his great faults to those who are not acquainted with them. This may be done even by gestures.

2. Exciting others to do the same: such as by questioning them about matters disadvantageous to one's neighbour, encouraging them, or continuing the conversation upon the same subject.

One is bound to repair this, by disabusing their minds as to the bad impression he has given concerning one's neighbour.

3. Listening with pleasure to slander though one has had no hand in it.

4. Not discouraging it by putting a cold and serious face upon it, and reproving those over whom one has any authority, or whom one might hope to influence against repetitions of it.

Secrets of others learnt against their will.

1. Listening to their confessions,—which is sacrilegious.
2. Listening to persons who speak of important matters.
3. Opening letters, reading private papers, such as written confessions.

Violation of secresy.

Exposing to others the secrets which have been entrusted to one, and the injury consequently inflicted.

Reflections and Lamentations.

Reflect upon the number of sins which thy tongue has committed. It was given thee to praise GOD and make Him praised, and has been often consecrated by the touch of CHRIST in the Sacrament. Repent of the offences thou hast committed against the charity which thou owest to thy neighbour, and resolve to repair all the wrongs done to him by thee in regard to his character. Beseech the LORD to "set a watch before thy mouth, and keep the door of thy lips."

(13) On the Tenth Commandment.

Penitents must be asked if they have sinned in heart by impurity—by desiring to commit it; by regretting the loss of any opportunity to commit it; by triumphing over past acts; by resolving to commit them anew; by taking pleasure in the recollection of past commissions, or in thinking over what they could or would commit.

They should be asked moreover whether they have sinned in like manner by thoughts of injustice to their neighbour; and by rejoicing over the wrong they have done him; whether they have desired their neighbours' goods in any way; whether they have wished the death of those to whose property, benefice, office, &c., they hoped to succeed; whether they have wished that people should be reduced to poverty and sell their possessions; or that dearness should raise the price of merchandise; or that sickness should bring about employment for physicians, quarrels for lawyers, &c.

The Tenth Commandment orders and prohibits explicitly what was implicitly ordered and prohibited in the former commandments,—namely, all that tends to prevent or to excite concupiscence.

Sins by way of Omission.

1. Not being content with our own and the position which GOD gives us.
2. Not stopping desire for what is another's.
3. Not labouring in that vocation which GOD has given us.
4. Not fighting against fleshly lusts, nor striving to mortify, crucify, and subdue them.

5. Not stopping sin in the beginning, nor persevering till it is extinguished.

Sins by way of Commission.

1. Envying the wealth and success of another.
2. Desiring to possess what is another's.
3. Pursuing greedily riches, honours, and pleasures.
4. Being oversolicitous, careful, vexed, distracted, and disquieted about earthly things.
5. Having sufficient, desiring more.
6. Being idle and not labouring to get one's own living.
7. Encouraging sin in the conception and birth, and allowing it to come to perfection.

Reflections and Lamentations.

Reflect upon the little care thou hast taken to check corrupt desires and affections. Bewail that thou hast not been pure in heart, that thou hast not been inwardly true, honest, charitable, meek, and patient. Resolve that thou wilt for the future watch the first beginnings of evil in thy soul and check sin in its fountain. Resolve to be contented with thy position in life, to be diligent in thy calling, and to envy no man.

TRANSGRESSIONS OF THE LAW OF THE CHURCH.

CONFESSION.

The Church commands every one whose conscience is troubled to resort to the priest, when they are in health: when sick and dying he is to move them to confession, if troubled in conscience about any weighty matter.

Hence the desire and intention of the Church is that the great majority of her children should frequently confess their sins. And without it very few ever break themselves of bad habits and practise Christian virtues. And in order to obtain absolution it is necessary to come properly disposed to the priest. Alas! how many sins are committed before confession, in confession, and after confession.

Sins before Confession.

By delay:

I. Passing a whole year with weighty matter troubling the conscience without making confession at any of the three great feasts, of which Easter is one.

II. Not confessing through sheer negligence of salvation.

1. At the time fixed by one's Priest.
2. When in danger of death.
3. When one has committed grave faults and feels the need of reconciliation with GOD.

By making choice of a too easy or less experienced Priest.

Choosing such as are not likely to find out one's bad habits and condition: or to send one away unabsolved: or to compel one to make restitution or be reconciled to enemies: or are likely to give a lighter penance.

By lack of self-examination.

1. Not examining oneself.
2. Examination without imploring the aid of the HOLY SPIRIT: without taking time enough: without really getting to the bottom of oneself: without desire of self-knowledge: and by seeking even to deceive ourselves on certain points.

By neglecting to excite oneself to contrition.

1. Not praying at all or doing any good thing with the view of obtaining contrition.
2. Being content with making a formal act of contrition without exciting oneself to contrition or without taking sufficient time for that end.

Sins in Confession.

1. Not speaking the truth upon important matters of confession.
2. Not avowing a mortal sin which is on one's conscience, or at least believed to be thereon.

3. Only half accusing oneself, disguising his faults, through not wishing to be thought as bad as he is.

4. Not thoroughly giving up all attachment to the sin which one confesses, and saying inwardly that he would commit it if he had the opportunity.

5. Confessing without having a true resolve to die rather than commit mortal sin : without wishing to fulfil the penance imposed : without intending to be reconciled to enemies, quit the occasion of sin, and make restitution, though ordered to do so by the Priest.

6. Not submitting to the directions of the Priest without disputing and murmuring.

Sins after Confession.

1. Not performing the appointed penance : neglecting to do it at the time fixed : not fulfilling the other orders of the Priest.

2. Falling back into one's old faults to such an extent as to cause fear that the confession was ill made.

Reflections and Lamentations.

Reflect that JESUS CHRIST has provided through His love to you the remedy of His Precious Blood, and that you ought to derive great profit therefrom. Lament the number of times that you have profaned this Blood by misuse of this Sacrament of Reconciliation.

COMMUNION.

Sins against Communion.

1. Neglecting to obey the Divine command to communicate.

α. When come to the age of discretion.

β. When in danger of death.

γ. Frequently during life.

2. Neglecting Easter Communion, because one did not choose to go to confession, or because the Priest did not find him duly disposed.

3. Not anticipating the Paschal Communion by a previous Communion when one foresaw impediments to the Paschal.

. Not taking means to communicate at an after period, when advised to defer one's Paschal Communion by the Priest.

5. Communicating at Easter out of human respect, without the due dispositions, after making a bad confession.

6. Communicating only at Easter through negligence of salvation, and so perhaps unworthily.

7. Communicating in a lukewarm manner, and risking sacrilegious Communion.

8. Frequently communicating without due devotion: with any affection for venial sin and without desire for the perfection which such frequent Communions are intended to procure.

9. Not following the advice of a Priest as to the time and manner of communicating.

10. Communicating without producing in our hearts the different religious acts which such a proceeding demands.

11. After Communion forgetting Whom we have received, and living in dissipation of thought, and even falling into serious faults.

Reflections and Lamentations.

Reflect whether all your Communions have been made with piety and devotion. Bewail your lukewarm Communions, lest haply you have like another Judas made them unworthily. Pray that you may die rather than make a sacrilegious Communion.

Fasting and Abstinence.

The Priest should inquire whether such persons have observed the rule of the Church as to fasting in Lent, on evens of Feasts, and Fridays: and whether they receive the Holy Eucharist fasting. As to days of Fasting and Abstinence, inquiry should be made in regard to the number of full meals taken in the day: to the quality of food taken at all meals.

The Law of the Church is infringed by not fasting on feasts occurring in Lent on any day but Sunday: by taking more than one full meal a day: by taking wine or beer out of meal times, the sin being greater or less according to the quantity taken:

by not fasting a part of Lent, when unable to fast the whole: by not fasting a little, when unable to fast strictly: by being too easily satisfied that one is unable to fast when he has not made trial of his strength in fasting at all.

Persons are dispensed from fasting who are under age: sick, infirm, convalescent, and aged: women with child or giving suck: persons engaged in hard labour: and such as never know what it is to get a full meal, and in general when health is likely to be injured.

People sin against the rule of fasting, not only by eating freely without permission, but even with permission, if the permission has been obtained on false pretences.

People sin against the spirit of fasting by not abstaining from sin, and from whatever is likely to minister fuel to their passions: by eating so as to escape the pain of fasting or indulging sensuality in the number and kind of dishes: and by not sanctifying the fast by offerings, prayers, alms, and mortification.

Reflections and Lamentations.

GOD requires of thee corporal and spiritual fasting. How often hast thou neglected the corporal fast which the Church commands thee to keep! How often hast thou neglected to practise the spiritual fasting without which it is not truly Christian! Beseech GOD to forgive you, and bestow on you grace to obey the laws of the Church in letter and in spirit.

The Priest should at the commencement of the confession of such persons, or of such as confess seldom, ask, if he do not already know, their state, condition, profession, trade, and mode of life: how long it was since their last confession, laying stress upon the good of frequent confessions: whether the last penance was fulfilled: if they know the Creed and Commandments: if they have duly examined their conscience, as is meet for so important a business. Upon all or any of these points the Priest should instruct the penitent as he finds necessary; specially to examine himself as to his whole life, distinguishing childhood, youth, &c.: distinguishing single from married condition: prosperity from adversity, health from sickness, times, duties, employments, companies, places, countries, dwellings, inns, thoughts, words, and works. He should instruct the penitent as to the necessary conditions for a good confession, as are briefly set down thus:

> "Sit simplex, humilis confessio, pura, fidelis,
> Atque frequens, nuda, et discreta, libens, verecunda,
> Integra, secreta, et lacrymabilis, accelerata,
> Fortis, et accusans, et sit parere parata."

It may be necessary to refer to past confessions in order to learn if anything rendered them void, and if on that account they needed to be gone over again, such as the having confessed to some one who had no authority to absolve, or did not use the right form; to a Priest so ignorant that he did not understand or know what was necessary in ministering this Sacrament; if the penitent had designedly suppressed some deadly sin in his confession, or the specialty of it, by calling parricide homicide, adultery fornication, &c.; or halved it by confessing part to one Priest and part to another; if he had confessed without any sorrow for his sins, without intention to amend, or having applied himself with diligence to bear them in mind. It is because persons sometimes do not confess in a right manner, but only through habit, and not with a distinct knowledge of their sins, and desire to amend, the Priest should in proper time and place exhort his penitents to make a good general confession in order to repair the failures of past confessions, and to enable them to turn to GOD with greater fervour.

After these introductory and preparatory questions, the Priest must as much as possible get the penitent to accuse himself first of all the sins which he remembers to have committed. After this finding, as often is the case, that the penitent needs questioning in order to recall to his memory many things which he has forgotten or has mentioned confusedly, the Priest should urge the penitent to recount the number of mortal sins committed by him, as nearly as possible. He should proceed with his questions in due order, beginning with the Ten Commandments, under which heads all sins may be reduced: yet as he has to deal with persons who rarely come to confession, it would be well to go over the seven capital sins, the five senses of man, the commandments of the Church, and the works of mercy. The Priest should try to discover the sins into which penitents are most prone to fall, and the circumstances which change the character of the sins or aggravate their guilt. These are set forth in the line:

"*Quis, quid, ubi, quibus auxiliis, cur, quomodo, quando.*"

Quis marks the quality of the penitent, whether learned or unlearned, married or single, lay or religious.

Quid, the amount and kind of sin, great or little, &c., in relation to the person injured, and to the wrong done him: whether to a father, a Priest, &c. How long sin has been persevered in: whether the penitent have blasphemed once or a hundred times, or habituated himself to it.

Ubi, whether the place were sacred or otherwise, public or private.

Quibus auxiliis, the quality of persons, instruments and means made use of by the penitent to effect his sinful object: holy things, deceit, spiritualism: his children, his domestics, &c.: whether he have struck a person with his fist, or with a stick, or a deadly weapon.

Cur, the end for which sin has been committed, stealing to gratify gluttony, drunkenness, or debauchery: backbiting for the sake of amusement or for the sake of injury : lying to deceive, or hinder mischief, &c.

Quomodo, manner of the act, whether committed with passion and maliciousness, in an unkind manner or otherwise, &c.

Quando, whether in the day or night-time: on a Festival or week-day : after Holy Communion, or otherwise, &c.

All these circumstances tend to create three different effects of sin: changing one sin into another; augmenting the gravity of sin; diminishing its enormity. As to the first, a man who commits a larceny offends against justice; if it be of sacred things, against religion; if it be by a religious, against his vows; if publicly, it creates scandal; if by force, it includes a twofold act of injustice. Thus one larceny may comprehend several shades of crime. As to the second, an educated person sins more than an ignorant person. As to the third, an ignorant person sins less than a learned person.

CHAPTER V.

HOW TO DEAL WITH DIFFERENT CLASSES OF PENITENTS.

(1) HAVING learnt by the self-accusations of the penitent or by his replies to the inquiries made of him, the Priest must proportion his counsels, his remedies, and his directions to the needs of the soul in question. And here it is that so much need of the greatest discretion exists in order to know both to bind and to loose, to retain and to remit. Here comes in the difference between the *rigid* and the *lax* Priest. The one scarcely absolves any one: the other absolves almost all who come to him. The best minister of confession will absolve more than the one, fewer than the other. The one is full of detestation for vices without compassion for the vicious: the other full of compassion for the sinner, without due consideration of the grievousness of sin. Thus by way of healing the one only applies the acrid wine of rebuke, while the other uses the oil of gentleness. The good confessor will pour into the wounds of the stricken traveller, after the manner of the Samaritan, both oil and wine. Let him be full of compassion for the sinner, as befits a father, and exhibits the mind of the SAVIOUR; here is the touchstone to distinguish between the zeal of JESUS CHRIST and the zeal of the

Pharisees. But he must preserve a true hatred of sin, for the good of the sinner, and charity will guide him in uniting to the strongest and most energetic remedies all the gentleness of compassion. Thus while the penitent humbles himself and becomes penetrated with compunction, he is not discouraged or irritated: on the contrary he regards the Sacrament of Penance with affection, and trusts in it and in its minister. "It is Confession," says S. Augustine, "by which the latent disease is probed with hope of pardon."

(2) The Priest who is too indulgent in giving too ready a credit to the reality of penitence, confounds willingness with will. The rigorist is slow to believe in true contrition, because he confounds efficacious will with its highest development: the real and sufficient will, however vulgar and ordinary, with the full and extraordinary, singular and heroic. Both extremes must be eschewed. True contrition is not easy to be excited ordinarily, without praying to obtain it and dwelling on the motives for penitence which faith suggests; but for him who prays and reflects, it loses its difficulty. GOD in short bestows the power of conceiving it. He who possesses a wise discretion honours both the justice of GOD which demands humiliation on the part of the sinner, and His mercy which hears his prayer. Contrary to the way of the lax confessor, the Priest must not recognise as a real act of the will, but only as a simple willingness, that motion of the soul which produces none or scarcely any result, such as is evidenced by taking steps to amend and diminish the number of ordinary trespasses. Contrary to the way of confessors who are always undecided, he should accept as

true, efficacious, and sufficient that will, which produces really observable effects during a certain period, even though it does not extend to producing them all and to preserving them always. He must not require a highly efficacious, extraordinary and heroic will, which produces an entire, perfect, unwavering, and constant change. Would to GOD that all sinners had such a will! all ought to desire and seek for it, but it is not all that have it. It is not necessary for their true and actual conversion and justification; it is enough that their repentance is efficacious, however common and ordinary, inferior to that singular contrition which transforms sinners into penitential heroes.

(3) A lax confessor is content to absolve a sinner because he protests his repentance without paying attention to any contrary presumption. A rigorist, not content with the absence of any well-grounded reason for suspecting the penitent's word, requires an evident certainty of his disposition. That the sinner has sinned in the past, and can sin in the future, are sufficient reasons in his point of view for testing the penitent longer and further. The Priest however before trusting entirely to the apparent good disposition of the penitent, should be careful to see that there is no circumstance which would fairly warrant a suspicion to the contrary. Should there be any, he should aid him in getting into a better state of mind, and if his efforts fail defer absolution. But if he find no sound grounds for distrusting his protestations of repentance, he should absolve him. When there appears nothing to the contrary, and the penitent says he repents, is resolved to amend, ready to accept the remedies and penances

prescribed, the Priest has all the certitude which can be desired, since the penitent is the most interested in making a good confession and obtaining a full and just absolution.

(4) One confessor is influenced by the fear of repulsing the penitent, if he send him away unabsolved, and thinks only of the immense loss which an abandonment of the Sacraments causes to souls. The other only thinks of the respect due to the Sacrament, and all impressed with the dread of making it of null effect, pays no attention to the inconveniences arising from sending away cases unabsolved. The Priest should fear equally these twofold dangers, of obstructing free resort to the Sacraments, and of compromising their validity. He must exercise all his charity as a father, adroitness as a physician, and discretion as a judge, to get the penitent into such a state as to be able wisely to absolve him either there and then or in a little while. By this he will be able at once to console the penitent and attach him to the remedy of confession, and secure the validity of Absolution as well as the respect which is due to it.

Practically, as we have said, one sort of confessors absolve almost all the world, and another sort absolve scarcely any at all. The Priest should be more closehanded than the one, and more liberal than the other.

How to deal with Children.

(5) In regard to *children* of from seven to ten or twelve years, according to intellectual development, the lax confessor proceeds with them as quickly as he would

with an adult guilty of the same faults, without giving himself the trouble of supplying the lack of the proper dispositions arising out of ignorance and infirmity natural to their age. It is seldom, generally speaking, except at the time of a dangerous illness, that young children receive absolution, because the nature of their faults is of so slight a kind, that it is scarcely possible to excite in them sufficient penitence for receiving absolution. Even when mortal sin has been incurred, it is difficult to inspire in them the needful contrition to justify their being absolved. It is also far from easy to make them understand the difference between temptation and consent to sin. The rigorist has a settled theory of dismissing them all alike with a blessing alone, because he thinks that they are incapable of that sublime and highly efficacious repentance which seems to him to be indispensable. The Priest should render them most special aid, and trust that they are capable of sincere repentance, though it be not of an extraordinary character. The Roman Church anathematises all who deny any but *idiot* children the right of Communion at Easter. And the English Church ordains that children able to say the Creed, LORD's Prayer, and Ten Commandments, and understand the Catechism, are to be confirmed without regard to age, and that if they be willing and fit to be confirmed, they may receive the Eucharist prior to Confirmation. How much more must the like principle be applied to Confession! Children therefore may receive absolution with much spiritual benefit, all the more that in some parts of the Church they are taken to confession after seven, and in some parts after five or six years of age.

The sooner, at any rate, children are instructed in the meaning of confession, and have it explained to them how to avail themselves of it the better. After a sufficient preparation for confession and Communion, and having made their confession two or three times, their absolution and Communion ought not to be deferred except for some very grave reason. Fathers and mothers, who do not bring them even at Easter to confession, are very foolish, seeing that true sufficient contrition is the work of grace, which abounds where there is least sin and where baptismal innocence yet lingers. Moreover, a good confession is more easy to a soul, which possesses less intelligence, if its will be still good and flexible, than to a soul which is more enlightened, if its will be perverse and obstinate. This is why adults are often less satisfied with their confessions than with those which they made in the age of innocence, from which they went away filled with compunction and consolation. On the other hand, in order to supply their defects, the Priest should pray for them, aid them in self-examination, and in repentance, by setting before them motives for contrition adapted to their age. After this, if they seem serious and show signs of understanding and actual devotion, they should not be deprived of the great blessing of absolution: if on the contrary they be actually thoughtless and unimpressed, it will suffice to dismiss them with a benediction. In all cases good thoughts should be suggested to them, so that they may depart with feelings of devotion and with the first motions of respect and love for confession. As their holy angels always behold the face of our Heavenly FATHER, so the Priest may be sure that they take account of his charity towards children of an age to which it is of the utmost importance for the soul to conceive immense horror of evil, and great esteem and affection for goodness.

(6) The Priest should exercise towards children the greatest possible charity and gentleness. If shamefaced and appearing on that account to hide some fault, they should be told that sins must not be kept secret through the feeling of shame in confessing them, that they are all known to GOD and to their Guardian Angel: that the Priest is bound not to repeat what he hears in confession, and that any sin kept back will be hereafter a cause of great distress and mischief, and will be after all to be confessed. He should ask them if they know the great truths. If they do not know them, he must patiently instruct them there and then, if time allow, or send them to some one for instruction at least in what is necessary to be known for salvation. In confession he should begin by making them tell him the sins which they remember, and then make them put their confession into the proper form, "I accuse myself of so and so,"—just as, if it be the first occasion of their coming to confession he should bid them repeat all that is necessary after him. Then he may ask as follows: (1) Have you concealed any sin through shame? (2) Have you said bad words, sworn, or forsworn yourself? (3) Have you neglected coming to church, behaved ill there, or worked on Sundays and days of obligation? (4) Have you disobeyed your parents, have you failed by disrespect towards them, raised your hand against them, abused them in their presence or in their hearing, or

made fun of them? (5) Have you neglected to say prayers morning and evening? (6) Have you quarrelled, told lies, insulted others? Have you committed any act of indecency? Here the greatest caution is required. The Priest should at first test the child by somewhat vague and indefinite questions.[1] "Have you said bad words? Have you played with other little boys or girls? was it in secret?" They should be then asked if they have uttered impure words or done dirty actions? It is often useful even though they deny having done so, to ask, "How often have you done so and so?" They may be asked with whom they sleep, and if they have played with their bedfellows? touched each other designedly and unbecomingly? But such questions as these should be put in the most guarded manner, and only when there is good reason to fear that the child has been exposed to temptations of this sort. It is better that a confession should be materially wanting in fulness, than that a child should learn or imbibe a desire to know what hitherto had been hid from its understanding. (7) They should be asked if they have taken what did not belong to them: or done any mischief. (8) They should be asked if they have said any harm of any one. The Priest must however be careful not to be too importunate in his questions, lest he disgust the child with confession for good and all.

(7) In absolving children great care is required.

---

[1] The Priest must proceed or not with such questions respectively, according as he has, or has not, reasonable grounds for suspecting evil, either from previous information, the manner in which each question is answered, and the like.

Sometimes they commit mortal sin in a case which would properly only involve venial, and incur the peril of venial sin only in a case which would properly involve mortal. It is therefore of consequence to discover how far they were conscious in each alternative of having rendered themselves liable to condemnation. It is easy to determine what to do when it is clear that they have a sufficient amount of understanding, by confessing with clearness, and answering questions correctly, that they are ashamed of having told falsehoods or of having done anything bad; that they have a due regard for obedience, and godliness, and know what is to befall good and bad people hereafter, and that they comprehend that by sinning they have offended GOD and have merited hell. In this case, provided they are duly disposed, absolution may be given them. But if they have fallen into mortal sin, they must be dealt with as adults, and if they do not manifest distinct tokens of contrition, their absolution must be deferred. If they seem to have little understanding, showing inattention by looking about, playing with their hands, and saying what has nothing to do with confession, but at the same time are in danger of death, or ought to communicate at the great feasts, they should be absolved conditionally, especially if they confess some doubtfully mortal sin. The same should be done in a relapsed case, for absolution should be deferred for those who have perfect understanding only when there is hope that the delay will enable them to come back in a better state to receive it. Care should be taken to ascertain whether they have made any effort to amend,—as whether they have refrained from lying when tempted to utter an untruth: or have checked themselves, when inattentive at church or in their prayers: or have resisted a lazy fit by returning to their studies and the like. But it is difficult to entertain any hope from delaying absolution in the case of such as have not the full use of reason. In order to ascertain their capacity for absolution, they should be bidden to make acts of faith, hope, charity, and contrition. If they can do so, the Priest should ask them whether they have felt contrition before they came to him, in order to assure himself that they do not come as mere machines. If they do not know how to make an act of faith, the Priest must instruct them, inquiring as to what they believe, and when needful, supplementing their defects by teaching them the doctrines of the Holy Trinity, the Incarnation, the Redemption, Rewards and Punishments,—going through the Apostles' Creed with them, and explaining to them the meaning of "Forgiveness of sins" with special reference to Absolution. They must be excited to contrition in the way most suitable to their age. Thus: "You love GOD Who is so great and good, Who made you, Who died for you, &c., and it is this GOD Whom you have offended. He is willing to forgive you, hope that He will forgive you for JESUS CHRIST'S sake, but you must repent. Do you repent that you have offended Him? You know you deserve hell for what you have done against GOD. Are you sorry that you have treated Him so ill? Never more, &c." After thus urging motives for contrition the Priest should try to elicit a sincere act of contrition and give as slight a penance as possible, and enjoin them to fulfil it without delay, lest they forget it.

(8) The Priest should remember that most people carry with them to the grave the sins of their youth: and on that account should use every effort to restore the young to GOD or preserve their innocence. He should neglect no opportunity of gaining their friendship: his happiness should consist in conversing with them, and entering into their ideas, and concerns, and occupations, as well as into their amusements and pleasures: directing them in all to the best of his power for their good. He should endeavour to keep them up to their confessions and communions, seek them out, pray for them, and urge them to pray for recovery of their first fervour. When he recovers them he should take the utmost care of them, and not content with this, should commend them to the oversight of some trusty and pious person, who will watch over them and keep them from dangerous companions. Meanwhile he should have great patience in bearing with them, though their conduct may be disturbing to himself when not displeasing to GOD, and so gain their hearts and confidence. It would be well to encourage them to confess often: and to inspire great humility in them before communicating: knowing that the devil is always most busy on the days of communion. For this reason he should induce them to let him have notice of their intention to communicate four or five days before, in order that he may stir them up to thirst with desire for the Sacrament, and get them to make acts of thanksgivings, and say other prayers, for some days afterwards.

Children who have sinned should be urged to avoid sin on the ground that it renders the soul as foul as the devil, while goodness and grace render it like the Holy Angels: that GOD clearly sees all things and is present everywhere, wills to crown the good with everlasting rewards, and to punish the bad with everlasting torments; and that He bids us avoid sin, obey parents, shun bad companions, and the like. It is one great benefit of bringing children to confession early, that, though they may not be deemed fit to receive absolution or the Holy Eucharist, they are thus brought into communication with the Priest, and are trained to self-examination, and so learn both to know their faults and to be ashamed of them, as well as the means of successfully combating them, of performing their duties, bearing their trials, and the like.

How to deal with Adults.

(9) Adults should be examined as to their faults in the same manner as has been suggested in the case of children, if their confessions do not seem satisfactory.

i. Specially they should be asked whether they have given way to bad thoughts, have spoken indecently and obscenely, whether they have wasted time, their parents' money, or pilfered from them, gone with bad companions, listened with pleasure to foul conversation, and laughed at it. As before noticed, in all matters relating to purity the greatest caution possible must be observed in putting questions.

ii. They should be specially advised to read the Holy Scriptures, such as one or part of any one of the lessons for the day: to cultivate a great horror of foul conversation, of equivocal language or *double entendres*, of gazing at persons of the other sex and familiarities with them: to unfold with confidence their temptations, so as to learn the best mode of meeting them: to shun bad companions, as the emissaries of the devil: to come to confession and the Holy Eucharist monthly, weekly, &c., as their different circumstances and dispositions allow: to examine their consciences every evening, and to have before them continually the presence of GOD and of their Guardian Angel.

(10) *As to vocation.*

In dealing with *adults* it is not the business of a confessor to decide on the state of life which young persons should embrace: but only to advise them according to the notes of vocation, which they exhibit to him, what they may reasonably judge to be the call of GOD.

Should persons wish to enter a religious order, advice can be given only after inquiry as to the particular order which is selected, because as a general rule it is better to remain in the world than to join a lax order, where people are sure to do as the rest do, and lose what little they had hitherto gained, and so deteriorate in practice and theory. The Priest should in such a case discourage such an idea, particularly if he be urged thereto by parents and guardians. If the order is strict and fervent, he should test the vocation of his penitents well, see if there be any impediment, such as want of health, or of talents, or the poverty of parents; he should also examine above all their intentions, whether they be to contract a closer union with GOD, to repair the disorders of their past life, and escape the dangers of the world. If their chief intention be worldly, such as to lead a pleasanter life, evade the disagreeables incident to their condition, or please parents who urge the step, the Priest should beware of promoting the object—there is no real vocation in the case, and the affair would end badly. But if the purpose of the penitent be good and there be no just impediment, neither the Priest nor any one whatever can without mortal sin oppose the resolution to enter a religious order. Sometimes it may be well to delay the carrying out of such an intention, in order to test the case, especially if there be reason to suspect want of stability, or that the resolution has been formed during a retreat or a mission, in which case people often make fine resolutions which vanish as soon as the first ardour has passed away.

(11) If a young man have formed an intention of becoming a secular priest, the Priest should not encourage him in his purpose except after he has been long and duly tested in regard to knowledge, capacity, and intention. Secular clergy are often involved in the same obligations—nay in higher than such as belong to religious orders, and nevertheless abide in the midst of the dangers of the world. Thus in order to be a good secular priest, he ought to have led a very regular life, severed from pleasure and idleness and bad company, and given to prayer and frequent use of the Sacraments. For lack of this he is in great peril of damnation, especially if he undertake the priesthood in order to further the views of his relations, the advancement and maintenance of his family. Parents must be discouraged from forcing their children to take Orders or religious vows. And in like manner young persons

should be dissuaded from making vows of perpetual chastity until they have been well rooted in the practice of virtue and formed in the habits of the spiritual life, and above all constant in prayer. They may however be permitted by way of beginning to consecrate their virginity to CHRIST for a certain period, as from one festival to another.

(12) With regard to those young persons who wish or *ought* to marry, on account of the danger of incontinence to which they would be else exposed, as parents would be in fault if they hindered their children contracting suitable marriages without just grounds, so children would be in fault if they disgraced their family by the marriages they contracted. Hence the Priest should do all he can to stop such marriages, and that too even if no dishonour be entailed, but only great vexation and annoyance result to the parents thereby.

(13) Generally in regard to *vocation* it may be said that the first point to be decided is whether the penitent is old enough to enter upon that subject. If he be so, the Priest must urge the vast importance of the matter, and show the grounds upon which any choice must depend. The Priest must remind him that he was created for GOD as the end and object of his being, and that all which is not referred to that end is worse than useless. This being so, that he must offer himself to the LORD GOD without any regard to aught beside, and be ready to embrace that state, which he believes to be most conformable to the Divine will, and most calculated to secure his salvation. He must be advised frequently to elicit an act of hearty desire to learn what the will of GOD concerning him is, to say during the

Holy Eucharist or at Communion-time, "LORD, what wilt Thou have me to do?" or, "Speak, LORD, for Thy servant heareth." He should take into consideration his talents, constitution, bodily powers, inclinations, means at his disposal: advantages and disadvantages, difficulties, perils, opportunities of serving GOD and of attaining to perfection. By putting all these together he may arrive at some conclusion what is most likely to contribute to his salvation and to the glory of GOD. Besides this, he should proceed to ask for illumination, and with the utmost care take heed not to commit even venial sin, lest it prove a bar to his enlightenment. The Priest should aid him, if need be, in these provisions, and not urge him to have any preference to one state above another, but let GOD guide His creature as He will. When he has made his choice, the Priest should exhort him to adhere to his purpose; and instruct him how he may best carry out his design. Should it happen that circumstances prove that the choice has been ill made, i.e. from some human or worldly motive, the Priest should dissuade him from forming any determination save with a view to the glory of GOD and the good of his own soul. Above all, the Priest must beware of allowing any one to take a vow of chastity except for a time or in the case of persons of mature age, less likely to break it, lest hereafter it become the subject of regret, and either be broken or be kept only with grief and anxiety.

(14) In regard to *females*, the Priest cannot be too cautious not only for fear of evil itself, but also for fear of the very semblance of evil. He must avoid steadfast gaze, soft words and tones. He must not trust too much

to their tears and complaints, but bid them pray for patience, nor trust too much to their revelations, but bid them keep the commandments of GOD. Not only in but also out of church must he avoid being with a female alone, nor touch her hand nor allow her to touch his hand. In questioning them, he must be more on his guard if possible than with young children, so as not to add to any knowledge of evil which they already possess.

He must bear in mind what are the special faults of women,—such as feed vanity and pride by spending too much time at their toilette, making themselves conspicuous, aiming at being admired, and showing jealousy when others are admired: dressing to excess and exhibiting more of their person than is decent, wasting time in visits and gossip, neglecting Divine Service and preferring late Celebrations to early Communions. In like manner matrons are liable to think more of personal vanity than of domestic duties. Such persons should have the Blessed Virgin proposed as an example of modesty, and humility, and purity. The Priest should in giving penances have regard to the best mode of correcting these feminine weaknesses.

If the Priest be inquired of respecting *their dress,* he should say that it should be suited to their condition, age, and position: and not be adopted out of vanity or desire to assume the appearance of beauty: that it should not cause family difficulties through its expensiveness, nor sin in others by its immodesty. They should not go into public with the view of exhibiting themselves to those who have wrongly formed attachments to them, but they are not, if their intention be pure, bound to shut themselves up on account of the wrong feelings they may produce. They must not however accept presents from such persons, nor allow endearments from them, however innocent on their own part. In regard to balls and dancing, the Priest must be careful how far he gives permission to attend them, both as to place, persons, and kind of dance.

(15) *When an engagement to marry has been made*, great care is demanded of the parties to avoid everything contrary to modesty and unbecoming. They should not be too familiar with each other, especially in the absence of others : everything should be avoided which tends to disturb the passions, and excite bodily emotions. After an engagement has been made marriage should not be too long delayed. Care must be taken that both parties enter upon marriage in a state of grace; live in peace together, bear each the other's burdens, remembering that they are human and liable to fail. The wife should obey in all things lawful: yield to her husband when angry, counsel him gently when doing wrong; bring up her children as the gifts of GOD and as being accountable herself to Him therein. They should be advised to have prayers together with their household at least every evening before bedtime, and to frequent Divine Service. Much of this applies equally to the husband, but he is specially to be exhorted to treat his wife as a partner and not as a servant.

(16) In regard to the *stupid, ignorant, and less instructed*, if their confessions seem defective, they should be examined by questions as to their occupations and the breaches of the Divine Law likely to be committed

accordingly: as for example, whether they have given way to foul thoughts; indulged hatred, envy or malice, or wished people ill, or rejoiced at their misfortunes? whether they have blasphemed, sworn, cursed, slandered, made imputations upon them, quarrelled? how, when, and whom, &c.? whether they have fallen into sins of commission or of omission? laboured on Sundays, or come late or not at all to Church? whether they have been drunk partly or entirely, and what they did in that condition? whether they have caused damage to any one, defrauded any one, cut down other people's trees, or pastured on other people's land, &c.? If they only admit having sworn or cursed their cattle there is a high probability that they are very ignorant, and inquiry should be made and instruction given accordingly.

Hence they may be bidden prefer the salvation of the soul to all else, and having regard to the shortness of life think that it is the service of GOD alone which is profitable now and for ever: remember that CHRIST spent His life from His childhood in toil, that GOD has appointed them also to toil and promised rewards thereof: that holiness consists in doing our duty, whether rich or poor, in that state of life to which He has called us, and in fulfilling His will: that it is grace alone which makes one really greater than another, and that they should seek for true riches in the Sacraments, by which grace is imparted. To complaints of poverty the Priest should reply that GOD could have made them rich as easily as He made them poor, and that GOD loves the poor in giving them poverty, since riches might have caused their destruction. Man knows not what is best for him. GOD feeds the ravens, and will feed them who are of more moment in His eyes. They should rejoice in being poor like JESUS, and unlike the rich man in the parable. Many would be now in heaven, who are in hell, if they had been poor; many would not be in heaven, if they had been rich. Hence it is that the Saints have always chosen poverty. Life is a play, in which each sustains a part for a while,—of a king, or of a beggar: he who best plays his part will be praised and rewarded. They should think how good GOD has been to them: how merciful and patient to them when neglecting His service: how kind to them on their return to Him. He has given us His SON and all things with Him. He Who gives Himself, what can He refuse or keep back? He is truly rich, who has GOD.

If they cannot make acts of love, hope, and faith, and contrition, the Priest must get them to repeat them after him. At the close of the confession he must inspire sorrow for sin in a way suited to their capacities, rousing their fears by the thought of death, judgment, heaven, and hell: expounding to them GOD's love and kindness in bearing with our sins, and His desire to save us: how much we ought to have loved Him and served Him. The Priest may compare the ingratitude of a rebellious son, of an obstinate servant, of one who has behaved ill to a benefactor, and inquire what they merit for such ingratitude? And if the father should be willing to receive his son again, what ought to be the feelings of the son, what shame, what confusion? We are such sons—and have offended a Good FATHER in spite of His repeated pardons and longsuffering. "I have been a very Judas to CHRIST, a very Esau. LORD JESU, for the sake of Thy Incarnation, Birth, Sufferings, and Death, forgive my sins. I am grieved that I have sinned so repeatedly against Thee. Help me to serve Thee and follow Thee."

If the unlearned person say, I do not remember my sins,—we are all sinners,—I have nothing particular to confess,—he must be questioned in the simplest manner as to whether he have ever told lies, disobeyed his parents, been in a passion, stolen, neglected his prayers or going to church, slandered others, and so on. If he confess none of these, he must be questioned about necessary truths, for it is probable that he is not acquainted with them. If he prove ignorant and cannot be taught then and there he must be sent away with a warning not to communicate, and with a direction to obtain the necessary knowledge. It may be well that the Priest should take some steps in the matter in regard to his being instructed in all things needful to make a good confession. If he be duly acquainted with necessary truths or can be readily instructed at the time he must be taught to make acts of faith, hope, charity, and contrition, and of due purpose of amendment, and be induced to grieve for the sins which he has in the past committed. If he appear to be contrite and duly disposed, and has not been for half a year or so to confession and be not likely to come again, he should be counselled to pay more attention to his soul's interest, and may receive absolution: for it is certain that when a penitent cannot otherwise accuse himself it is sufficient for him to confess himself guilty in words in order to be validly absolved, especially when the necessity of the case and inability to confess more than this demands. There may be cases where the penitent cannot comprehend the necessary means of grace,—it is for the Priest to discern whether this dulness be the result of past sins, or arise from natural constitution of mind. In the first case absolution might be deferred till the penitent be withdrawn from his sins; in the second, provided the penitent seem well disposed and to have led a godly life he may be conditionally absolved and admitted to Communion. Natural dulness may be concluded when the penitent seems equally obtuse in temporal matters, and, if he be not so, his dulness may be ascribed to his sins. He ought then to be questioned with great caution on the subject of impurity, as being a common cause of spiritual obtuseness. In the case of extreme stupidity he must be dealt with as a fool or a child: if the penitent's dulness proceed from age, he may be absolved if it appear that he once knew what is necessary to be believed. If not, he must be speedily taught, lest increasing years bring increase of stupidity. *Penances* for such persons should be such devotions as they can perform on the day itself or on the next festival. Thus if confession have been neglected a suitable time should be fixed for their next confession : if they have sworn or cursed they should say for a fixed time three Our FATHER's in honour of the Holy Trinity, offer their labours and toils to GOD as an act of satisfaction, and beseech grace to amend, asking pardon for their sins every evening : as often as they swear or curse strike their breasts and ask pardon. Should they forget to do so, they must be told that it will suffice to make up for their omission when they remember. In the case of many sins having been confessed it may be enough for want of a more suitable penance to enjoin the penitent to offer the Holy Sacrifice on certain Sundays and festivals up to a fixed period, as a satisfaction for his sins : to make acts of faith, hope, charity, and contrition before and after Communion. They should be urged moreover to be on their guard against some special sin and offer their resolution on this head to CHRIST after Communion.

(17) *Duties of Married Persons.*

To entertain mutual love towards each other, and to correct each other's faults in the spirit of love, and not in exact proportion as their faults deserve. The mode of correction of wives depends upon the customs of the place and condition of the wife. The wife sins by arrogating too much authority,—and the husband by treating her as a slave and not as a partner, by not providing for her according to custom, by leaving her without due reason, such as cruelty or adultery. The wife is not bound to follow her husband wherever he choose to go to her disgrace or serious inconvenience, unless previously arranged at the time of marriage. If the wife leave her husband without just cause he is not bound to maintain her. The wife is not bound to render due benevolence, if grave damage be apprehended for herself, her husband, or her offspring, as the result: nor if her husband be afflicted with contagious disease, unless it were known at the time of marriage and were not of a very grave nature; nor if she herself were ill in such a way as to be likely to suffer : nor if she cannot have any but stillborn children : nor if her husband be mad or drunk or brutal: nor if divorce have been pronounced, or vows of chastity have been made with mutual consent : nor if he have been unfaithful : nor if he seek it unnaturally. It must be held that anything done to hinder the procreation of children, or to risk their being stillborn, is sin. Certain provisions of the Jewish law, though they are best observed for the sake of the offspring, prohibiting the wife to render due benevolence at certain times; are not absolutely obligatory. On the whole we may say with Bishop Jeremy Taylor (Holy Living) that " he is an ill husband, that uses his wife as a mistress or harlot, having no other end but pleasure. Concerning which our best rule is that although in this, as in eating and drinking, there is an appetite to be satisfied, which cannot be done without pleasing that desire, yet since that desire and satisfaction was intended by nature for other ends, they should never be separated from those ends, but always joined with all or one of these ends, *with a desire of children, or to avoid fornication, or to lighten and ease the cares and sadnesses of household affairs, or to endear each other;* but never with a purpose either in act to desire or separate the sensuality from those ends which hallow it. *Onan* did separate his act from its proper end, and so ordered his embrace that his wife should not conceive, and God punished him." Married persons are to be exhorted to use moderation in the use of their lawful pleasures—" according to the following proportions—to consist with health, not to be too expensive of time, with temperate affection, without vio-

lent transporting desires, or too sensual application"—
"Let each of them be temperate, and both be modest."
With the above limitations it may be said that many
things in thought, word, or deed, are allowable in the
case of married persons which are sinful in the case of
unmarried.

(18) *Property of Married Persons.*

Husbands are bound not to alienate nor impair the
property which has been tied up to their wives or bequeathed to them, except with their consent freely and
fearlessly given. At the same time the husband may
make use of the interest arising out of the property,
which has been given with the wife by way of dowry.

Property acquired by their common labour or industry is held in common, during their cohabitation.

The husband sins grievously by allowing through his
own fault any grievous loss to befall his wife's property.

The wife, when the husband fails to provide for her,
may spend the husband's money for food, clothing, almsgiving, and such recreations as are permitted respectable
matrons, unless the state of family affairs require otherwise. She may lay out his money if needful for his
spiritual good, or to avert some great family misfortune,
or for her children's benefit; or to prevent her husband
reducing them to indigence by his extravagance and
excesses she may save what she can without his knowledge,—and she may take out of the common property
an equivalent to the husband's waste by drink, &c., as
having a right to half of it, even though there be no
imminent danger of their coming to poverty. She may
also take money given her by him to pay debts for

serious family necessities. She is not bound to pay his debts contracted before marriage out of the money tied up to her, but she ought to contribute half out of any other money within her power towards liquidating debts contracted during marriage for the good of the family and by mutual consent. She may aid her poor relations and children by a former husband, even in spite of her present husband, with moderate alms according to her condition. If her husband die in debt, she may take what is necessary for her own sustenance and that of her children.

It is to be borne in mind that much depends on the laws of different countries as to such points.

(19) *Obligations of Parents*

Are threefold—care of the bodies of their children, of their minds, and of their souls.

Hence they sin—the mother by giving way to passions of the mind, when she is *enceinte,* and by using too great bodily exertion: the father by exasperating the mother to anger, &c., and endangering the child's life or health by cruelty. So, if the mother cannot herself suckle her child, and does not provide a proper and healthy wetnurse. Parents sin, if they neglect to provide for children unable to earn their living, or waste their goods, or pay no attention to their affairs, and so fail to leave a sufficient means of livelihood behind them: if they expose their children at the doors of hospitals when able to bring them up, and especially in any case if they neglect to see that their exposure has no risk of death attending it: if they disinherit their children wholly or in part without just cause: if they compel their children to enter into the Religious Life, or hinder them when so minded, or forbid their marrying altogether without just cause: if they do not take care that they be baptised and Christianly and virtuously brought up, and if they allow them to consort with bad companions: if they send them to heretical or secular schools: if they do not correct their faults, or if they punish them without charity or without righteous zeal, but only out of passion and disproportionately to the offence: or call them by opprobrious epithets. A father may exclude a son from his house, &c., who has contracted a disgraceful marriage, for a time, but not for ever. Parents ought not to make known to externs the otherwise secret faults of their children or domestics, except there be some good reason for doing so, but may tell each other of them: and the mother ought to do so if she cannot herself keep them in order. A parent is not bound to proceed as in a court of justice in the correction of his children, but may be content with less evidence than would be demanded therein. But he must also take care that the punishment shall not be so grievous as the fault deserves.

The Priest must take into account the sins of parents, who offend in the above particulars, according to the gravity of the matter, the injury and loss caused, and the circumstances of the case.

Widows sin by appropriating clandestinely their husbands' goods beyond what is their right by custom and law: by not inserting such effects in inventories, or by putting a lower value on them than is just.

Widowers by not giving their wives' heirs what is justly due to them : by cooking inventories either to benefit their new wives at the expense of children by the former marriage, or *vice versâ :* or by mismanaging their common property and their children's.

(20) *Of Temptations likely to befall the above.*

These arise either out of their faults, out of the bad conduct of their children, or out of an inordinate anxiety about maintaining and enriching them.

When a wife complains of her husband, the Priest should be willing to believe that she has not much reason on her side, and not condemn the absent; and it is best to counsel prayer, patience, and meekness. A woman's tongue is often the cause of domestic strife and unhappiness, and should be therefore restrained. If she complain of her husband's severity and passionateness, she should be told to pray for him, be more than ever watchful to please him and generally complaisant, and precise in her obedience to his wishes. When her husband is in a passion, or overcome by drink, she should be silent, or at least give a soft answer, and behave as if she had been in the wrong; when a good opportunity arises for giving him counsel, she should do it with gentleness. Patience is after all the best and only remedy when all else fails, and she may hope hereafter for a plenteous reward, and for present interior consolations. If she attempt to rule her husband, he should be advised to reason with her gently and firmly : doing as he thinks right in spite of her, though yielding to her when he can with propriety, so as to keep her in good cue. If the husband complain that his wife drinks, he should be asked if he be himself always sober, and be directed to set her a good example, allowing her at the same time what is usual and fit for women of her station. He must hope that by gentle admonitions, patience, and good example, he may at last succeed in persuading her to amend. But if the husband drink, he must be counselled to avoid all places and persons and things likely to lead him astray, and ordered to abstain on such days as may be foreseen to be accompanied with temptations, or not to drink more than he knows he can carry, or he should pledge himself to abstain altogether for a time, or never to enter a public-house, or never to drink more than he knows is safe. He should not promise to abstain longer than he is likely to keep his promise, or can safely do so without peril to his health by going from one extreme to the other. It is best to give it up by degrees: he should ask his wife to help him to keep his pledge and hinder his violation of it. He should take care to breakfast early, not to drink before eating, and to eat or drink something sour: not to drink several kinds of wine: not to eat windy kinds of food while drinking, to drink slowly, to drink water largely after he has indulged in company with others. If the father complain of his children being disobedient, and of their provoking him to impatience, cursing, &c., he should be counselled to avoid sin and obey GOD himself: to examine himself whether it be not through his own fault and bad education of them, whether he has not dealt too harshly with them, and exasperated them: he should be reminded of what he was in his youth, and bidden to wink at small faults and rebuke greater with more mildness. He should urge his children to be good by kind words, take away indulgences from the bad-behaved, and bestow them on the good. If parents complain of the want of means to provide for their children the Priest should exhort them to bring them up in the fear of GOD, as the best inheritance: to have faith in GOD, and His Providence: and remind them that children belong more to GOD than to their parents, and that He will care for them: that an ample inheritance is often a loss to children both here and hereafter.

(21) *Advice to Parents.*

Parents should be counselled to take care that their children be well trained and taught according to their station: sent together with domestics to Church and Catechising: and to examine them on their return: to set a good example in words and deeds: and not to find fault if they be detained at Church longer than usual. They should not allow servile work to be done on Sundays more than is necessary: they should take care to have prayers said at least every evening: bid their children and domestics go to Confession and Communion at certain times: have pious pictures and crucifixes in their houses to the exclusion of such as are of questionable benefit: try to preserve unity, peace, and concord: not preferring one child to another. The mother should not interfere when the father punishes in a discreet manner: nor caress the punished as if not in the wrong. The parents should on this head not rebuke one the other except in private. They should set an example of goodness towards the poor, and sometimes make their children their almoners, by way of training them in works of mercy and charity. The mother should be a pattern of modesty, industry, and diligence.

(22) *Duties of Children in regard to Parents.*

They should be reverent, loving, and obedient: support their parents when old and destitute, in sickness or in misfortune: not oppose their making pious legacies, nor neglect to carry out their last dispositions, and bury them with customary propriety. They must not exhibit anger or hatred, nor treat them harshly and rudely, nor illuse them, save to preserve their life and limbs. They must not wish them dead, nor charge them with crime, except in the case of public safety, &c. They must obey their parents in all things relating to the government of the home, not contract ill assorted marriages against their will, or without consulting them. All rebellion and contumacious conduct in regard to express commands of parents is grievous sin in itself, though excusable in some cases on the ground of age, infirmity of character, education, &c. The child ought not to do what he knows will exasperate the parent, though the act may in itself be innocent. What is respectful or otherwise to parents may be further determined by the custom of the place or people. Many acts of disrespect are more grievous in the case of children's behaviour to their parents than in the case of others—since parents stand to their children next to GOD.

(23) *Of Children's Goods and Rights.*

These may be divided into earnings, and acquired property, as by will or gift. The capital belongs to the child, and so long as he is a minor, the interest may be expended by the father. The child sins by spending while a minor such interest without the knowledge, connivance, or will of his father, and is bound to restitution, if his father be not likely to condone his expenditure. So also by taking what his father would be likely to refuse him for drink, gambling, &c. The extent of the fault depends on the means and condition of his parents, the number of children, and general treatment of the children by the parents. Boys at school or college may spend a certain part of their allowance for expenses upon their amusements unless their parents prescribe otherwise. The amount expended must depend on what is customary and likely to be approved by their parents. A son sins if he expend without his father's consent, implied or given, on his own amusements, &c., what he acquires by labouring on his father's property, and acting in any way as his clerk, agent, deputy, &c. Unless a fixed salary be agreed upon, he cannot claim more than board, lodging, and clothing. If a son have the management of his father's property and his father die without giving him compensation, or putting it in his will, he is not justified in settling his father's affairs to take a larger portion for himself except with the consent of the family. If a son have taken anything from his father in his lifetime, he is bound on the division of the inheritance to make restitution to the other children, unless his father have remitted the obligation to do so in his lifetime, or unless the others when acquainted with the facts condone his acts. In dividing an inheritance, there must be a deduction on account of the expense which each child has caused his parents, unless the parents have otherwise directed. A disobedient child should be reminded how much suffering has been endured by his parents on his account, in order to bring him up honestly and respectably: and that a child ought to try to diminish rather than increase their cares. If he sit and eat with his parents he ought to show them honour and respect. To disobey parents is to disobey GOD, and how can disobedient children look for His blessing? If he have been rude and insolent he should be advised to return home and ask pardon; or if this be too difficult, to show by his conduct and words that he is willing to be amenable. If he complain of a parent, in being harsh to him and kind to others, he should be asked if it be not the result of his own behaviour, and urged to show himself more amiable and respectful, so that his parent may be moved with more affection towards him. If he complain of his parent's dissipation, improvidence, and bad management of affairs, he should be told to be more diligent in attending to his own business and consult his friends or pastor how to get his parent to a better mind—pray for him, bear with him, and so, if all fail, secure himself a reward in the world to come, as well as GOD's blessing here.

(24) *Of the Duties of Superiors.*

Those who are over others as masters and the like, are bound to take care of those who are under them as servants and the like, and to do for them according to agreement expressed or understood, as being in the place of parents to them.

Masters therefore sin by not taking care that their servants keep the laws of GOD and of the Church: by not removing them from all risk and opportunities of sin, as far as possible: by not rebuking the sinful: by not instructing the ignorant, and counselling them in all things needful for salvation: by not giving them sufficient food and just wages at the proper time and as expressed or implied when they were hired: by dismissing them without due reason before the close of their engagement, or treating them so that they are obliged to leave them, and that without paying in full all that was due to them: by refusing to pay their wages or any portion of them, because they do not require their services or do not choose to avail themselves of them: by not duly supplying them with food and medicine when they are sick for a short time: by refusing to give characters out of spite, and so keeping them out of situations without due cause. Masters are not bound to pay and maintain them, if they are long ill, except by agreement. They should however generally be exhorted to treat their servants kindly and liberally, to be gentle and moderate in finding fault, and often to wink at slight failings: not to publish their errors, except when called upon to give a character, and then not to say more against them than is needful to caution their future employer.

(25) *Of the Duties of Servants.*

They ought to obey in all things relating to good behaviour, and to the terms of their agreement: to be diligent in discharging their duties, to remain as long as they are bound by their covenant, except some reasonable ground of leaving arise, and not to waste or destroy their master's property. Servants therefore sin by negligence in their duties, by leaving their service before the proper time: by not doing their best to prevent loss or destruction of their master's property, especially such as is directly intrusted to their care, in regard to which an obligation of restitution will lie: by asking for higher salary than that to which they are entitled or their masters could be expected from their station to give: by discontentment with the wages agreed upon and by secretly increasing them at their master's expense on pretence that their labour deserves a higher recompense than that which was covenanted: by feeding cattle more than their masters order or expect, (though this unless excessive is not a deadly sin, nor requiring restitution:) by spending more on journeys and refreshment than is needful or allowed by the master: by cheapening at market and charging the master a higher price than they actually pay: by selling at a higher price than the master fixed and retaining the surplus: by buying at a lower price and retaining the surplus: by keeping back money with which they were furnished by the master to avert any loss or injury when they were able to settle the affair without money payments: by giving away or selling food to any considerable extent to people out of the house, when the master would be displeased on becoming acquainted with the facts: by taking dainties, such as are wont to be reserved for the master's table, and not allowed to domestics: by giving alms to the poor at the master's expense, either in money or in kind, without his permission expressed or understood: by labouring on Sundays unnecessarily when ordered to do so, to avoid scolding or abuse: by entering the service of dissenters, specially when not permitted by them to go to church and attend to their religious duties, or in danger of being perverted by them, while other places of service were open to engagement: by becoming parties to their employer's sins, and forwarding their wishes in regard to them.

Servants should be cautioned to obey their masters and mistresses for the LORD's sake, and not to repeat out of doors or to strangers what they hear or see: nor to speak ill of their employers to others.

In regard to such cases as when a servant accuses himself of lying because in obedience to orders he said his master was not at home, contrary to fact—he must be told to use such words as do not involve a lie.

(26) *Duties of Parish Priests.*

The Parish Priest is bound to have or gain a suitable amount of knowledge for the discharge of his duties: if this is not possible, he must employ a curate who can supply his deficiencies, giving him a due salary. He is bound to reside as the law commands, and not to be absent from his parish more than three months in the year, except for some reasonable cause of which the Bishop approves, and not without leaving a fit substitute. If he be absent without leave, he is bound to make restitution by devoting the revenue of his living for the time of absence to some charitable purpose. He ought not to be frequently absent from the parish on nights however disconnected without good cause,[1] or provision for all contingencies and duties, else they ought to be reckoned in the time of absence. He is bound to see that no child depart out of this world unbaptized, and teach midwives and others who frequent lying-in-women, how in cases of emergency to baptize: to baptize conditionally when any doubt exists of the child being baptized in the proper form and manner: at all times to confess and communicate such as desire it, provided he be not of opinion that they come too frequently for their soul's good, and there be no one else to minister to them: to remain at his post when sickness breaks out in his parish, or else provide a fit substitute, lest any die without the Sacraments through his absence. He must take care not to be absent from his parish when a death is expected, without providing for such a contingency, nor to render himself by excess in food or drink incapable of rising to attend to the dying. He must not trust too much to the chances of a sick man outliving a night, and so delay the Sacra-

---

[1] E.g. charity to one's neighbour, pressing necessity of health or business, obedience to the Bishop, obvious benefit to the Church or State.

ments, especially that of penance, because even though the body may not succumb the mind may. Nor may he leave those whom he has fortified with the Sacraments, but either himself or by means of others keep up their spirits against the assaults of the devil who comes on them with greater vehemence, knowing that he has but a short time. He is bound to instruct not only those who come to church, but those also who are unable to come, such as herdsmen : to prevent sin even at the risk of his own life : to set a good example to his flock in all things, shunning all avarice, and the least appearance of intemperance or impurity, all quarrels and litigations, except when compelled against his will to defend a suit. He should be charitable and not hoard up money, which seldom profits those who inherit it, and always do what good he can in his parish so as to acquire the love and veneration of his people. He ought to celebrate the Holy Eucharist as frequently as possible, not only on account of his people, as the intercessor of the parish, but also on account of his own needs : he should take every opportunity of collecting his people for Celebrations and Offices and Instructions, lay himself out in short by establishing guilds and societies for teaching and building up his people in the fear and love of GOD and of His dear SON.

Sin is incurred by those *who propose to receive Holy Orders*, if there be any bar to their doing so and any lack of the proper dispositions; temporal views; want of vocation; human respect; negligence in gaining necessary knowledge, or due piety, and in learning plain chant and ritual; by leaving off meditation, holy reading, and use of the Sacraments; by reading heretical or immoral books out of curiosity and with pleasure; by spending money on pleasures and amusements rather than on good and useful books, and by keeping company with others who are unsound in the faith or irregular in their morals.

(27) *Sins of Priests.*

They sin by neglecting pious exercises so as to be unable to celebrate the Holy Eucharist, or say their Offices (as in the Psalms by not stopping in the middle of the verse) with due attention and devotion and to the edification of the people: by getting into the habit of celebrating without preparation and recollection and thanksgiving: by not pronouncing with exactness every word and by not adhering to the ritual and the rubrics: by not taking care to keep the altars neat and decent, as well as the ornaments and other things belonging to the Holy Sacrifice: by celebrating or performing other functions with a view to temporal interests: by hearing Confessions without trying to become fit to do so with ability, or by excusing themselves from hearing them through false humility or indolence: by undertaking parishes without having the requisite strength or discretion: by neglecting to get the books necessary for instruction in their duties which they are able to buy: by contenting themselves with saying their Offices and celebrating without applying themselves to study though they need it for instructing their flocks: by giving up preaching, absolving, and other duties, because they have no need of salary on account of their patrimony being large enough without it: by wasting time in sleep or company: by attending to temporal affairs to the prejudice of their spiritual duties.

(28) *Sins of Parish Priests.*

They sin by celebrating the Divine Offices with negligence without observing the rules of chanting or the ceremonies of the Church: or with dirty and worn out vestments and ornaments: by neglecting to preach and catechise: by rarely going to hear confessions and by putting difficulties in the way of their people who would else come to confession: by taking no pains to bring people to confession, both young[1] and old, or to urge them to receive Holy Communion, and specially at Easter, or to put an end to scandals, quarrels and suits in their parishes: by being too much taken up with their temporal affairs to the neglect of their spiritual: by not giving alms in proportion to their incomes, and by neglecting the sick and poor, and not taking advantage of their misery to draw them after JESUS; by persevering in doing what is a scandal to their weak parishioners: by taking no care in preparation of their sermons: by administering the Sacraments without instructing the recipients how to benefit by them: by keeping the Sacrament when reserved for the sick too long: by letting the fabric of the Church become decayed, and the rights of the benefice fall into abeyance: by absenting themselves without good reason and

---

[1] All ought to be brought not later than twelve years of age at the least.

without leaving in their place a suitable deputy: by giving certificates and testimonials too readily out of human respect.

(29) *Sins of Confessors.*

They sin by repelling penitents through severity and unsympathising manners: by discouraging them while confessing their faults by speaking harshly, or after confession by reproving them with asperity: by questioning more closely than is needful: by rendering the conscience false or scrupulous so as to lead to exaggeration or misconception: by questioning to please their own caprice or taste: by not examining those who seem to omit momentous faults: by absolving unfit persons through inattention to their dispositions: by failing to require restitutions, reconciliations, and reparations: by not testing those who indulge in habitual sin, nor showing them how to amend: by letting persons remain exposed to occasions of mortal sin, when they might escape them: by giving too heavy or too light penances: by not showing how relapses may be avoided, and how progress may be made in virtue: by indulging in too great familiarities:[1] by making concessions to persons of position: by repelling those who wish to receive the Sacraments, and not aiding them in the grace which calls them to perfection: by confessing persons in a state of life with the duties of which the Priest is unacquainted: by speaking indiscreetly of what they have heard in confession.

[1] A Priest who should be so wicked as to abuse his office to tempt another person to impurity would thereby render himself incapable of performing all priestly functions.

(30) *Sins of Bishops.*

A Bishop sins not only by ordaining candidates of insufficient attainments, but also if he do not take all possible means of inquiring into their moral and religious fitness as well as into their orthodoxy: by not employing his resources in due proportion to the relief of the poor: by absenting himself without good reason from his diocese: by not doing his best to put an end to scandals amongst his clergy, and by not showing a good example of holy life and conversation: by not affording sufficient opportunities of Confirmation, and by confirming otherwise than singly.

(31) *Duties of Schoolmasters and Pupils.*

These are much the same as those of parents and children. Hence schoolmasters are bound to do all they can to get the pupils on in learning: train them in sound moral principles, and if they fail in these points through want of fair diligence they are not justly entitled to the stipend which is paid and ought to make restitution: to place them out of the reach of temptations to sin: to punish their faults, set them a good example, and be content with fair remuneration. In like manner pupils are bound to obey their master as being in the place of a parent, in all things relating to study and sound morals, to make good use of their time for learning, pay the fees which their parents give them for the master: and by neglecting any of these things they commit grievous sin.

(32) *Duties of Guardians and Wards.*

A guardian is bound to take the same care of his ward's property as if he were the parent, and to make restitution if through any neglect or fault of his own serious loss accrue: such as when he appropriates to his own use, sells or alienates any of his ward's goods, or the ward loses by his neglect of the estate. He is bound to keep a proper account of what has been committed to his care; and see that his ward receives a good and moral education, suitable to his condition in life. On the other hand a ward is bound to obey his guardian till he comes of age, and not to give away or alienate any part of his property without the consent of the guardian.

(33) *Duties of Merchants.*

Merchants are bound under pain of restitution not to overcharge beyond the legal or natural or conventional value. They must not mislead the buyer by pretending that the goods are intrinsically more precious than they are; nor take advantage of his ignorance. Retail is more costly than wholesale, because of the extra trouble in retailing. When goods are sold by auction, so long as no tricks are employed to enhance the value of them, any price may be fairly accepted. The value of goods increases or decreases according to the abundance or fewness of buyers: according to the scarcity or plenty of goods: according to the mode of sale or feeling of the vendor, expenses, dangers, toils in procuring or preserving them: and according to the cost or loss sustained in trying to meet the wishes of the purchaser. It is right for a purchaser to give less for articles that are exposed to sale for what they can fetch, or because the seller wants to get rid of them; except when it would be wrong to take advantage of his poverty and necessity. Hence it is wrong to ask an immoderate price for houses or land, merely because they are contiguous to the property of the purchaser. Merchants may raise their charges to strangers when there is an extraordinary influx and scarcity is thereby produced. It is allowable to buy in the cheapest market or time; to sell in the dearest, as well as to sell at a high price when a depreciation of the article is expected. At the same time charity forbids this being done in the case of poor buyers, since this would be to ruin one's neighbour for the sake of gain. To persuade others not to buy in order to create a monopoly for oneself, is a sin against rectitude. Combination to sell at a certain price is an offence against charity to others; and against rectitude if fraud be employed to accomplish that end. To sell at a higher price than the value in the market because the buyer offers more is unjust, unless indeed the excess may be regarded rightly as a gift by the seller, as the sheer result of kindred or friendship. Traders are bound to shun cheating, and to point out such defects in their merchandise as could not be known by the buyer. They sin by giving false warrants of soundness or quality, express or implied : by selling what is obviously useless or injurious to the buyer and contrary to the end for which he wishes to make a purchase, and especially if they make no reduction in price in selling an article which is inferior in value, or defective in kind or quality. The seller must not take advantage of the buyer's ignorance or stupidity. Defects however need not be pointed out by the seller, unless they are clearly useless or injurious to the buyer, since such a proceeding would go far to prevent all sales taking place. Ignorance however on the part of the seller does not excuse him from compensation.

Hence whoso knowingly sells an article defective in matter, quality, or quantity, he sins against justice, and is bound to make restitution. He sins also by selling what is sure to spoil before the buyer can use it: by selling property under litigation without stating the fact: by selling at a very low price but giving scant measure: by selling liquors which will not bear being transported to a distance, when the buyer expects them to do so: by mixing or adulterating, while making no reduction in the price: by manipulating articles with water, &c., so as to increase their weight and cost.

(34) *Duties of Buyers.*

The buyer is bound to pay the ordinary fair price for goods purchased, and point out to the seller, if a defect have escaped his notice, the cause of depreciation. He is not however required to increase the payment, if what he buys proves to be worth more than he gave. Nor is he bound to pay more for a field than it is commonly taken to be worth because he knows that there is a treasure lying hid in it, such as mines and the like.

(35) *Duties of Workmen.*

They are bound not to sell their handiworks above the fair price: to take care of materials intrusted to them, and not to use more than is needful : and to give up whatever is left, and to complete their work at the fixed time, or in good time to prevent loss to their employer.

They sin by swearing or saying they will bring the work done by a fixed time, when they know they cannot: (if it is only an error on their part, they sin by taking God's Name in vain, and if they break their promise to another's loss they are bound to make it good :) by getting others by fraud and misstatements to leave their employers, in which case they are bound to make good any loss which accrues to them. If they do it by fraud, &c., it is an offence against justice: if through hatred or vengeance, against charity.

They sin by using more materials than are necessary, or bad materials, or if they do not finish their work thoroughly, but scamp it.

The following tradesmen sin :—

The *Goldsmith,* by selling brass for gold : or by mixing more brass with gold or silver than is usual or needful, and by concealing the mixture from the purchasers: and by buying stolen goods.

The *Bookseller* by binding books badly, and charging all the same for them : by selling indecent, heretical, and pernicious books, and by passing off defective copies for whole.

The *Publican,* by selling liquor to those who he knows will become drunk : he may however be excused in cases of great difficulty, such as his rendering himself liable to great abuse and illusage, and to ruin of his business.

The *Butcher*, by cutting up meat so as to favour his friends to the loss of others : by passing off bad meat for good.

The *Tailor*, by buying cloth for another at a higher price than he need : by keeping back what is left without leave, except where the custom allows him : by taking a reduction of the price of the cloth from the vendor for his own use, when it will be added to the sum paid by the buyer who employs him.

The *Baker*, by making bread under weight and size, or adulterating it with inferior or injurious matter.

Workmen, by working over night, so as to break the Sunday or festival; except in cases where they have promised to complete their work, and cannot do so without so labouring.

All of them sin by not using proper diligence in preserving what has been intrusted to them, and are bound to restitution.

In regard to fasting, those who are employed in severe labour are exempt, such as blacksmiths, &c., but not tailors, &c.

If bad money has been given them as wages they must not pass it. And if they have accepted too low wages they must not increase them by secret peculations.

(36) *Duties of Officers and Soldiers.*

Officers must be faithful to their Sovereign or State : take care of their men's souls and bodies : not exceed their powers: keep to their agreements with the soldiers. Any breach of these is a sin against justice and calls for restitution: such as when they permit the enemy to get the superiority: neglect to keep up the number of soldiers for which they receive pay: leave sick soldiers behind: supply them with bad food or drink: single out through spite or wantonness any under their command for harder or more dangerous service: do not restrain them from thefts, rapine, and blasphemy: and do not make them obey the commands of GOD and calls of religion as far as they can. By overrunning the country with larger forces than is fair: receiving bribes from private people or villages, not to quarter soldiers upon them but send them elsewhere, or to hinder the soldiers harassing them, or to lead the army in this or that direction: by rashly giving battle and exposing the lives of their men: by enlisting men by violence, or fraud: by not allowing them to retire when their time is expired: by subtracting from their pay or delaying payment: by not providing them with clothing; by keeping back from the heirs the money due to them from a dead soldier: or by depriving private persons of land for the purpose of erecting forts without giving them compensation.

(37) *Duties of Soldiers.*

Soldiers are bound not to enlist for carrying on an unjust war: to perform strictly the duties to which their engagement holds them: and to be content with their wages. They sin by disobedience to orders: deserting their post: not fighting bravely: not defending the fort intrusted to them: in leaving the camp or army without permission, and the service before the expiration of their term : by taking away or extorting anything from non-combatants, except in time of great distress and famine : by inflicting damage upon the inhabitants of a hostile country without orders, while the latter are making contributions in order to be exempt from such losses : by serving in an unjust war : by slaying one who is serving in a just war except in self-defence : by killing innocent persons, after a siege and the place has been given up to rapine, such as children, religious, women, and travellers, who have not taken any part in hostilities, though their goods are liable to spoliation : by blasphemy, oaths, fornication, and duels.

Truces with the enemy must when made be adhered to, even when he conducts an unjust war, and injustice may have been committed in forcing on the truce.

(38) *Duties of Judges.*

They sin by pronouncing judgment contrary to justice through passion or vincible ignorance: by neglect of study : by delay of decisions without sufficient reason to the loss of the parties concerned: by yielding to bribes and influence brought to bear upon them : by advising one party to compound the cause to the interest of his opponent: by granting or refusing costs unfairly : by letting a criminal off through negligence or respect of persons : by allowing advocates free licence in blackening the characters of those against whom they are retained.

(39) *Duties of Advocates.*

They sin by undertaking to defend causes and to give advice when they are ignorant of the points of law relating to them: by giving advice contrary to justice: by pleading causes which they know to be unjust: by uselessly enlarging the briefs and lengthening the pleadings: by demanding too high fees: by refusing to defend the poor: by wearying out the opposing parties through stratagems in order to delay the course of justice.

(40) *Duties of Suitors.*

They sin by promoting unjust lawsuits: by employing bad and false means to support them: by chicanery in order to elude the just claims of others: and by being influenced by hatred or vengeance: by refusing to come to any terms: and by persuading others to perjure themselves.

(41) *Restitutions.*

A person is bound to make restitution either in kind of the thing of which he has unjustly deprived another, or in equivalent, provided that the first is impossible or is not required by the person to whom it is due. This does not apply to cases in which unintentionally loss is inflicted upon others. Else even if one person alone out of a number who have inflicted damage upon others be able to make restitution, he is bound to do so entirely and not in proportion: unless indeed the damage would have been all the same whether he had been present or not. Persons may be excused from making restitution when great length of time has elapsed, when the creditor has condoned the matter, when compensation has been otherwise made, or when there is an impossibility to restore absolutely or relatively to loss of character or of just position, and in the case of bankruptcy. In case of slander they may be excused when character has been cleared in other ways, or the slander has been done away by the slander becoming forgotten: when it has been or is believed to be condoned by the slandered, and when reparation can only be made at the cost of greater injury: or when character has been forfeited in some other way, or when the slandered person refuses to make restitution to the slanderer who has suffered alike from the slandered.

The Priest should take care that the restitutions which he requires of the penitent should not cause him to fall into disgrace thereby, but should bring it about that they be accomplished secretly by means if need be of some discreet third party. In case of slander the slanderer must be enjoined to take every opportunity of producing an opposite impression on those whose minds he has formerly empoisoned. In case of usury, unjust legal proceedings, &c., the Priest may have to take other advice, and then he must be careful to give no hint or clue as to the person in whom he is interested.

When the Priest sees that the penitent sees and recognises the duty of restitution, it is well for him to say—" I do not doubt that you know your obligation, and resolve to discharge it." In case of doubt, there is no obligation to restore, if the doubt be favourable to the penitent. But if the penitent be rich and the creditor poor, the penitent should be exhorted to do as he would have done to himself. If the obligation be clear, the penitent must not be allowed to plead difficulties,—such as the pauperising his family, &c. If Absolution be given prior to restitution, upon its being agreed to, the penitent should be told not to communicate till it has been carried out, but this does not apply when a person has the property of another in his possession. When the penitent does not know to whom the restitution should be made, he must make it in almsgiving to the poor.

Restitution should have a fixed period given for its being carried out, and the penitent should be urged to pray daily for courage to preserve his good resolution.

The sick should be counselled to make restitution while they have the power to do so. If it be needful to do so by will, it should be left to the Priest to carry out their intentions, or to some trusty friend in a codicil, without mention of the object.

(42) *How to deal with Accused Persons.*

By the English law no accused person is required to criminate himself. It is therefore a conventional mode of pleading when the rightly accused answers "Not guilty." This is especially the case in matters of life and death. Even after he is proved guilty he is under no obligation to make a public confession, nor to remain in prison, if he can escape. Nor are those who are not intrusted with his imprisonment prohibited from assisting him to escape.

(43) *How to deal with the Tempted.*

The Priest should urge—Temptation cannot be escaped, because we are partly inclined to evil, and the devil seeks to destroy us, and this induces a state of warfare and trial. Temptation teaches watchfulness and humility; GOD proves our love to Him thereby, and our fidelity. Heaven is the reward of warfare and victory. CHRIST rejoices to see us play the man and fight for the glory of His Name: He is at once spectator and combatant within us. Man burdens not his beast beyond his power, GOD does not impose on us trials beyond our capacity. Temptation is a sign of GOD's love to us, and of our predestination. And the devil rages ever violently against such as have escaped his power, and troubles not those who are his prisoners, but, as a hunter, pursues the fugitives, not the captives.

(44) *How to deal with Shamefaced Penitents.*

The Priest should kindly remind them that they do not shrink from revealing their bodily diseases to friends and physicians, and that as the soul is of more consequence than the body, they should not shrink from disclosing the disease of the soul to its physicians. Better the confusion of a few minutes than of eternity. Delay will only make it more painful and difficult. Man who has had no shame to sin in the presence of his Creator, should take it as great kindness from GOD that in place of eternal shame, He only demands brief shame in the presence of a fellow-creature. The Priest knows less of what he hears in confession than what he hears elsewhere: for he must commit all to oblivion and silence. Better confess to him now than hereafter to men and Angels. Already our sins are known to GOD and the Angels: what great matter then is it, if the Priest also know, obliged as he is to silence? The Priest should remind him that there is probably nothing new in his confession, nothing worse than what the Priest has heard before from others: he should speak of his own frailty as a sinner, of the blessing of penitence, the joy of a cleansed conscience, and peace with GOD.

(45) *How to deal with those who despair of amendment.*

The Priest should remind the penitent that no sins are beyond the power of GOD's grace to overcome them: that if the devil has power to destroy, GOD has much more power to revive. This is why CHRIST suffered so much that He might provide us with a costly and sufficient antidote to the poison of sin: and with ample strength to resist the world, the flesh, and the devil. Falls may have been frequent: they have been permitted to show man his weakness and cure his pride and self-reliance. If he cease not to relapse, he must not cease to rise again. The vessel often fouled and often cleansed is cleaner than that which is fouled but never cleansed. We clean our shoes, though they become dirty again: the soldier heals his wounds, though he may receive fresh: the prisoner leaves his prison, though it may be to return to it. He is not conquered who is often wounded and overcome, but only he who falls at last. It is better to fall and to rise again than continue in sin. By rising again we gain strength.

(46) *How to deal with the Feeble-minded.*

The Priest should remind them that GOD is their FATHER, Who, as the Parable of the Prodigal shows, is ready to meet them halfway, yea, before they have made their confession in words, receives their penitence: that GOD has given His SON and cannot refuse aught to them: that He knows whereof they are made, and remembers that they are but dust—CHRIST the Good Shepherd—CHRIST the Good Physician, healing the sick, seeking the lost. This feeble-mindedness comes from the devil, who would destroy us. GOD's holiness is greater than man's unholiness: GOD's mercy than man's sin: CHRIST's merits than man's demerits, and the like. Feeble-mindedness and want of faith is a great wrong to GOD, inasmuch as it imputes falsehood to GOD in His Word, or incapacity to pardon.

(47) *How to deal with Penitents whose language is unknown to the Priest.*

Before undertaking to hear confessions, the Priest must have made himself acquainted with the language and dialects of the people, so as to be able to understand the necessary matters to be confessed. If however there be no one else better acquainted with them within reach, the Priest may upon the confession of one or such mortal sins as he comprehends to have been committed, give absolution in case of necessity. The penitent however should be directed to confess such sins as the Priest cannot comprehend to some other Priest who can, on the first opportunity. If the Priest be entirely ignorant, he may in similar cases absolve upon the penitent making his sins known by signs. When death is expected, the penitent must confess by means of an interpreter, signifying to the Priest by pressures of the hand the kind and number of his sins.

(48) *How to Absolve Adults.*

i. The severe Priest treats adults who are virtuous and habitually free from mortal sin, though guilty of many slight faults, as we have seen he treats children. He does not give them absolution because he says they do not repent of any of these faults and do not amend; but he hastens to absolve them if they fall into mortal sin, as if the wickedness which causes a grievous sin to be committed facilitated repentance for a transgression of a more heinous kind. On the contrary, the lax Priest absolves all his penitents without any difficulty, while he alleges that though the same faults do always recur, yet that none of them are mortal. The Priest should absolve them, but he should use great discretion in doing so, lest they come to confession out of mere custom, to no purpose or even sacrilegiously, in which case there is danger that they lack true contrition, and come without the necessary dispositions. Still absolution should be given since the Priest has a ready and easy means of securing as much as possible the validity of the benefits thereof, and he ought to hold for an infallible prescription the duty of never depriving a soul of the great blessing of absolution, except when necessity or great good require. Now in this case no necessity exists, since he has a remedy at hand, which consists in recommending all whenever they come to confession to pray and humble themselves with the view of thoroughly repenting, as well as especially to direct their contrition and firm resolutions to some particular sin, whether past or present, grievous or more noteworthy among their voluntary venial sins, since it is more easy for them to feel the penitence which is necessary and efficient in order to secure for this sin at any rate the virtue of the Sacrament. They should accuse themselves of this particular sin at the close of their confession by specifying it—such as much murmuring, or by generalising—such as notable sins against charity and purity, &c.—for it is not necessary particularly to explain what has been already confessed. This is the way, in the first place, to deal with persons whose venial faults are not considerable, not only in regard to the matter of them, but also in regard to the wilfulness with which they were committed: sins rather committed than premeditated, sins of the moment, the ill-intention of which consequently is of short duration, interrupted as it is by the sudden stoppage of evil—such as a little curiosity or vanity, or a brief impatience. In the second place, this is the way to treat those whose venial sins are small as to their matter, but great or notable in regard to the amount of premeditation—such as polite falsehoods, of which the badness is increased by their being studied and prepared, and such as slight impatience which lasts some time. In short, the will exhibits more evil when it reiterates its opposition to the remorse which makes its sting felt many times during a long interval. More vigilance is required in regard to those souls which fall back into these notable venial sins, and that very frequently, and they must be warned that except they show some fruitful repentance for their faults and correct them in some degree, they cannot obtain pardon for them when they receive absolution. The Priest may sometimes threaten to refuse them absolution, in order to awaken them; provided they are disposed to bear with such a loss as a means of healing. If however they should be troubled and discouraged by such a threat, the only resource which the Priest has to secure the validity of the Sacrament would be to induce them to accuse themselves of some past or present faults for which they truly repent, provided there is no ground for presuming that this fault is a bad habit which still survives and is not corrected.

ii. In the case of penitents guilty of grievous faults, the mischief of rigorousness and laxity is equally apparent. While the one is too ready to absolve, and the other too reluctant to absolve, neither really effects the glory of GOD or the salvation of souls. The Priest should, as a main principle of procedure, exact of the penitent sufficient signs of his state of mind in order to found a solid and wise decision as to his actual contrition, and his determined and sincere purpose. So long as he can form such a judgment of the case he may and ought to absolve, except when greater benefit is to be derived by an opposite course.

iii. It is here that so much wisdom is needful in order to decide whether delaying absolution will be for the edification or destruction, the salvation or the ruin of the penitent. Should delay seem more beneficial, and the penitent be able to come back in a little while, absolution should be deferred. Such a course should be tempered with gentleness,—showing (1) the penitent that it is only adopted with reluctance in regard to his good and the Priest's duty, and that an actual concession of absolution would be attended with discomfort and discontent: (2) teaching him how he ought to prepare better by prayer and good works analogous to his needs and condition: and how to guard against relapses in the mean while : and, if a general confession be requisite, how to make it briefly and easily : and (3) advising him to come back on a fixed day within eight or ten days, adding that any relapse within that period should cause no discouragement, but rather urge him all the more to resort to the physician, and encouraging him with the promise of renewed and greater aids. So the penitent may be enabled to go away without despondency and with the full hope of approaching absolution and reconciliation with GOD.

iv. In some cases where delay of absolution may be thought ruinous a Priest may find the lax or rigorous line convenient to himself but ruinous to the penitent. By the lax line he may get rid of the case by giving absolution, without taking any trouble to induce the penitent to repent, on the strength of his mere protestations of regret. When a suitable penance is enjoined and wholesome advice is bestowed, to absolve is better than the rigorous procedure whereby a penitent is curtly dismissed without prescriptions or counsel, and merely told to prepare better and come back in a fortnight or month's time.

v. In cases where circumstances require prompt absolution it is necessary to be content with such dispositions on the part of the penitent as are real and efficacious, without exacting such as are extraordinary and overflowing. A penitent is about to marry, and the day is fixed: a priest has to celebrate the next day: a traveller has to start on his journey, and the like. To remit is to run the risk of invalidating the Sacrament: to retain is to expose to the danger of fresh commissions of sin; of sacrilege; of non-return to confession, or of return after a long interval with fresh sins; and of increased difficulty of confession in consequence. To expect them to leave their business and employments, to wait at any cost, and then after all prepare for a further and better confession, this is to expect heroism, and special grace, and that too all on a sudden. Rather should the priest strive to win them to such repentance as may justify absolution being given, implant and irrigate good feelings in the heart of the penitent in the hope that GOD would give the increase. In such a case the Priest should (1) beseech from the bottom of his heart the Divine assistance: (2) dissemble his trouble and embarrassment, while offering it to GOD: (3) stir up in himself great pity for the sick soul: (4) like an adroit physician in a case where danger lies in delay use the most prompt and efficacious remedies, make up for lack of time by fervour, and turn the very circumstances which are contrary to useful account. He should speak to the penitent thus,—" What a good thing it is you have come to confession at least to-day! If ever you needed to make a good confession it is now. What happiness is in store for you if you enter the married state, proceed on your journey, with the grace and blessing of GOD. On the other hand, what good can you hope will befall you without GOD? Nay, what perils of soul and body await you, if you continue in a state of sin! Take courage. I will assist you." This is the way the priest should begin by way of securing a complete and unreserved confession. When the confession is over the Priest should add,—" Now you have the most important part to perform—contrition. Hope in GOD to obtain it, for it is not in vain that GOD has waited for you and brought you to-day to be reconciled to Him. It is true you need extraordinary grace, and you have made yourself unworthy of it by your delay, and perhaps by the want of good intention in your coming to-day, but be not discouraged—you have still time. Still to appease GOD and gain His aid you must use all the means. Just as you would do to save your life if you fell into a river, so must you do to save your soul. JESUS is the SAVIOUR of sinners who desire to return to Him. I give you an hour, go and cast yourself at His Feet, and think upon what you ought to do in order to gain the grace of sincere repentance, and tell me then what you choose to do—in the way of prayers or of alms. Beseech JESUS to have mercy upon you; be severe with yourself: reflect and reproach yourself with the greatness of your faults and the outrage you have offered to GOD by your delay up to this moment. Make many acts of contrition, and then come back, and I will soon finish what we have begun and give you consolation."

vi. In order to make sure of his repentance when

he returns the Priest should inquire what the penitent has promised to JESUS and how he has employed his time. It is to be expected that he will have done more good during this hour than he has ever done in a week: for he has been shown the importance of contrition as well as the means of exciting it, and been encouraged by the promise of approaching absolution. Ordinarily it will be found that he is quite changed from what he was, no longer unfeeling and hardened, but contrite, humbled, docile, and ready to accept any penance. To make still more sure of his good will, a penance may be given him of a somewhat severe kind, but not such nevertheless as to alarm him, and if he accept it the Priest, as a discreet confessor, may diminish it by-and-by. His promptitude in accepting it enables the Priest to obtain what he aimed at, the knowledge of his good will. It is thus that the Priest may by the grace of GOD with the help of these little attempts which the LORD will vouchsafe to bless, obtain sufficient *data* on which he may form a prudent and certain judgment. Now then he is in a good state for absolution, and may be absolved, and GOD Who has by the labours of the Priest recovered this wandering son, will find a means of richly recompensing him. If any doubt still exists as to his penitence the Priest should have recourse to prayer with fervour and confidence, and so absolve and console him. If in spite of this the state of the penitent cause any disquietude, though not profound or considerable, yet still in a slight degree, then is the time to recall to mind S. Chrysostom's words,—that it is better to have to give account for too much mercy than for too great severity, and what S. Paul said—"I would to GOD that I were accursed for my brethren's sake." The Priest need not fear to be accounted faulty before GOD so long as he can make these three protestations,—(1) "LORD, Thou knowest why I absolve him instead of sending him away: it is to save him from manifold faults and Thee from many insults; (2) Thou knowest how I have acted in this matter, I have spared neither prayers nor toils; (3) Thou hast made me in this Sacrament a minister of Thy love, and if Thou hast also made me a minister of Thy justice, it is not of a vengeful justice which punishes and destroys the wicked, but of that paternal justice which wills his amendment and salvation." Let not the Priest be afraid, but trust abundantly that GOD will recognise Him as His faithful servant.

vii. If notwithstanding all efforts the penitent evidently is reluctant to repent and to satisfy what is required of him a last endeavour may be made by the Priest. He may offer to GOD to share in the sinner's penance: or promise to perform some great work in order to win this soul. He should arm himself with holy indignation: imitate the language of Nathan to David, and as if about to dismiss the penitent depict the eternal and temporal punishments in store for him, —the latter often most affect obstinate souls. Then he should return to consoling truths; set before him the thousand blessings—even temporal—which await his return to GOD: in order to lead him to act upon the slightest motive for good and try to win him. If the Priest fails—be his grief at failure what it may, he must then dismiss him unabsolved, bidding him to return when he will and is penitent. The Priest should instantly intreat GOD to bring back this soul at some other time, or direct him to a more worthy minister, and save him. The Priest should as much as possible exhort his penitents to come with exterior as well as interior marks of preparation. As to the first[1] excessive ornaments and finery in dress are inconsistent with deep sorrow for sin. As to the latter no confession is satisfactory which does not bear the marks of careful and exact self-examination, of duly proportioned sorrow, and of firm resolutions of satisfaction and amendment. Where these are wanting penitents should be persuaded to withdraw for the purpose of preparing more worthily. Such marks may be justly suspected to be lacking when penitents have just left some temporal occupation without time for prayer : when they appear to have no knowledge of their sins : when they are known to persevere in forbidden ways : when they have no intention to give up some sin or the proximate occasion thereof : nor to make restitution when able to do so. Yet the Priest should be on the look-out to notice when penitents show *some diligence* in preparation and take advantage of it when the necessary dispositions seem lacking through incapacity or other cause to supply the deficiency by exciting them to sorrow for sin. This he should do by representing the

---

[1] When excessive dress is adopted for ulterior purposes, such as to excite impure affections, mortal sin is incurred. The like may be said of those who cause thereby others to break the law of the Church by omitting to attend Divine Service ; by expending more than they can afford, and by giving rise to quarrels upon the subject ; by retrenchment of alms, withholding just payments, and by unjust gains.

enormity of their sins, as offences against God, and so meriting punishment of an infinite degree; and the immense loss incurred thereby, even eternal condemnation. So he may inspire them with such sorrow for all and each of their mortal sins as to be able to absolve them with a clear conscience. Besides this he should take care to instruct penitents according to their needs, especially such as rarely confess, in the dispositions and modes required for making a good confession, laying special stress upon its being complete and upon other circumstances.

viii. When the penitent is ignorant of the Creed and the Commandments and refuses to be instructed in them, absolution must be deferred. So also when fathers and mothers do not take care that their children and servants be properly instructed, or hinder them from being instructed, or practising what they have been taught. In like manner when they do not give them time to attend Church on Sundays and Greater Festivals: or when they set before them such food as is incompatible with days of abstinence: or throw difficulties in the way of receiving Holy Communion, and that fasting. And further when they do not correct them for breaking the Commandments, and in all these cases decline to adopt a better way of managing their households, absolution must be withheld.

(49) *Penances to be enjoined.*

Such penances should been joined as tend to create good habits, or to root out bad habits: such as to say morning and evening prayers at the proper time; examine conscience every evening; be present at Divine

Service (specially at the Holy Eucharist) for so many days with the special object of obtaining some grace or virtue, and of conquering some vicious propensity: in order to avoid drink, to avoid all places of temptation such as public-houses for some fixed period, as well as companions who are likely to persuade indulgence; to abstain altogether on certain days, such as Friday, in honour of the Passion of our LORD, and the like: and similarly in order to avoid gambling: in order to get rid of sloth, to rise for a fixed period at a certain hour, and read a religious book during a fixed time; beseeching our LORD to pardon misuse of time, and to give grace to use it for salvation: in order to be cured of negligence in Divine things, to be present at special services, sermons, and the like—always bearing in mind, that contraries are to be cured by contraries.

(50) *How to deal with cases of a more difficult nature.*

i. *Scrupulous*[1] persons—next to prayer need adherence and obedience to their Priest. He may discern whether they be scrupulous, if they be every now and then doubting whether this or that act be good or bad, or thinking this or that act to be sinful without just cause: if they continually change their minds upon slight grounds as to the lawfulness of this or that act: if they run wild about minute circumstances and act with blind perturbation: if they give way to

[1] The word *scruple*, properly signifying a pebble which by insinuating itself into the shoe causes much inconvenience to the traveller, is applied to some groundless or unnecessary fear about acts of omission or commission involving sin.

overgreat excitement about their mistakes or venial sins : if after taking counsel with several priests they are all the more distressed : if they anxiously inquire about things which are known to everybody and propound them as abstruse questions to more than one and more than once : if they conclude certain acts to be sinful upon grounds which would not occur to a sane person : if they judge things to be sinful which are done by eminent persons without any suspicion of evil attaching to them : if the examination of conscience bring with it greater darkness of mind : and if after confession one doubt crops up after another. Scrupulous persons are often difficult to deal with, because the devil strives to make them obstinate and perverse, and resist the Priest's conclusion that they are tormenting themselves unnecessarily.

Scruples arise from three causes,—from God, man, and the devil.

God inflicts them sometimes by withdrawal of light from the sinner as a punishment for resisting past illuminations, that he may learn all the more to loathe his sins and implore the Divine aid. Or they arise out of natural temperaments of different men : out of brain affections or injuries. Or the devil excites them, lax consciences to greater laxity, rigid to greater rigidity ; but he does not attack great saints or sinners, but chiefly beginners and newly converted : often taking advantage of misfortunes, distempers, or griefs, and so delights to fish in troubled waters. The tokens whereby we may know that scruples proceed from God are when they bring with them horror of sin, anxiety to shun it, and to change their ways : when they do not last long and leave behind a calm in the soul, having effected the end for which He sent them. But if they last long, and without any lull in confessions, it is clear that they are not from GOD, and if so it is little matter whether they proceed from the devil or from nature. In short, the devil acts by means of natural temperaments. In like manner it is evident that scruples come not from GOD, when a person yearns for perfect subservience to GOD, watches against all sin, and yet is worried about trifles, and if the scruples are contrariant and antagonistic. Scruples may be taken to have a natural origin when apart from any of the above causes the heart is in pain, the brain clouded, the limbs tremble, and especially if scruples follow upon every act, eating and drinking or abstaining, speaking or not speaking, going out or remaining at home, and the like. That scruples come from the devil is seen when a person is thereby induced to lukewarmness and loses firmness of character, and is drawn away by degrees from the pursuit of virtue. More particularly this is the case when despair of salvation is the result. The same is also evident when they intervene in the holiest acts, if they are only perceptible in relation to one or two kinds of sin, and if they show themselves in regard to little faults but not to more important sins. Hence scruples which proceed from GOD are useful, but injurious when they are derived from nature or from the devil. Nevertheless, even these last may be overruled to man's good by GOD, enabling them to sympathise with other scrupulous persons, and stirring them up to humility and confidence in GOD: while He comforts them so that they can patiently bear their affliction.

The Priest must distinguish between those who are really scrupulous and those who are reasonably anxious and doubtful as to restitution, former confessions, and the like. To have a scruple on one point does not constitute scrupulousness. Scrupulous persons may be allowed to reiterate their confessions upon those points which they are sure that they have omitted formerly or lately, but not otherwise. The Priest ought to (1) speak often to them of the great confidence we ought to have in our LORD JESUS CHRIST, Who died to save us, and so exhort them to live in tranquillity so long as they have recourse to Him. (2) He should warn them against reading books likely to revive scruples, and against conversing with scrupulous persons. Such as are grievously tormented should be dissuaded from attending preachers who dilate upon alarming truths, and from examining their conscience upon points which give rise to ill-founded scruples. (3) Should the scruple consist in the dread of consenting to bad thoughts—such as militate against faith, purity, or love, the Priest should deal boldly and freely with all this, and say that these thoughts are temptations and sufferings but not sins. So long as a person is one who fears GOD there is every reason except in very plain cases to the contrary to conclude that mortal sin has not been committed, since such a monster cannot enter the soul which loathes it, without being clearly known and felt. Such souls must even sometimes be forbidden to confess like sins, so long as they are not sure of having committed them and could not certify on oath that they had done so. It must be noted that scrupulous persons must be guided by general rather than by special rules, since they often doubt whether the latter are applicable to the case in hand. It is not good to give reasons in dealing with them, lest their scruples gain new force by argumentation.

ii. As to the scrupulous, who torment themselves about their past confessions, and fear that they have not explained all their sins or the circumstances of them, or that they had not sufficient contrition when in the act of making their general confession, and that during a fixed time they repeated the sins of their past life, the Priest should urge them never intentionally to think of such things, or to confess their past sins so long as they cannot be sure that they were mortal sins, and that they have never confessed them. If the penitent does not obey, the Priest must be firm in repressing him, must deprive him of Communion and assign him grave mortifications. The scrupulous must be treated with great severity, for if they lose the anchor of obedience they are wrecked, become insane, or disorderly. The Priest should not appear to give much weight to scruples; listen, but not ask for information, answer only to the points raised, and having answered, not allow the point to be reopened. Sometimes it is well to deal pleasantly and jocosely with them.

iii. Others there are who fear to sin in all their actions. Such must be ordered to act with freedom and cease from scruples, so long as they do not see clearly that their action is sinful. An ill-founded fear is not a dictate of conscience: and so long as they are not certain that an act is bad they do not oppose conscience, but an ill-advised dread of carrying the act into execution. Scrupulousness is a malady with which a truce only and not perfect peace can be made, and for which humility is the only sure remedy. Hence it may not be possible always to lay aside such fears; the only thing to be done is to disregard them, and act independently of them.

(51) *General Remedies for Scrupulousness.*

' Great humility, confidence in GOD, resignation to His will, and prayer for peace of mind and illumination. Obedience and adherence to the same Priest. Consideration of the loss inflicted by scrupulousness on the soul. Persuasion that it is scrupulousness, and not just and reasonable anxiety. Use of medicines suitable to relieve the physical tendencies. Aversion to the company of scrupulous persons, who infect others. Contempt of scruples and bold opposition to them, resisting openly the devil, without entering into discussion as to their grounds; avoiding solitude. To inform the conscience on this head there must be cited the teaching of holy men and theologians, the dictation of the confessor, the ill results of yielding, and the misery resulting, all which exhibit the probable will of GOD—that scruples should be thus dealt with, as men deal with them in the ordinary affairs of life. The scrupulous person should be reminded how often he has found that to be false which he had before thought true, and that he would reply to an inquirer differently to the course which he himself pursues. Too great anxiety is as vicious as too little, and leads to despair. GOD requires only prudence. The traveller who is overanxious easily goes astray, and makes more mistakes than one who exercises only a reasonable caution.

The scrupulous may assume that they may act without sin if they have no insight or fear in regard to the sinfulness of the action, and they need not balance the reasons for and against it. Especially if they would naturally advise another person that such an act was lawful, or were aware that other persons, whose discretion might be trusted, would act in the same way. Even should such a person find that he has erred, he need not distrust this principle of action, since it is impossible to examine into all doubts and fears which are raised, nor does GOD require it of us.

Even if on reflection a man seem to have had doubts when he acted in the matter in which he has erred, it is not always necessary to conclude that he committed sin by acting in spite of his doubts; since his doubts have been purely of a speculative character, and he is not bound to confess such doubts, therefore it is better for him to make no further mention of them, and not to examine himself in regard to them whether he have sinned or not, but only indulge in a general kind of sorrow that he has offended GOD, and resolve within himself either that he has not sinned, or that he is at least not bound to confess them, being ready to confess them when he has overcome his fears and become alive to the necessity of confessing them.

(52) *How to deal with persons who are tormented with scruples that they have yielded to inward temptations.*

They should not decide that they have consented to mortal sin unless they are quite sure, nay, could swear that they had consented to it. Certainty would be requisite in judging another—it is no less required in judging oneself. Especially if they had often seriously resolved never so to sin, or even to die rather than so sin: if they were frightened by the temptation, and instantly repudiated it. Even if they afterwards felt they had acted with too little courage, or were not aware whether they were asleep or awake, sober or drunk, or were doubtful immediately after the circumstance took place whether they gave their consent, it may be assumed that full consent was wanting. If it be clear that the general habit of mind is to choose death rather than to sin against GOD, it may be assumed that consent is wanting.

(53) *Fearful persons.*

Fearful persons, whom the least semblance of evil alarms, are called by GOD to the greatest perfection. Such have much need to resort to a Priest for obtaining peace and tranquillity. They should be advised to (1) make a general review of their past life and a general confession, and (2) to divest themselves of attachment to the world. As to love their neighbours as themselves is the duty of all, so they must not forget the charity which their own souls need in attaining to a pure conscience, and laying hold of eternal life. So long as the conscience is oppressed with a sense of faults, they are, as it were thorns, which voluntary confession changes into roses and sweet odours. Human wickedness attracts them into the heart, Divine goodness extracts them. As need demands confession should be made to Priests, who are in good report, without scruple; if they cannot hear confessions, they can but decline to do so. As they are not needed for a general confession it is of less consequence. If any deadly sin deter from communion, the loss must be endured till a fit opportunity arrive for confession. When however there be due contrition and purpose to confess on the earliest opportunity, which may be distant, Communion need not be deferred. It cannot be too often impressed upon the penitent that the seal of confession justifies all concealment, even to denial of what has been said to the Priest, as though nothing had been said at all. Nor should the penitent be distressed at not having observed all his falls. He must be content with confessing what he has noticed, and leave the rest to the mercy of Him Who raises the fallen even when they do not perceive their falls. For persons who fear that they may not remember what they have to confess it is good to write down the matter of their confession—else it is best to confess by heart.

(54) *Annual Confessions.*

Annual confessions are useful, inasmuch as they help to realise sinfulness, and to test progress or relapse, and give fresh vigour to good resolutions. But they must be made without disquietude and scruples, more for the sake of encouragement than of absolution. In such cases the confession need not be minute and in detail: it is enough to give the salient points of it. Annual confessions, unless they are made in this way, are undesirable.

(55) *Conclusion.*

The scrupulous person may be consoled, if the Priest

see fit, after such a general confession, to the following effect :—" Be of good courage, your general confession bears all the marks of sincerity and completeness. If you have omitted anything through inadvertence or forgetfulness, dismiss all scruples and doubtfulness; and should anything hereafter come into your mind which you have now forgotten, you can amend this confession on the next occasion by adding what you have now forgotten. If your omissions have been involuntary there is no need of going through your general confession again. Be sure to confess your faults whenever you feel specially burdened." In certain cases confession every eight days is advisable.

(56) *Annual Review of Confession.*

In regard to the review of the penitent's interior condition: (1) He should get ready all that is requisite for making such a journey fruitful, and sufficient for many years. (2) He should commend it in prayer to GOD. (3) He should unfold all the windings of the soul, and view its recesses, and consider what needs to be replaced, amended, and restored. (4) He should have vast and absolute confidence in GOD's mercy, as well as in the benevolence of the confessor. (5) It may often be useful for the penitent to note down on paper what has been suggested to his mind after consideration. (6) And it will be all the better for the penitent all the more that he feels abnegation of or indifference to his own will : so as to wish and resolve to obey the inspirations and instructions which are vouchsafed by GOD, Who operates on such souls as are solely His, and are not already taken up with their own will and other affections.

(7) Above all disquietude must be avoided in this preparation for review. It must be done with calmness and freedom.

(57) *Forgotten Faults.*

Slight faults, whether remembered after a confession has been made, or committed after the same, do not require that the penitent should go again to confession before communion. Rather, we may add, it is best not to go again to confession, but to reserve them for another confession, with the view of rehearsing them then if they be remembered.

The doubtful should be consoled with the assurance that in receiving absolution they may put aside all the cruel disquietudes which afflict them in regard to the forgiveness of their sins: that they need not distress themselves because they have not sufficiently gone into the details of their faults, since it is not material whether a murder be committed with a sword or otherwise, or a house be set on fire furnished or unfurnished. All that need be said is that murder was committed in a passion or by way of revenge, or that arson was accompanied with homicide or otherwise.

It is not necessary that what has been forgotten in a general confession to one Priest should be confessed to him. It is enough that it be added in the next confession, to whomsoever the penitent may chance to have recourse.

(58) *What must be mentioned in Annual Reviews.*

There is no need to confess those little thoughts which pass and repass like flies before the eyes.

The annual review of the soul is to be made to remedy the defect of ordinary confessions, so as to excite deeper humility and renewal of good resolutions in regard to propensities, habits, and other sources of offences to which the penitent finds himself more liable.

It is best, if possible, to make this annual review to the Priest who has already heard the general confession, but it is not absolutely essential to do so.

There is no need to note therein more than the principal falls, the chief disorders of the mind; not how often, but how much and how long, and what were the provocatives.

People may fall into mortal sins, so long as they had no intention to become corrupt, or to be hardened in evil, without loss of devotion, since what is lost by sinning may be regained by true repentance: and hence annual reviews are very salutary to souls labouring under infirmities; for if the first good resolutions do not confirm and strengthen them sufficiently, the second and third may do so. By continually making fresh resolutions the soul at last becomes firmly resolved and acquires courage together with a holy humility in regard to its weakness, self-accusation, prayer for pardon and for the help of GOD.

There is no need to confess the having had a strong feeling of anger or of any other sin. It may be spoken of in a review by way of learning how to conduct oneself; but not by way of confession, unless there has been consent. It is not necessary therefore when a person has been tempted for two days, but has only given way or not sufficiently resisted for a quarter of an hour during that time, to say more than that "I relaxed in my resistance to such a thought for a quarter of an hour." As for temptations thus resisted, they must be endured like other things for which there is no remedy.

So when persons make up an account of their faults for confession, they should not trouble themselves with thinking "what the Priest will say or think of me if I confess so and so?" They should say to themselves, "let him think or say what he will, so long as I obtain absolution, and have discharged my duty." Just as after confession there is no time to examine whether all has been duly said which has been done, but it is the proper time to think only of our LORD, to Whom they have been reconciled, without disquiet, and to thank Him for His mercies; so it is after making up their account. They must say simply what comes into their mind, after which they need not be anxious. And while persons must not shrink from looking into their own souls, notwithstanding the dread which they entertain lest they should find something therein which they do not like to express, so they must not be so weak as to want to say everything, however trivial, and to rush to the Priest on the recurrence of every little ache or pain, which may last for a quarter of an hour. People must learn to endure with courage these little things, for which there is little or no remedy, since they are the result of the imperfections of human nature, such as the inconsistencies of humour, wills, and desires, which cause often much vexation.

The Priest must beware of making particular inquiries which are not really essential—such as whether the penitents' names are this or that, whether they perform penances, practise virtues, and what, and whether they are subject to temptations, &c. It is true that the penitent may, though not obliged to do so, respond to such interrogations, but the Priest renders himself liable to such an answer as was given by a penitent who was asked his name, "You have not to do with my name, but only with my sins."

(59) *Distinctness in Confessions.*

Penitents need to be told not to repeat what the Priest has said to them in confession. The seal of confession obliges both parties. The Priest should take care not to press his counsels always upon penitents as absolutely essential; he should change his directions if it appear that they are beyond the ability of the penitents, or contrary to the obligations under which they are bound.

Penitents should be urged to confess distinct acts of sin. There is no need to confess feelings of anger and the like, if it were not in their power to stop them. When anger leads them to disorderly acts, sin is committed. They should therefore particularise something which is of the nature of actual sin, rather than the sense of being sinful.

They should be reminded of the duty of being true, simple, and charitable in their confessions: true, by opening their grief without reserve and dissimulation; charitable, by making no mention of their neighbour as the cause of their faults; simple, by stating the fact of their sin, and not mixing up with it the cause or the promoter of it.

They should not be allowed to accuse themselves generally or uselessly. If they have had disparaging thoughts of their neighbours, of vanity, or worse, or distractions in prayer, provided that they have yielded to them, or not sufficiently resisted one or the other or all, let them confess such yielding or non-resistance, but not else. Sweeping accusations are of no use in confession.

Slight imperfections need not be, nay, ought not to be confessed unless they be resolved to amend them.

(60) *Sorrowfulness necessary in Confession.*

People should be told that there is no need of a long time to make an act of contrition. All that is required is to cast oneself at the feet of GOD in a spirit of humility and repentance for having offended Him. The sorrow of true penitence should not be called sadness so much as disgust or detestation of sin: not a feeling of annoyance and vexation, nor such as stupefies the mind, but such as renders it active and zealous: not such as depresses the heart, but such as uplifts it by prayer and hope; and causes to be felt within it the outbursts of devotional fervour; such in fact as by reason of its bitterness produces always the sweetness of incomparable consolation, according to the precept of S. Augustine—"The penitent should always be sorrowful, but always rejoice in his sorrow."

"The sorrow," says Cassian, "which works solid penitence not to be repented of, is obedient, affable, tractable, gentle, meek, and patient, as being the result of charity, in such sort as that though comprehending all pain of body and contrition of mind, it is in a certain way joyous, animated, and reinvigorated with the hope of harvest : it retains all the sweetness of affability and long-suffering, having in itself the fruits of the HOLY GHOST, love, joy, peace, long-suffering, gentleness, goodness, faith, meekness, temperance." Such is true penitence, and such is the good sorrow which is in truth properly neither melancholy nor sorrowful, but only bent on detesting, rejecting, and resisting the evil of sin in the past and in the future.

(61) *Deaf and Dumb.*

Deaf and dumb penitents must be received where they can be properly communicated with by signs so as to obtain some security for their due contrition for sin. It would be well to gain some information from persons with whom they live as to their faults and how to arrive at a proper understanding with them. Should the Priest be able to ascertain what their faults have been, even though he can get at the knowledge of only one fault, and they exhibit signs of repentance, he may absolve them. But this should only be done conditionally, if there be not a moral certainty of their state of mind. If the dumb can write, it is right to require a written confession, unless there should be great difficulty in their doing so, or if there be any danger of its being read by others. So with very deaf persons, it may be needful that care should be taken to put off their confessions till an occasion offer of more privacy. If the deafness be not perceived at first, it may be injurious to tell them with a loud voice to go away and come back, lest bystanders should imagine that they were dismissed in disgrace. In such case after any deadly sin has been confessed absolution should be given to persons rightly disposed, or at any rate should be given conditionally.

(62) *Condemned to Death.*

In dealing with prisoners under sentence of death, great charity and patience are required. On his first visit the Priest should try to gain their affections by tenderness in words, and if possible in almsgiving, if needful: inquire their names, their birthplace, their religion: suggest the good providence of GOD, Who in manifold ways brings back His lost sheep to Himself, urge them to repentance and trust in JESUS: and exhort them to patience in submitting to the hardships of the prison life. It is well for the Priest not to hear their confessions until the trial is over, lest the criminals should entertain earthly hopes from his intervention, and so be tempted to make the best of their sins to him. He should make it plain that he has nothing to do with their earthly life, but only with their souls. He should examine in confession whether they have wrongly accused others as guilty, in order that they may be induced to recall their false testimony, if any have been given. He must be careful not to induce them to accuse themselves falsely for fear they should be deprived of Absolution and the Viaticum. He should enlarge upon the certainty of death as the gate of eternal life, and urge that the sentence which has been pronounced by an earthly judge is an act of GOD's grace Who wills the salvation of the condemned. He should speak of the bliss of the saints and of the misery of the reprobate. He should exhort that thanks be given to GOD, Who has waited for this special moment in order that the prisoner might die in a state of grace, instead of cutting him off in the midst of his sins. Then he should prevail upon him to accept death in union with That Which the LORD suffered through the love He bare him. He should revive his courage by telling him that if he accept death he will be saved, and find an abundant entrance into the kingdom of GOD. Then he should persuade him to confess all his sins without fear or reserve. The penitent should be asked if he retain hatred against any one, prosecutors, witnesses, judge, &c. After receiving absolution, he should be brought to communicate several times, with the view of making a good death. It is not recommended to give communion to persons before their trial, except to such as suffer persecution for CHRIST's sake. To the latter it may be given even on the day of execution, and by way of viaticum, even though they be not fasting, and if death be near.

The criminal should be counselled to spend his time as much as possible in holy reading, and meditations and prayer: to assist at the Divine Sacrifice in spirit whenever he is aware of its going on near him: at the striking of the clock implore a happy death, patience, and resignation, and with the different hours connect the different acts of the Passion of CHRIST. The Priest should guard against making himself the bearer of the news of the doom to which the criminal is sentenced, but be content with preparing him for his end. At night he should be told to try to sleep, and some one should be with him to aid him spiritually in case of sudden temptations. On the morning of his execution he should be encouraged to consecrate the day to GOD, and unite his sufferings with the Passion of CHRIST, and care should be taken that nothing be given to stupefy him, and render him incapable of winning a crown of glory by a good death. The Priest should take heed not to hurry the criminal and hasten his death: but accommodate his pace to that of the criminal; pray softly with him, bidding him guard his eyes and look on the ground, and salute none save the Crucified One. As the condemned goes forth from prison to the place of punishment the Priest should say, " Follow now, my son, JESUS CHRIST, Who ascended Calvary to die for you." Arriving at the place, the Priest should reconcile and absolve him anew and say, " Be of good cheer, you are in a state of grace and favour with GOD; already heaven gates are opened to receive you, where JESUS CHRIST, and His Saints wait for you. Unite your death to that of the SAVIOUR Who died through His love for you, amidst humiliations and tortures. You love Him, do you not? Say then after me, acts of faith, hope, and charity, contrition, oblation, &c.: LORD, I love Thee above all things: I accept death in order to accomplish Thy holy will: I accept it in expiation of my sins. I hope that Thou hast pardoned me. I repent anew of the offences I have committed against Thee. I desire soon to be reunited to Thee in Paradise, to love Thee through all eternity." As his eyes are being blindfolded, and he ascends the scaffold, the Priest should say, " My son, ask JESUS to come to thy aid. Receive death as the forfeit of thy sins. Renounce all temptations of the Evil One." As he is on the scaffold and the instrument of death is about to descend, the Priest should say, "Behold the SAVIOUR stretches forth His arms to embrace thee:" and bid the penitent pray, "LORD, I have offended Thee, I repent, I love Thee with my whole heart. GOD of my soul, Thou callest me. Lo! I come. JESU, be with me. FATHER, I give Thee my heart and my soul." After the fatal instrument has descended the Priest should pray for the soul of the departed.

Should the condemned obstinately refuse to confess, the Priest should pray for him, beseech the prayers of confraternities, brotherhoods, or sisterhoods: remind him that whether he confess or not the law will take its course: inquire if he despair of his salvation because he has so long given up his soul to the devil, assuring him that GOD is ready to forgive his long rebellion if he have the will to repent: or if it be some settled feeling of hatred against any one which keeps him from confession. Care must be taken at first not to press confession too much. It is more profitable to speak much of the mercy of GOD, of the bliss of heaven, of the pains of hell, and of death. The condemned should be told about such as under like circumstances have died penitent or impenitent. Then let him be left to his own reflections. By-and-by the Priest may return to him, and see if he has changed his mind, and say, "My son, death is at hand, what will you do? Choose now hell or heaven. Remember if you now die impenitent, you will have to repent uselessly through all eternity." If he continue still hardened, let some litany be said by the Priest and such as will join in it for his conversion,—let the Priest lovingly and earnestly beseech him not to destroy himself for ever. If he still remain unmoved, the Priest must pray on, as they proceed to the scaffold. The last attempt may be made on the scaffold by warning the unhappy man that he is throwing away his last chance for ever, and that hell is yawning before him, but this tone of severity must be tempered with affection. Should he relent, time should be asked to enable him to confess, and if he confess with sufficient contrition all his grievous sins, absolution may be given.

(63) *The Dying.*

It is a great work this which demands of the Priest wonderful tenderness mingled with firmness, so as to obtain a good death for the dying. Not only in the prison, but in the hospital, there is need of a Priest who can get quickly at the heart of the dying : make them by a few words feel sweetly the importance of a due preparation for death : urge them to make an act of faith with such earnestness as if their salvation depended on it : and lay before them the condition of some one in a similar condition, so as to render their confession more easy and insensibly get to learn the state of their conscience. He should say to them, "Your life has been misspent and sinful,—but you are heartily sorry, are you not? You wish now that you had led a purer and holier life? and never done so and so? You would rather die than sin thus again, if GOD were to spare you? suffer anything rather than displease

Him any more? Be of good cheer,—upon this moment eternity depends. You loathe your past life? you offer your life as forfeited to GOD? and consecrate it to Him for ever?" Lastly, the dying man must be prevailed on to pardon all who have wronged him and caused his death.

(64) *Persons tormented by an unclean spirit.*

If a penitent who is tormented by the spirit of impurity presents himself, the Priest must devote all his care to fortify him in so terrible a conflict. There needs powerful grace on the part of GOD in such a case, and great resistance on the part of the sufferer. He must persevere in rigid mortification, and in manifold prayers, commending himself frequently to our LORD with tears and groans. If he relax in these things he runs a very great risk of falling into some secret indulgence of feelings contrary to purity. If the penitent be not to blame, so far as the Priest can judge, he must exhort him to prayer with frequent invocations of the Name of JESUS: avoid as much as he can the pleasures of the senses: frequent the Blessed Sacrament: often protest that he never wishes to consent to the suggestions and delectations to which the evil spirit moves him: strengthen himself by making the sign of the Cross, or by wearing a cross: bid the evil spirit depart in the Name of the Holy Trinity: and finally make many acts of outward and inward humility, for the LORD often suffers these kinds of temptations to assail souls in order to cure them of secret pride and self-conceit.

Physical aids, such as cold baths at night, tying the hands to prevent involuntary movements, and such as a physician might advise, should be recommended in more obstinate cases.

There are persons, however, who appear to invite such attacks, and are therefore most difficult to be healed. The Priest must, however, not despair even in their case, who need extraordinary assistance from GOD, because the devil has gained possession of their will, and they have become too feeble to resist. He must deal with them in the largest spirit of charity—encourage them by telling them that so long as their will is not compromised they do not sin, and that every time they resist, guilt is not incurred. The same remedies as prescribed above must be enjoined, and absolution generally should be deferred until after due probation, because conversions are rarely experienced in such cases, and perseverance is still more rare.

(65) *Difficult cases.*

As we have just spoken of cases which require all the best qualities of the Priest in absolution to be brought out we will take three classes which are often most perplexing. These are (occasional) such as are subject to occasions of sin; or (habitual) under the influence of habits of sin; or (relapsing) liable to relapse into sin.[1]

It must be noted that habitual and relapsing differ in

---

[1] An occasion of sin is some external circumstance, which is likely to lead to sin; such as living together, keeping company, trade, &c. Danger of sin is everything within and without which tends to sin.

this, that though every habitual sinner is a relapsing sinner, every relapsing sinner is not habitual; since that depends on the frequency of his relapses within a given period.

(66) *Those who are subject to occasions of sin.*

Generally speaking, persons should not be absolved unless they engage to withdraw from such persons, places, and associations, as they know by experience are dangerous in presenting fresh temptations to sin. Indeed it is not safe to give absolution unless such withdrawal is actually consummated. In cases where this is physically or morally impossible, as where the temptation arises from a fellow-member of the same family, or cannot be effected without some scandal or disgrace, or some very great inconvenience, it may suffice to urge such means of security, as may render the likelihood of temptation as remote as possible. A person who is evidently bent upon amendment and is willing to take such precautions as are advised, such as not to be alone with such a one, perform some act of mortification, above all betake himself frequently to prayer and to confession, may be absolved upon his promise to act in this way, especially when some difficulty is likely to occur from delaying his absolution.

Absolution may be thus given once or twice upon the promises of the penitent, where his sincerity seems clear. At the same time every effort should be made to produce in him a deep and earnest contrition. But if the penitent have failed several times before to fulfil his engagements, absolution must be delayed until he have fulfilled them. Still the Priest must use every encouragement to induce him to return, and promise to aid him in his difficulties.

In order to do so, the Priest must learn what was the obstacle which hindered the penitent from fulfilling his promise at the first time. Here must be observed the difference between an obligation to make restitution or to render the temptation more remote. In the latter case greater strictness is required, because two souls are imperilled, and it is a question of offending GOD, and so it is no material but a formal act of sin continually urgent and pressing which is likely to result. Nothing but physical or moral impossibility can justify indulgence on the part of the Priest here. But in the case of restitution there may be sufficiently lawful reasons to allow of delay though not of neglect; it is then that the Priest by insisting upon immediate restitution might hurt the debtor without benefiting the creditor. The penitent should have a time fixed for payment of his debt and for coming back for absolution, and be urged to pray for recollection and courage to discharge his liability. The Priest should moreover suggest means of removing any difficulties in the way. Sometimes where the penitent shrinks from meeting his creditor, or the person whom he has offended, he may get some one to intercede and prevail in obtaining a kind reception. The same rule applies to cases where reconciliation with an enemy is required. In the case of malicious misrepresentations, it may suffice that the offender retract his observations in the presence of those to whom he has made them. And a dangerous person should be persuaded to leave the house where the penitent lives, but not forced to leave it for fear of giving rise to or confirming possible suspicions.

The Priest must take care not to insist on the fulfilment of obligations which he enjoins, unless they are entirely necessary, when he finds the penitent obstinately set against them, and does not acknowledge their necessity. Otherwise he must be refused absolution as unworthy of it. The same caution must be observed where the penitent labours under invincible ignorance, such as when he has contracted a marriage which is null and void on account of some secret impediment, likely to lead to grave disorders.

(67) *Two kinds of occasions of sin.*

We may divide the occasions of sin into two classes —those which depend *on the will* or voluntary, and *on necessity* or involuntary. The first may be physically and morally, i.e. by natural strength and without sin and great difficulty, avoided,—the other cannot be, physically or morally, avoided, without grave inconvenience or scandal, such as is beyond the ordinary power of human strength to endure. We may subdivide them into *near* and *remote*. *Near* is that which generally causes men to fall, or accidentally does so, being only relatively, and in particular cases, dangerous, since what is near to some is remote to others. We may define the *near* occasion as being that temptation which has caused men to fall often before. What is near to a careless person is remote to one who is religious: and the same may be said of mankind according to their propensions. Hence men are bound to flee those occasions which though remote to others are near to them.

(68) *Marks of near occasions of sin.*

The occasion of sin may be said to be near in the case of those who have persons in their houses with whom they are in the custom of sinning: or who are led in particular games or amusements to swear or to cheat: or who by frequenting places where they are prone to get intoxicated, quarrel or indulge in impure thoughts and words. Thus, a servant-maid who is vehemently pressed by her master, and feels that she may be insensibly drawn into sin, is bound to leave his employment, if possible, or at the worst to think herself always in danger. A person who though he only enter a house once a year, yet if he always sin by doing so, may be said to have there a near occasion to sin. And though certain acts may not be occasions to sin to some persons, yet if scandal ensue thereby, absolution is rendered difficult.

(69) *How to deal with occasions.*

Those who are betrothed to each other need to be very cautious in their intercourse with each other, since it is difficult for them to restrain looks, and thoughts, and words, and even acts which border upon dangerous if they be not absolutely so. It would be unjust to hold that lovemaking is always sinful, but it would be equally bad to regard it as always innocent. Innocent in its commencement it often becomes sinful in its progress. The transition from pleasure in the society of each other to passion and sin is not so uncommon as some might suppose. Absolution must be withheld where persons will not desist from secret or untimely interviews, unknown to or forbidden by parents, and from such behaviour as may be hurtful to either party or exciting sinful emotions.

(70) *Important distinctions.*

We have said that the Priest may absolve once or twice the penitent who is liable to a voluntary occasion of sin before he has removed it. But not when it is actually at work, as when a man keeps a mistress in his house or a servant falls into sin with her master, and the like. Excuses and reasons for not removing occasions of sin which are frivolous or not of sufficient importance must be always cut short by the confessor. Such are the inconveniences arising out of the necessity of discharging a servantmaid. If the Priest sees that the master is ready, when required, to discharge a servantmaid, he may permit him to keep her for a limited period, since his readiness to discharge her may be taken as a proof of solid repentance. Ordinarily, however, in regard to both impurity and covetousness fire and sword must be the order of the day, and promises are little to be trusted.

It is otherwise in games, publichouses, and conversations. Here the promise to withdraw from such places of temptation may enable the Priest to give absolution on the instant two or three times. But in the former case it is almost invariably requisite that the penitent should get rid of the near occasion of sin prior to receiving absolution. The only exception is when he manifests extraordinary signs of contrition, such as warrant the Priest in concluding that he has received such abundant grace as to be able to withdraw himself from the cause of temptation. And these are all modified according to the facility with which the penitent may return to be absolved without having to go to another Priest for confession.

(71) *Necessary occasions.*

When the occasion does not depend on the will of the penitent, but is matter of *necessity*[1] *physically*, as when a person is in prison and at death's door, and has neither time nor power to send away his mistress: or *morally*, as when it may involve scandal, or a grave inconvenience affecting life, reputation or fortune,—the penitent may be absolved without withdrawal of the occasion of sin. But if the exterior occasion cannot be removed, every effort must be made to weaken the interior occasion. In such a case he must avoid familiarity and the sight of the sinful partner: receive the Sacraments: perform acts of mortification and penance,—such as self-denial in food or sleep, suited to his bodily powers, and counselled by his Priest: commend himself frequently to GOD, renewing daily every

---

[1] Necessity may be defined in three ways. It depends on the man or woman separately or conjointly. It may be that a son cannot leave his father's house on account of a maidservant who is the cause of his falls: that a wife cannot send away from her house the friend of her husband: or that a male and female member of the same family cannot separate without the scandal of exposure. A wife cannot refuse due benevolence when the husband is an Onanist. The Priest must apply himself to decide whether the occasion be voluntary or involuntary, and whether the impossibility of separation be real or pretended.

morning his resolution to sin no more and avoid every occasion of sin as much as possible. As the occasion of sin is not in itself sin, where it cannot be avoided sin is not incurred by its existence. GOD will aid in such a case all who observe the needful precautions.

Where no amendment follows it is to be feared that necessary occasions of sin have become wilful occasions of sin: and the difficulty is to distinguish between cases in which the moral impossibility of resistance is real or apparent. Where the occasion of sin is less readily removed than sin is avoided, when the occasion offers, the impossibility is real. Else the danger of multiplying sin by the very means taken to destroy it would be increased.

This rule applies to all who cannot leave their duties or employments or houses in which they are prone to sin, so long as they are truly desirous of amendment and use the means of amending. Delay of absolution in such cases however is very salutary in order to stir up the penitent to observe the needful precautions.

The remedies with these almost despaired of sick folk are three—" If thine eye offend thee, pluck it out, and cast it from thee." Through flight, fire, and sword,—though the occasion be dearer to the penitent than the apple of his eye,—he must get rid of it. "If thy hand offend thee, cut it off." Though another occasion defile thee with games, feastings and debaucheries, cut it off. "If thy foot offend thee, cut it off, and cast it from thee." Though another occasion be this house, this publichouse, this company, leave it, cost what it may. No person can be absolved who being able to avoid a near occasion of sin refuses to do so.

(72) *Interior and exterior marks of occasions of sin.*

The near occasion of sin is not identical with the danger of sin: nor is the near occasion of sin identical with the near danger of it. The near occasion of sin depends necessarily and always upon some exterior circumstance, which does not carry with it the danger of sin, however near it be. David, for example, saw Bathsheba at a distance. Here was the near occasion of sin, but no danger until moved by his lust he sent for her. Hence the near occasion of sin arises from the interior inclination to sin, and the exterior circumstance which suggests and gives facility to sin. It is David's living with Bathsheba afterwards which justifies our calling it in his case a near occasion to sin. Thus it may be defined as being that which, having regard to the circumstances of the person, place, and past experience leads to frequent and constant sin. And the remote occasion is that which under like predicaments leads but seldom to sin. Thus what is a near occasion of sin to a young man, is but remote to an old man. The exterior occasion of sin may in itself be a very holy action—such as hearing a confession, but if the confessor give way to evil thoughts, confession may be to him a near occasion of sin. He must, if such be the case, either relinquish his office, or employ the best means of amendment. Hence exterior occasions of sin may be as many as there are things in the world. But if the interior occasion of sin—that which men inherit from Adam as our natural propension to evil, be checked, no exterior occasion will much affect them, and unless they do so check it, they are unworthy of absolution, so long as they cannot abandon the society or place which is to them a continual irritament of their carnal mind.

(73) *Frequency of relapses.*

Thus what is properly called a near occasion of sin is that where people sin always, or all but always, or at least frequently. Hence we must explain the two words, *fall frequently*. As to the first it is a great mistake to suppose that that only is a near occasion of sin wherein a person is led to fall disgracefully into glaring acts of vice, and not also when he yields to sinful words, looks, or touch: or as to the second, when a person sins but seldom, though he sins whenever he is exposed to the temptation. A skilful confessor will not therefore take into consideration merely the number of falls, but learn by examination how far the sin depends upon the occasion, and what is the amount of influence exercised by the occasion upon the sin. If the occasion be clearly seen by the Priest to be involuntary and unavoidable, the exterior circumstance not being removable, he must do his best to weaken the interior, viz. the imminent danger resulting from the inward propension to sin. In cases where through lack of fit dispositions or progress of amendment, the Priest does not feel himself justified in giving absolution together with sufficient directions to avert the evil, he must urge (1) avoidance of all intercourse with the dangerous object as much as possible, (2) prayer for aid, (3) frequent Confession and reception of the Holy Eucharist under the direction of the same Priest, and following all his prescriptions, and (4) acts of mortification with his sanction. If no sign of amendment result, absolution must be refused, as it is most likely that the involuntary occasion has become voluntary. This is the point where the Priest needs illumination to come to a wise decision. In regard to voluntary occasions, a distinction must be made between *urgent* and *non-urgent*. Urgent occasions are such as result in falls chiefly in the case of avarice and impurity, and need to be dealt with severely and promptly. Excuses must not be listened to, however secretly weighed by the Priest. A servant must be dismissed in spite of inconvenience or loss or even scandal, especially where suspicion may be already presumed. Non-urgent occasions allow of more concessions to human weakness, such as places of amusement and dancing, and love-making. There are, however, cases under the last head which are absolutely unlawful, such as where they are accompanied by the excitement of lustful emotions, or occur between persons of unequal conditions of life, who cannot hope to be married, in church, contrary to parental rules, secretly or in night time, and manifestly producing in one or other of the parties bad symptoms.

The same rules must be observed in regard to other professions in life, where persons are exposed to the danger of falling into blasphemy, dishonesty, hatred, perjury, and the like, in order to decide when to give or refuse absolution, especially where the occupation or employment cannot be abandoned.

(74) Those who are in the habit of sin, or who relapse.

These must be dealt with in a different manner. A single and predetermined act is not sufficient to stop bad habits and relapses. They require a long series of difficult acts in opposition to successive frequent and unlooked for attacks. The sufferers are in danger of despair at their failures, or of presumption in excusing themselves for their weakness. They cannot receive absolution if (1) they have neglected some or most of the means prescribed: if (2) the number of their sins be not diminished: and if (3) they give no extraordinary sign of contrition. But if absolution be delayed, the Priest's zeal should be directed (1) to suggest the best motives and means to excite true repentance, and (2) to induce the penitent to return within eight or ten days at furthest. It is good for the patient who is very ill to see his doctor frequently. And hence, if he come back without sufficient evidence of change of heart, he should be remanded, but for a shorter time—and so on till some signs of amendment be discovered. S. Bernard is said to have cured a young man of gross sensuality by obtaining from him a promise to abstain for three days in honour of the Blessed Trinity from such sin. On his return S. Bernard, finding that he had so abstained, bid him do so for three days more. And at the end of the second three days' time having succeeded, he was ordered to repeat his abstinence from acts of sin, and at the close he came voluntarily and offered to abstain for the rest of his life. This is acting in the spirit of S. Chrysostom, who says that "We ought to be ashamed of ourselves if we despair of the salvation of our brethren when the devil never despairs of their damnation, but ever is on the look-out for it. What excuse shall we have if, in the face of so much watching on the part of the devil for our destruction, we never exhibit anything like that vigilance for the salvation of our brethren, especially when we have GOD always on our side." "He shows the most ardent love of the brethren who against and without hope perseveres in his care in their behalf."

The priest should receive such penitents with open arms, without betraying any signs of disgust or astonishment because they have relapsed so soon and so miserably. He should rather commend their haste to return to him. He must learn what orders they have neglected, the time and manner of the assault and victory, so as to become better acquainted with the cause and remedy. A Priest is said to have cured one patient by bidding him come to him for confession as soon as he had fallen into sin, and not to wait for a second fall. By absolving him, and giving him the same penance, he was cured in a few months. Hence it is possible that a penitent may for a while fall daily or weekly, and yet present sufficient signs of penitence to enable him to be absolved. Humility and earnest desire to amend are often as clearly manifested by the coming of the penitent to confession as soon as he falls as in other ways, such as when he manifests actual diminution of the number of his falls. And this because confession is not merely a trial of the penitent, but also a remedy for his disease. And since Penance contains sanctifying grace for justifying the sinner for the past, and sacramental grace for preserving him from future falls, we must distinguish between what is a proper disposition to receive absolution, and what is its fruit. Else we may act like doctors who content themselves with purges without taking care to order the supports needful to sustain the effects thereof, and so kill their patient. This is why communions should not be withheld from habitual sinners, when they are thought capable of receiving absolution.

(75) *When the relapsing should be absolved.*

If the Priest desire to perceive clearer marks of contrition than a firm and solid purpose of putting in force the prescribed means, such as a clear diminution in the number of acts of sin, he must not proceed absolutely in the spirit of arithmetical computation, but relatively, by taking into consideration the particular circumstances of the case. First he should try to discover whether human weakness or whether wickedness is the cause of relapses. Thus some sin from old habits, others from natural violent propension: others from the frequent assaults made on them from within and without. These deserve more compassion, though their falls be equal in number, than those who sin under circumstances more favourable to virtuous conduct. Interior relapses of consent to sin have less malice of sin and deliberation and choice than exterior developments. And sudden and hasty acts such as blasphemy have less wickedness than deliberate acts, such as drunkenness: and sin is of less magnitude when solitary than when committed with another, and in the seduced than in the seducer. Consideration should also be given as to the mode of treatment, whether severity or gentleness is more likely to be beneficial to the particular case. Sometimes it is desirable to bid the penitent take half or a quarter of an hour to excite contrition. As in bodily disease where abstinence may or may not be good for the individual; so in spiritual maladies sometimes absolution or communion must be withheld or conceded.

(76) *Precautions to be observed with the relapsing.*

In order to rightly estimate whether the penitent's amendment justify absolution being given, it should be considered by way of comparison how often he has fallen into his old sins. If one, for instance, had been in the habit of sinning in speech six times or more in the day, and during eight days had sinned but three times a day, while another who had been in the habit of sinning in act almost daily, and during eight days had fallen but three times; it would be better to absolve the first and defer absolution for the second, because the first exhibits more efforts and efficacious amendment than the second in proportion to former bad habits. Yet cases may arise in which the second may be absolved, such as when delay might be accompanied by some great spiritual loss, the penitent being overwhelmed by some temporal calamity, and less capable of bearing up under the denial of absolution, as an additional cause of pain, or being likely to leave for some other place where he would not have courage to reiterate his confession.

(77) *How to deal with young people.*

In regard to young people—experience proves that it is better to be prudently liberal with absolutions and communions, with the view though not perhaps of preventing the occurrence of sins altogether, yet of greatly diminishing their number, than to deal with them as one would with persons of maturer and stabler age. This is because the passions of the young, who are in the flower of their age, are as strong as in manhood, but have not the same thoughtfulness or steadiness. They are more fickle in changing from evil to good and from good to evil. Moreover, they are subject to parents and teachers, and liable to the remarks of their companions, which render it more important that communion should not be withheld from them for so long a time as upon similar grounds it would be denied to older penitents.

(78) *Of general confessions in the case of the relapsing.*

As to confession in relapsing cases, it would not be safe either to insist upon the repetition of general confessions when the penitent comes to a particular Priest, on the ground that his previous confessions had been made without the proper disposition, or to dispense with a general confession on the mere assumption that it had been so made. The main ground of requiring a general confession would be that there was good reason to believe that something material had been omitted by the penitent, or that there was a well founded doubt on the subject. But confessions which have been followed by no amendment even for a short period may be regarded with reason as insufficient, and needing reiteration. But this ought not to be the case whenever the penitent has sensibly diminished the number of his faults, even though he may have relapsed. Like medicine, after which the patient seems to be better, though the fever recur afterwards; so with confession, which, though it blots out all sins of which a person accuses himself with sincere grief, does not remove all subsequent evils, such as weakness and inclination to fall away. It diminishes but does not entirely subdue the power of bad habits. This complete cure ordinarily is the result of persevering in confession, which by slow degrees purges from sin and strengthens the spiritual constitution till the health of the soul is re-established.

(79) *How to deal with sacrilegious Confessions.*

If the penitent say that he has made an imperfect confession, he should be (1) told to confess all his sins since his last confession, and then to add what he omitted before: (2) asked whether he knew, or thought, or was doubtful at any rate that it was deadly when he suppressed it. Should he say no, he should be asked whether he suppressed it with such ideas afterwards. If hitherto he has not done so, there is no need to repeat his confession: but if he have, his confession must be gone over again from that point, as being invalid. If he only knew that his act was generally speaking of a bad character, without distinguishing its small or great importance, and was likely not to have concealed it had he known its gravity, he probably need not repeat his confession unless he think it a duty to do so. Thus the conscious or doubting omission of one deadly sin invalidates all confessions dating from that time, and requires that all confessions from that time should be reiterated—unless they be all made to the same Priest, and he remember the state of the penitent, in which case it may suffice to say, "I accuse myself of all sins committed from such a time." When the penitent has scruples on this head, though he have omitted nothing wilfully, he may be allowed to make a general confession, if there be reason to think that it would be profitable to him.

Where, however, the Priest requires or advises a general confession to be made, instead of exacting a detailed statement of the quantity of sins, he may be content with three points (1) the length of time since the penitent fell into the faults: (2) the frequency of falls while the bad habit lasted: (3) any explanation which may be necessary. Thus the Priest will secure the knowledge of three things, (1) the state of the soul; (2) the penance and remedies required; (3) the propriety of giving or refusing absolution. If it be impossible to get the penitent to make such a confession, he must be brought into such a state as to entertain a general sorrow for the past, and have time allowed to give spiritual strength.

(80) *General Confessions.*

The making a second or more General Confession has been compared to beating a forest for game, because it is possible to confess without obtaining the full knowledge of faults. General Confession may be *hurtful* to some, *useful* to most, and indispensably *necessary* to others.

Hurtful (1) to scrupulous persons, just as rubbing the eyes often makes ophthalmia worse, especially when they have repeated their General Confession already, have amended their lives, enjoy peace of soul, and are not conscious of having omitted anything material in their past confession. It is sometimes well to advise them to make a review of life since the last General Confession, so as to be better informed as to the state of their conscience. Such persons had best be advised to make frequent acts of contrition, as being enough for all who have done their utmost to make a good confession.

Useful (2) both in life and for the hour of death. During life a good General Confession is like a new and clean dress, about which the wearer is more careful. The sight of all one's sins at one view is more alarming and exciting than of them singly; and it is on this account that some holy people make their General Confessions once every year, to stir themselves up to deeper sorrow for the past, firmer resolutions for the future, and more affectionateness to our merciful FATHER. *At the hour of death* all will be happy who have not put off their confession until the time when it is always most difficult to make it truly and perfectly.

Necessary in seven instances : (1) when persons know or think that they have from shame or some other motive concealed some deadly sin without having in successive confessions disclosed it: (2) when they have confessed without examination of conscience, or with negligent examination so as to have exposed themselves to the risk of imperfect confession: (3) when they have designedly told parts of their deadly sins to one Priest, and part to another, so that they were not all known to the same confessor: (4) when they have confessed without contrition, through habit or respect of persons, or have purposely gone to Priests who they knew were less likely to deal wisely with their cases: (5) when they have confessed without real purpose of amendment: (6) when they will not quit occasions of sin, while continuing to go to confession: (7) when they wilfully refuse to make restitution or to be reconciled while still going to confession. All such persons ought to make a General Confession of all the deadly sins which they have committed since they first commenced the habit of wilfully and knowingly confessing so badly, and to take as much care in self-examination as if they had never confessed before. Persons have been known to conceal a particular sin, though it has surged up to their remembrance while making many a confession. Sometimes they excuse themselves on the account of the tender age at which it was committed, though upon inquiry whether they concealed it from others and feared to be punished if found out, it is clear that they were conscious of its badness, and need to make a fresh General Confession. Two classes need to do this— those who have never made it before, and those who have gone a long time to confession without giving any signs of amendment, such as even abstinence from sin for a brief period, or some resistance to it before relapses.

In examination of conscience previous to a General Confession, the Priest should advise the penitent to draw up an abridgment of his self-accusations, so as not to confess in a confused or lengthy manner, and to avoid dilating on details, and making four long stories out of four sins which might be expressed in four words. This is especially needful in regard to transgressions of the seventh Commandment, where any unnecessary explanations and interrogations must be strictly restrained. Nor is it necessary to divide sins according to the different periods and conditions of life, since sin is not changed by the difference of age. Venial sins should not come into the examination at all for fear of rendering the whole confession too wearisome and vexatious.

In regard to the number of sins, if people cannot recollect them with any accuracy, it is best to ask about their frequency and continuance, and so excite them to contrition and amendment.

(81) *Remedies for the relapsed.*

Remedies for relapsed Christians, specially such as relapse into sensuality, are (1) to enter on a course of spiritual exercises, and if possible to make a general confession (if it has not been made for a long time,) taking some days previous for preparation by prayers, frequent acts of contrition and of mortification, and by a thorough self-examination. The sight of all his sins covers the sinner with holy confusion, humbles him, excites him to a more lively repentance, and disposes him to receive in the sacrament of penance such extraordinary grace as to prevent his relapse. (2) To confess thrice a week to the same Priest or oftener, and to say to our LORD night and morning—"*My Saviour, and my Judge, Who hast prepared for the devil and his angels everlasting punishment, and Who warnest us that the same doom awaits impenitent sinners, here prostrate before Thee* I resolve in honour of Thy Passion to abstain at least until the morning or until night from such and such sin." (3) To exhort the relapsed to commend himself to GOD frequently during the day, and not to allow the entering in of any temptation: and if assailed, to resist it instantly, without giving it time to gather force, with the thought of GOD's presence and power to punish the sinner in the very act of sin. (4) To urge him, if he fall away, to come as soon as possible to confession, without waiting until a second relapse befall him. He should be induced to lay aside his shame by being told that his having to come back is no source of annoyance to the Priest, and that it does not lower him in the Priest's esteem, but the contrary: and to put away negligence by being reminded that delay in such a case is a dishonour to GOD, a grieving of the HOLY GHOST, an encouragement to the devil, a confirmation of his passions, takes away the power of feeling ashamed of his faults and of amending them, and thus may be the cause of his gradually going down to hell when he least expects it. He should be told that humility and penitence may save him in spite of his relapse, if he come at once to confession, but that otherwise his case is desperate. (5) He must be reassured in the midst of the difficulties, which he experiences in extricating himself at once from his bad habits, so as not to regard as useless the efforts which he makes, by being told that it is of faith that he who prays with confidence, perseverance, and humility, and at the same time corresponds with the Divine inspirations, must sooner or later gain what is necessary for his salvation. Greater sinners than he have had hope and amended their lives, why may not he? Already he may see some fruit of his prayer, in any cessation of sin, and in having time and grace afforded him to confess.

(82) *How to deal with cases where extraordinary contrition is exhibited.*

There are cases where no appreciable diminution of faults is discernible, and yet absolution may be given. This is when extraordinary contrition is manifest. This result may be accepted by the Priest in the case of a person who has been vividly touched by a sermon, sudden inspiration, or circumstance in life, which has moved him to come straightway to confession—sometimes in spite of many difficulties, or notwithstanding the distance he has had to travel. It is as when Nathan took David's "I have sinned," as a sign of his true repentance. Eight tokens are commonly suggested. (1) Tears of sincere compunction and hearty words of penitence. (2) Diminution of sinful acts, when exposed to the same occasions and temptations, or at least falls only after long resistance. (3) Care in efforts to amend, observance of rules and prescriptions. (4) Desire for remedies and fresh means of amendment, and promise to use such as are ordained him. (5) Voluntary confession, specially if at the cost of a long voyage, of some loss, and after great struggles. (6) After a sermon, or death of a friend, pestilence, &c. (7) Confession of sins hitherto concealed. (8) Protesting deeper knowledge and horror of sin. Seven notes of insufficient penitence may be taken. (1) After being rebuked twice or thrice by a zealous confessor, return with undiminished or even increased number of sins. (2) No greater horror of sin than before, a confession of the lips and not of the heart. (3) Neglect of the remedies prescribed without regret. (4) A negligent mode of life with free indulgence of the passions, without any attempt to amend. (5) Coming to confession only at Easter, or through the advice or compulsion of relatives or masters, or any respect of persons. (6) Excusing faults, discussion with confessor, or objecting to penances and showing indisposition to amend. (7) A great propension to sin and disinclination to avoid occasions of it, so that little weight can be attributed to protestations of repentance.

Where a great change is visible in a person's present and former state of mind, as when he declares that he feels as he never had felt before, the gravity of his sins, and a resolution to amend, and makes his confession in a devout and penitent manner, to which he avows he had been hitherto a stranger, the Priest should take it as the work of GOD in the soul for the purpose of winning absolution. He must imitate his Master in generosity to sinners, and as liberally absolve as He gives power of return to Himself. In such cases souls must often be dealt with as those of men on their dying beds. Delay may be dangerous—only let everything be done at the time to secure penitence and firm purpose of amendment.

(83) *Use of Spiritual Retreats and Missions.*

Spiritual Retreats and Missions are often salutary in producing the necessary conversions, which check relapses. The Priest will find in resorting to the aid of other clergy means of breaking through the difficulties which some souls find in returning to GOD. To confess a long hidden sin, to make a long deferred act of restitution, to be reconciled to a person with whom one has been long at variance, to avoid some occasion of sin, to overcome some respect of persons, which keeps one back from declaring himself on the side of GOD, and to introduce fervour into a long continued lukewarmness in His service—all these are often put off till death, and in vain. But the novelty of the retreat or mission, the excitement originated by a stranger preacher of known or surprising power often prevails to open a door which remains closed to the efforts of the Priest, to whom the penitent has listened without success. Experience shows that they who remain unaffected by such attempts have not thrown themselves heartily and regularly into endeavours to utilise them.

(84) *Distinction between habitual and relapsing sinners.*

But a distinction must be drawn between *habitual* and *relapsing* sinners. Habitual sinners are such as have fallen into habits of sin without having confessed them. On their first confession absolution may be given, provided they appear to have the fit dispositions. But in the case of inveterate habits, the Priest should satisfy himself that the penitent has put in force the prescribed remedies, and conceived greater horror of sin. Five falls in a month suffice to constitute a bad habit of external acts, provided there be a sufficient interval between them. In grosser sins, once a month during the year is enough to stamp the case as habitual.

Relapsing sinners on the other hand are such as after confession fall back in a similar manner without amendment. Such should have their absolution, ordinarily speaking, deferred for a short space until some clear sign of amendment is discernible. All, however, that is requisite is that the Priest have a moral or relative certainty as to the dispositions of the penitent; and he need not torment either himself or the penitent to obtain further proofs which are impossible. It may be desirable in some cases to refuse absolution to a relapsing person though duly disposed: it is always useful to appear to be afraid to absolve them: but it is better to give than to refuse when extraordinary signs of contrition are manifested.

One may remark here, in regard to bad habits, that it is easier to absolve those who relapse into oaths and the like than those who fall back into such sins as hatred, dishonesty, and impurity, which involve the fault of concupiscence in the highest degree. Although the Priest be not obliged to give absolution without delay, yet it is rarely profitable to delay, except the penitent lack obviously the necessary dispositions: for the Priest should hope that the grace of absolution would profit him, when duly disposed, more than its being deferred, specially in cases where he has fallen through *inward frailty*. For it is different where one has relapsed through some outward cause, which is often more exciting than the mere inward propension. In that case the penitent has to remove himself from nearness to the dangerous occasion, society, or circumstances, before his condition can be safe for absolution.

(85) *Relapsing Ordinands.*

Greater strictness is required in absolving those who are candidates for holy orders, than laity. It may be necessary to give absolution to the former only on condition of abstaining from admission to holy orders for several months. Nothing but extraordinary compunction on the part of the ordinand can except him if liable to habitual sins, specially of the grosser sorts, from this rule. An exception however may be given when great scandal may attend adhesion to it.

(86) *How to absolve habitual and relapsing.*

Habitual and relapsing sinners are only to be absolved on the ground that the will is changed (1) when some hope of amendment is evident: (2) and when they are willing to avoid the proximate occasion of sin: and when they are acquainted with the mysteries of the faith, such as the Holy Trinity and the

Incarnation. When once a scrupulous person has decided that he has not consented to a temptation, he ought not to return to the question: for often such reconsiderations cause a return of the temptation. Two rules may be given to aid in the decision. (1) To see whether at the moment of temptation a lively attachment has been preserved for the virtue which is assailed, and hatred for the vice which is suggested. (2) Whether the person could take an oath that no consent had been given to the temptation. It is well to refer all scruples to the judgment of the Priest, who sometimes may do well to recommend less frequent confession in order that the penitent may forget and make less account of his scruples. It may be well also to dismiss persons without listening to their scruples, since scrupulousness, as we have before said, is a disease which allows of truce but not of peace, and can only be healed by humility.

Persons should be directed not to urge their Priest to allow them to do anything to which he has showed a repugnance: and if they cannot have recourse to him, to interpret his intentions in an honest way and conduct themselves accordingly. They ought not to be suffered to impose mortifications on themselves without his permission, lest they ruin their health or yield to pride. They ought not to attach themselves to means with the forgetfulness of the end, such as the love of GOD and of their neighbour and interior mortification. Nor should they take any vows without his advice, nor should he often give them permission to take vows, lest they be induced to break them. When they make vows it should be always conditionally. Every one should be advised to remain in that state to which GOD has called them: not to leave domestic or other duties for devout exercises which are not of obligation: to undertake little, but practise it without ceasing: to be on the watch against little faults, lest by negligence in minor affairs the heart become hardened, and greater mischief be the result. They should be counselled often to renew their resolutions and not to be discouraged because of the temptations which assail them: to trust in GOD, Who changes not, and not let their hearts be troubled, for GOD is wont, when He would vouchsafe some virtue, to permit us to be tormented by temptations to the contrary vice.

(87) *How to deal with the sick and dying.*

When the Priest is called in to visit a sick man on the point of death, all his charity, adroitness, and precision will be required. It is obvious that any false step either in the way of laxity or severity must, if ever, then be most deplorable. First of all it is clear that it must be out of the question to demand of the dying man the same exactness of confession and the same signs of contrition which would be looked for from a person in full possession of health. At such a time if the soul be stirred at all it is likely that the devil will try to cast him down to despair,—and what with the pains of dying and the fear of death, the penitent will have little need of so severe a treatment as the refusal or the delay of absolution. What is advisable to be done in the case of healthy persons, who need to be absolved without delay must be followed in respect of the dying: only let great precautions be taken not to weary the sick—such as speaking gently, and now and then putting in a word. It may be that the Priest must content himself with getting the formal completeness of confession, without resorting to such interrogations of detail, which help to make up its material completeness. It is more important to arrive at the conviction of the penitent's sincere contrition, than obtain a complete confession in all its minuteness. So long as there is no immediate danger of death, the absolution may be put off from morning to evening, and from evening to morning. The Priest should avoid alarming the sick man,—speak without embarrassment, and inspire hope of pardon inasmuch as GOD has not suddenly carried him off. In cases where the sick man can give no outward sign of contrition or of self-accusation conditional absolution may be given, especially in such cases as when the penitent has lived to all appearance in a Christian manner. If the penitent be capable of performing a penance, it should be of a light kind, and such as may be replaced by one more severe, if he recover and go to the Priest afterwards. In the case of women in childbed or wounded persons who cannot be left by the nurses and friends, it may suffice that they make a confession in general terms, particularising only some slighter fault, such as impatience, with the intention of making a complete confession when restored to health. If the dying man ought to make any act of restitution he should be persuaded to do it without delay, on pain of being refused absolution. It is often useful and necessary to obtain the assistance of a pious and prudent laic, when there is any difficulty in moving the sick to penitence, or in the priest's attendance.

(88) *Caution to the Priest.*

The Priest should take care (1) to learn from the medical man *privately* whether the sickness is likely to be fatal : (2) to obtain all the information he can from the relatives and friends as to the sick man's conduct, habits, and faults. In the case of such as have received their injury at the hands of others the Priest should speak generally on the subject of forgiving even without entering into particulars. Should the sick man speak of them, or of his property, children, and lawsuits, the Priest should change the subject. (3) When the Priest is apprised that the sickness is likely to be fatal, he should not speak there and then to the sick man about confession, but make inquiry as to his sickness and his sufferings. Then he should bid him resign himself to the will of GOD, unite his sufferings to those of JESUS on the Cross with an oblation of them to GOD by way of expiation of his sins. By degrees he may ask him whether he have ever confessed, and how long since : while urging him to trust in GOD for his cure, he should tell him that the sickness is of a grave kind, and that he must not attend to what the doctors or his friends say on this head with the view of not disturbing his equanimity. He should then press the sick man to lose no time in making his confession, while his mind is capable of making such a one as may be of service to his soul and even to his body. Cases are on record where a good confession has restored to health persons who had been despaired of. But if the sick man plead for delay, and be in no immediate danger of death, lethargy, or loss of senses, it may be granted him, so long as he will fix a time, at evening or on the morrow morning. If he be obstinate, the Priest must persevere, and put up publicly and privately prayers on his behalf. (4) When the sick man is far gone, he should be advised to put his affairs in order, if the needs of his family require it, still more if it be necessary in order to satisfy his conscience. The Priest must in such a case be careful to avoid any suspicion of personal interest. If the sick man have brothers and sisters in great need, it is right to admonish him that he is bound to provide for them in due proportion to their necessities. He should not charge his heirs with the obligation of having him remembered at the Holy Eucharist, but make himself due provision for its being done. (5) The Priest must be careful not to weary the sick man by speaking too much or too loud, but just enough to inspire compunction or consolation. (6) Besides the little print or figure of the Crucifixion which is placed, if possible, beside the bed of the sick man, it is well to have a larger Crucifixion placed where his eyes would naturally most often rest upon it. (7) It is proper to have all dangerous objects removed from the sick man's chamber, papers and books of doubtful or of unedifying kind, to say nothing of persons who might be occasions of sin and of pictures of improper design. As the end draws near, as few people as possible should be permitted to enter his chamber, especially such as are likely to excite his feelings. Silence should be the rule except in the case of prayer and holy reading.

(89) *Remedies against temptations.*

Against *temptations*—it is well to get the sick man to make the sign of the Cross,—and to invoke the Name of JESUS. But in particular in regard to temptations against *faith,* which attack people who have led dissolute lives, or have been self-reliant and self-opinionated, the sick should be advised to abandon arguments and reasoning, and to reply, " I believe,"—to thank GOD for having regenerated him in the womb of the Catholic Church, and to protest his determination to live and die in its faith. Besides this it is well to employ himself in making acts of contrition, confidence, and love of GOD, and the like, and the Priest should remind him how the proofs of our faith are such as render the truth manifest, propagated as it was by poor fishermen and sealed by so many thousands of martyrs in its defence. Against *despair.* This is the common temptation, whereby the devil assails the dying. Hence it is necessary to speak to them almost exclusively of the mercy of GOD, of the Passion of JESUS CHRIST, and the promises of GOD. Against *vain glory.* The sick man should be told that sin alone appertains to us, but that all good is from GOD. Against *impatience.* The Priest should rehearse the sufferings of the martyrs, above all of the King of Martyrs. He should warn the sick man that impatience may expose him to torments in the next life, while patience may save him for ever. Not only must he submit to the will of GOD, so far as relates to the pains which he suffers, but also in regard to the ignorance of the physicians, and the negligence of his nurses. In regard *to the young,* who feel it so hard to die, they should be reminded of the misery of human life, the sickness, the vexations, the disappointments, the danger of sinning and of losing eternal life. Thus the Saints always longed for death. S. Paul said, " I have a desire to depart and to be with CHRIST." Others have said, "While I live I may lose GOD," and so rejoiced at the striking of every hour. It is the consolation of the Divine Spirit—" Blessed are the dead which die in the LORD: even so saith the Spirit; for they rest from their labours." " Here we have no continuing city." The sick should be bidden to thank GOD that He has not cut them off in a state of sin, but called them out of this world at a time when they may depart fortified with the Sacraments and hope of salvation. In this life we daily offend GOD at least by trespasses or venial sins, and we ought therefore to accept and even desire death in order that we may be cleansed from them. We should resign ourselves to the will of GOD, who worketh all things for our chiefest good. "Who knows, my son," the Priest should say, "whether you will be saved if GOD prolong your life?" Should the sick man say that he would live longer in order to perfect his repentance, he must be told that there is no penitence more acceptable to GOD than the willingness to die, as an expiation of our sins: no more holy action than submission to His will in the act of dying. Against temptations *of attachment to creatures and* anoint the head alone, conditionally and with one form of prayer. It may be given to children, who have the use of reason, though they be not yet admitted to first Communion, and to insane people as in the case of the Holy Eucharist. If the sick become more or less unconscious, the Priest or assistant should whisper holy names and acts, since they often experience pain from loud tones. Sometimes it is better to speak near the head than into the ears. Short ejaculations from time to time thus softly uttered may be of service.

When the agony of death ensues, the Priest should put in force all that the Church allows to assist the dying. He may often make the sign of the Cross over him, and give him benediction, and give him often a crucifix to kiss from time to time; he should suggest to him some thought of contrition, resignation, oblation of his sufferings, trust in the Passion of our LORD, pausing at intervals, so as to afford time for reflection or rest. He should bid him often invoke the Name of JESUS, inwardly if he cannot outwardly, and often say the Kyrie Eleison. At the time of the last agony the Priest should say the Litany for the dying from time to time, or get it said by the standers-by. He should give the signal when the soul is actually departing, in order that all may pray fervently for its happy passage. As soon as the sick has lost consciousness, it is better to assist by prayers than by words; and when he seems about to breathe his last, the Prayer for the sick when there is small hope of recovery, should be said by the Priest on his knees at the foot of the bed. The dying should not be touched at all, still less often, with the view of finding if he be cold, lest it should disturb his mind. So long as he retains his senses he may receive several times Absolution after a brief reconciliation in order to secure his being in a state of grace, if his former confessions have not been satisfactory, or at least to increase grace in him. If he fall into mortal sin, he should be bidden to invoke the Name of JESUS, and if tempted again to the same, he should be stirred to confidence and contrition and absolved. If the dying be without consciousness, and give no sign of contrition or desire of Absolution, it is not well to repeat it often even conditionally. Moreover some little time should elapse between the giving of each Absolution, and the Priest must be guided by the knowledge which he possesses of the state of the sick man's conscience: as for example, if he have been in the habit of yielding to evil thoughts, to violent hatred or impure love: or if the sickness be very sore to impatience, Absolution may be the oftener given him: otherwise it should be ministered every three or four hours, but oftener if he be on the point of departure. It is well also to caution the sick man while he is in full possession of his faculties, that when unable to speak he should give some sign agreed upon when he wishes for Absolution and when the Priest wishes to give it him,—such as shutting the eyes, bowing the head, lifting the hands, and the like. Finally, when the soul seems to have passed away, the Priest should not be in a hurry to give notice of it, and still less to close the eyes and mouth or face, for in so doing he might hasten death. But when it is beyond all doubt that death has ensued, the Priest should bid the standers-by join in commending the soul and say on his knees the Commendatory Prayer, acts of faith, &c. The Priest should bear in mind that the dying should be chiefly moved to make acts of love and penitence, and at the moment of the last breath, of resignation of the soul to GOD—this without intermission and with a firm voice, "Into Thy Hands, O LORD, I commend my spirit: into Thy Hands, pierced with nails for my salvation. LORD JESUS CHRIST, receive my spirit," &c.

It is well that the Priest should be able to distinguish the tokens of approaching departure, in order to be of more service when it takes place. The principal signs are these: (1) when the breathing becomes more difficult and distressing; (2) when the pulse fails or beats with intermission; (3) when the eyes become hollow and glassy, or more open than common, or too brilliant, and see things different to what they are, or when the upper eyelid droops and overhangs the lower. To these may be added the sharpened nose with blanched point and panting nostrils, the contracted temples, the hands trembling, the livid nails, the yellow tinge of the face, the breath foul and cold, the body immoveable, the sweat cold, and clammy forehead, great heat of the body in the region of the heart, pulling or pinching the bed-clothes, coldness of the extremities. The signs of giving up the last breath are intermitting and less loud breathing, the loss of pulsation, choking of the throat, a low sigh or groan, tears spontaneously flowing, distortion of the mouth, eyes and body. Some however die with one or more of the above symptoms and with vigorous pulse,—some suddenly and in convulsions. In some cases moreover the tokens of life are so feeble, that men seem dead before death has actually supervened. The undoubted sign of death is the entire coldness of the whole body, specially about the heart: the cessation of the least breathing from the nostrils, and the ascertaining by putting a mirror to the lips that no breath remains. On the other hand the Priest must remember that people die without giving such clear signs of death, and that he had better lose no time in attending to the dying.

The Priest should suggest always to the sick that they are specially on the Cross with JESUS, and that obedience to the medical men is better than any prayers, meditations, and offices, when they forbid them to be made, or when the sick cannot collect their thoughts. Above all he should think of the sick as specially united to CHRIST crucified, and show them a particular reverence, as being most dear to GOD and objects of envy to the Angels.

The Priest, however, in time of contagious or infectious disease should take care not to inhale the breath of the sick, by coming too near, or the odours caused by the sick man's turning in the bed: he should sit at the head of the bed, not between the fireplace and window: on opening the chamber door he should hold his breath and wait a few seconds before going in; when he has gone in he should not swallow his saliva, but get rid of it. Some think that it is better to go to the sick fasting than after food, since the poison may be taken into the system with the food.

After death the Priest should do his best to console the relations and friends, and exhort them to prepare for their end. After death, at any rate, we can sin no more against GOD. This is matter of thanksgiving in all cases. Where it can be reasonably hoped for, death is the door of eternal bliss and rest in JESUS: we cannot desire to delay the hour of ceaseless union with GOD. We may soon rejoin the departed—to-morrow, if not to-day. GOD is more to us than father, mother, wife or husband, children or friends. The period of exile is over—the dead in CHRIST are gone home to their country.

(90) *How to deal with penitents who are liable to various temptations.*

Temptation is that which allures to sin, being some perceptible good which being tendered to the will inclines or allures it to infraction of the Divine commands, and may be heavy or light according to the power which sets it in motion. It is either due to our own corrupt nature, as when the imagination or intellect is excited to evil thoughts: or to the devil, as when he depicts on the fancy debasing ideas, urges it to the representation of perceptible evil objects and stirs up bodily emotions. It is a sign that the devil is the cause, when all this takes place with a violent onset which overwhelms the ordinary current of the passions by a crowd and heap of vivid conceptions. This is called the spirit of temptation: in matters of faith, the spirit of infidelity, and blasphemy: in perilous moral subjects, the spirit of fornication, &c. Not to give way when thus tempted is a great sign of past or future progress. Sometimes the temptation arises from a combination of ourselves with the devil, as when from the devil and our own concupiscence. GOD allows these temptations to assail us for our good,—(1) that we may increase in virtues, since the habit of virtue is increased by courageous acts: (2) that we may obtain great peace such as is produced by the consciousness of having conquered the devil: (3) that the soul may be more closely united to God and betrothed to Christ. Hence it often happens that when the cloud of temptations seems to separate us from God, we are in reality brought nearer to Him thereby. The means to be used against temptations are humility, prayer, and courage. Humility removes the obstacles which stand in the way of the assistance of Divine Grace: for even fasting, when used to subdue the flesh is often accompanied with spiritual pride, self-complacency, and self-reliance, if not exercised in company with humility. Prayer obtains the aids of grace, and courage enables us to make use of them.

(91) *Remedies against temptation.*

Hence when a temptation assails a penitent the Priest should counsel him, to fly to prayer, acknowledging his weakness and imploring the Divine aid, making acts of charity, contrition or the opposite virtue: in the latter case, however, taking care not to do it, if it cannot be done calmly and without excitement. Temptations should be regarded as signs of God's love, as calling us to love Him and to cast ourselves into the embrace of Jesus Crucified. (2) The penitent should be urged to put his whole trust in God, as knowing that in Him we can do all things. The devil is ever as ready to trample upon the cowardly and feeble-minded as he is to flee from the bold and courageous. (3) All contention or parleying with the enemy must be avoided : like our LORD we must answer him only with Scripture or with silence. Sometimes the tempted is beset by devils so that his only chance is, to sit still as a man surrounded by fierce dogs, knowing that the least motion on his part may draw their fury upon him, and so to preserve calmness and contempt for the Evil One. (4) The penitent should reveal his temptations to the Priest, because the devil dislikes nothing so much as this: and the tempted may so acquire more humility and receive also counsel how to meet the assaults or crafts of the enemy. (5) The penitent should constantly exercise himself in those virtues which are opposed to the temptation. (6) In the case of temptations to impurity, however, the only resource is to repress perturbation of body or mind, and fly to our Blessed LORD and His sacred Wounds: and protest a resolution to die rather than offend Him by any consent to the temptation: beseeching GOD to hear the prayers of the Immaculate Virgin Mother, and of the Guardian Angel. (7) In the case of temptations to vengeance, the mind should be diverted from dwelling upon the wrong inflicted and directed to the example of CHRIST's patience under injuries: and to the remembrance of his own frailty, and to pray for the offending person. (8) When the temptation relates to predestination, it should be put aside with the thought that means are man's, ends are GOD's: that his business is to love and serve Him, and that as long as he tries to do this he may hope in Him that He will not cast him away, and that none ever trusted in Him and were confounded. (9) If the temptation be prolonged, as to what he may be likely to do in a certain case, e.g., sin rather than bear a great misfortune, he should turn his thoughts to some other subject, and resolve to trust GOD at all hazards,—not making rash promises, but in humility acknowledging that without His help he must fall. (10) If the devil tempt by means of holy things, such as to thoughts of impurity when looking on crucifixes, &c., the person tempted must not give way, but show no signs of fear and persevere. The same is true of temptations arising from the same cause to heretical or blasphemous thoughts. In such cases the more he can show his scorn and contempt for the devil for thus trying to distress him the better.

(92) *How to deal with persons of higher degrees of perfection and devotion.*

The Priest should pray in this case for special illumination: endeavour to become closely acquainted with the spiritual constitution and mind of such persons, so as to adapt his counsels and instructions to their capacities. He should urge them to preserve a constant desire for perfection in the highest degree, that so they may by setting before themselves the highest standard, attain to some height. They should be led up by slow degrees, climbing step by step, beginning with the lowest, first learning to labour with a right intention and imitate the actions of JESUS CHRIST: first to suffer light things before they aim at weighty: first to endure with equanimity before they will to rejoice at adversities. They must not aim higher than GOD calls them, Who assigns to each his own measure of perfection, and degree of sanctity: always following the Divine lead, lest they upset the work of GOD by their own devices. For instance, if GOD direct the soul to fear, it should not be diverted from it, and though the yearning for greater perfection should be roused, yet it must be done in a suitable manner, so that those virtues be cultivated to which GOD moves the soul: for He sometimes leaves the exterior life for man's management, while He alone instructs what should be the interior course. Men should be taught that the perfection of every one consists in performing their ordinary works well; in rising well, praying well, reading well; in attending Divine Service, teaching, and labouring to the best of their ability: eating, drinking, taking recreation, and conversing in a becoming manner: examining their consciences thoroughly at night, laying them down to sleep with propriety—in short performing all their duties rightly. He who does all these things well is perfect; and he does them well when he does them as, when, where, and how GOD wills them to be done. Such persons ought to be tested as to what spirit they are of,—divine or mundane, fearful or loving, and what is the predominating affection that ought first to be mortified. Different people require different treatment; the phlegmatic,[1] the melancholy, the choleric, and the

[1] The phlegmatic are mild, easily moved, faithful, peaceful, malleable, but they are also feeble-minded, changeable, slothful, lukewarm: the melancholy are circumspect, moderate, thoughtful, consistent, but they are also singular, suspicious, and self-opinionated. The choleric are brave, bold, spirited, and nobleminded, but they are also rash, impatient, passionate, quarrelsome, proud, harsh, and inhuman. The sanguine are gentle, affable, spirited, obsequious, liberal, and tractable, but

sanguine must not be dealt with in the same manner: the weak and the strong require each special handling. Their testing, however, should be carried on secretly, and not obviously, lest they on perceiving that they are being tested adapt themselves accordingly. It should for this reason not be farfetched but applied on the spur of the moment. Common and easy duties should be enjoined so as to repress any desire for extraordinary, and check pride. When it is evident that they are prone to act on their own judgment and of their own head, they should be gently dissuaded from doing so. GOD has willed that they should learn humble obedience in order to attain perfection. Discretion teaches that while firm resolutions are made, the mind should not be obstinately bent upon doing or not doing anything without having regard to the variation of causes and circumstances. It is safer to trust the judgment of another person who is discreet than oneself: obedience is better than sacrifice, because by it the intellect, will and soul itself, are immolated to GOD. Obedience is the best test. They should be advised to search out their own motives and the supernatural springs of virtuous actions: often examine their doings as to the original motives of them: learn to act from supernatural rather than mere natural impulses,—in action to propose some virtuous motive, and act upon it. Natural motives should be corrected and diverted into the will and pleasure of GOD; and when occa-

---

they are also hot, contentious, voluptuous, and attached to creatures. These different complexions need to have their respective defects carefully corrected, since they are greater or less in one or other according to the predominance of this or that characteristic.

sion calls for the exercise of some virtue to which they are naturally inclined, they should not give themselves unreservedly up to its influence, but keep nature in check, and recall themselves to the pattern of CHRIST Who laboured to please the FATHER. Nevertheless, the virtues to which men are naturally prone may be cultivated in them, as being the means which GOD has bestowed upon them, and to which His grace accommodates itself for the easier obtaining the end, and men should press on more steadily thereunto,—only taking care not to let the satisfaction of having attained in some degree hinder them from further progress.

(93) *How to deal with the secret temptations of such persons.*

The Priest should watch against the wiles of the devil who is always lying in ambush as well against the more advanced as against beginners. When GOD takes away the pleasure we have in religion in order to lead us on to stronger food the devil often tries to distress and harass the penitent with the fear that it is no use to try to make further advance. The Priest should then instruct him in what true progress consists, that it and the contest appertains to GOD, Who knows when to give the victory: that the business of perfection is not accomplished in a day, but with slowness, as plants grow and fruits ripen. He must vigorously make use of the grace bestowed upon him, and wait patiently for the help of GOD. Should the devil insinuate a belief that his want of devotion proceeds from want of penitence and instigate him to greater mortifications, of extraordinary kind, he should always consult his confessor, for the devil seeks often to persuade people first to take on them austerities, in the hope that if they fail thereby to overcome their sins, he may ultimately induce them to relax altogether. The Priest must deal energetically with such results,—bidding the penitent not draw back from the plough nor look back, lest he emperil his final perseverance and eternal salvation. GOD has called some to the state of perfection without which they cannot be saved. Grace depends on His will, not on ours. In returning to the world and giving up a strict religious life the penitent may not have the grace which he hopes to retain. To miss of conformity to the will of GOD is to be lost.

The devil tries to persuade people to rest upon their oars and to be content with little progress, with the view to draw them back into lukewarmness, love of ease and comforts and indolence. The intellect first loses the high esteem of perfection and union with GOD, the light which directed it in all its operations, and the low esteem of mundane honours and pleasures. The will led astray thereby is captivated by a fresh love of earthly things, and embraces as great what it had before cast aside as trivial, dreads weighty duties and regards as weighty what it before embraced as light, through losing the vigour of charity. It does not at first leave off all means of perfection, but prays, yet without attention and reverence: it frequents the Holy Mysteries but without preparation: reads books, but without a right intention. At length it begins to leave all these habits off, such at least as can be omitted without incurring any unpleasant results. The devil is at first content with these successes, and then induces neglect of all spiritual exercises; finally assails with some powerful temptation and causes a lapse into some mortal sin, makes the lapsed person disgusted with himself and by kindling anger in his breast precipitates him from sin to sin: severs him either from faith or from the religious life. It is in this way that the lukewarm fall away, and it is most difficult to heal them and restore them to fervour, because the Gospel truths, in the full light of which they have sinned, no longer rouse them, and the last things do not alarm them. Hence the Priest should strive either to anticipate the evil, or apply a healing touch to the disease before it has become inveterate. The beginning of lukewarmness is not so easily detected as its progress. When prayer, mortification, resistance to temptations, readiness to receive the Sacraments, love of solitude, and desire of progress pass away, it will be evident whether men advance or recede in virtue.

The remedy which the Priest should propose is the resumption of all the devotional exercises which had been neglected and the good performance of them, and so the penitent will easily amend. He should recall the penitent to the thought of lost grace, and of its value, of the end for which GOD has granted us time, the loss and danger incurred by lukewarmness. If the penitent be one who has made formerly great progress, he should be counselled to perform his exercises in retreat.

But if the case be of a more seriously retrograde kind, the Priest must not despair, but choose a middle path between stirring up fear and hope. He must receive the person with kindness, and show his sympathy by gentle words and pleasant countenance. Severity in this instance only makes the poison more fatal. Bees are when swarming recalled to the hive more by making a subdued noise than by a loud clatter, and more flies are caught by a drop of honey than by a cask of vinegar. The Priest should suggest reasons for putting confidence in GOD, and show how this change as a work worthy of the Majesty of GOD will redound to His greater glory, as a manifestation of His omnipotence and mercy. To distrust GOD is worse than to forsake Him.

If the Priest does not succeed in this wáy, he must betake himself to motives of fear,—the dangers and losses of lukewarmness,—danger of dying in such a state,—indignation of GOD, and violence of the devil,—with death punishment and not conversion begins. The devil will tempt by encouraging the penitent to dwell upon the cases of others who live recklessly without despairing of salvation, and are good sort of people, who enjoy themselves in riches and comforts. Thus custom usurps the place of law, and one's own ill savour is not perceptible where the morals of all are corrupt, and people easily are persuaded that they live well enough if they accommodate their lives to those of the major part of the community, and specially of the higher order. The Priest must try to correct this pernicious error, and not suffer the blind to follow the blind, or one soul to take the multitude for its guide and so enter the broad way that leadeth to destruction. He must remind him that the day of doom will try each separately, and then of what avail will be numbers?

The penitent should be told to read and meditate with the desire of amendment, pray earnestly for the same, and learn to conquer his inclinations in little things at first before proceeding to greater things, especially in resuming the exercises which have been laid aside, for as by neglect of these he became lukewarm, so by diligent use of these he may return to warmth.

(94) *Of several temptations to turn back.*

The devil is wont to spread a net of pride and presumption for those more advanced: for when they experience a union of themselves with GOD in extraordinary love to Him and contempt of the world in comparison with that happy condition, he urges them to act upon sudden impulses of zeal without knowledge and to disregard little deflections from duty. Earnest prayer, self-examination, and consideration of their own frailty will be of much service to such persons, for it is not every such motive nor sudden impetuosity which is inspired by grace and the HOLY SPIRIT. Nature often prevents grace, follows it and turns it aside. If in such a case the result is some deadly sin, the Priest should receive the person kindly, and not show any signs of wonder or disgust, for fear of causing him dejection. For what is there wonderful in the fall of a creature who through in-born corruption is prone at every moment to fall? The grace of baptism and other Sacraments does not so build up the ruins of man's fallen nature, as that no place should be found for sin to enter. Far more wonderful is it that after a fall man should, though overwhelmed with shame, become his self-accuser. No one wonders that the blind fall into the ditch; no one is indignant at their fall; but every one strives to lend a hand to pull them out. Even when the fallen are angry with themselves, it is not always the result of grace; it may be a mere natural motion of pride because they think themselves humiliated by such a misfortune. Hence the Priest must labour to purge away all dross, and while permitting them to indulge in proper grief, remove all bitter feelings which take their rise in pride, and excite them to hope, charity and humility.

Hope may be inspired by suggesting that the fall may be the commencement of greater holiness, that as GOD knew how to elicit the greatest good from the fall of Adam, so He knows how to do the same in the case of all falls. By justifying the sinner GOD augments His own glory, since justification is a more excellent work than creation; for it raises man to sonship with GOD, and the sin to be removed is the obstacle to that operation. GOD turns the fall of the penitent sinner into his elevation to a higher eminence than before, and takes occasion thereby to embrace the true penitent with greater kindness than that with which He received him when innocent, turning ruin into splendour, loss into gain. Thus GOD's mercy is said to cast all our sins into the depths of the sea: and the example of David may inspire the sinner with confidence, who prays to GOD to be "merciful to his sin because it is great." Thus it is GOD's goodness which heals the sick, raises the fallen, and relieves the destitute. It is the Good Shepherd, Who rejoices more over the lost sheep when found, than over those which were safe all along.

(95) *Of secret temptations to turn back.*

There is no special favour bestowed by GOD on the Saints who lived innocently, which He has not equally conferred on true penitents. Such should be urged to great charity, as being called upon to make up for the past by trying to discover how they may serve GOD with renewed ardour. The lapsed should be like the soldier, who after having played the runaway returns to wipe off the stain of cowardice by fighting bravely. So GOD allows the fallen to extract medicine from the poison. Also they should be excited to humility, since pride is the cause of their losing charity. Hence they should humble themselves by recognising their own unworthiness, impotence, nothingness; coming to GOD like the prodigal son, or as the publican; accounting themselves unworthy to utter the Name of GOD, and worthy of everlasting torments. The ordinary pleasures of the world should be abstained from by them as being unworthy of the smallest comforts in this life. "Should I who have been GOD's enemy indulge myself in such things?" Carefully should they guard against all occasion of falling. The burnt child dreads the fire. Yet inordinate sadness must be avoided.

(96) *How to deal with persons who have illuminations, visions, &c.*

The first thing to be done is to distinguish between what come from Satan and what from the HOLY GHOST; for there is danger of confounding or mistaking them.

The devil tries to induce men to think they possess real virtues, when they are only shadows: and the heart of man, which is deceitful above all things, affords him much scope for delusion, so that he is led to call evil good and good evil, and the passions thwart the judgment. Moreover there is such a similarity between virtues and vices, such as between zeal and anger, liberality and profuseness, humility and feeble-mindedness and hypocrisy, confidence and presumption, firmness and obstinacy, love of GOD and love of self. The acuteness of man's intellect cannot of itself always penetrate the depths of the thoughts and affections in his heart. Hence he needs to watch lest either a manifestly carnal impulse carry him away, or lest a carnal impulse should disguise itself as a spiritual, and make his faults seem to be virtues. Hence he must try the spirits and learn whether they be of GOD, else he will be in danger of thinking the false spirit to be true and follow it, while he thinks the true spirit false and drives it away.

(97) *How to distinguish the motions, visions, suggestions, and illuminations of the Good Spirit from those of the Evil.*

The Good Spirit only inspires what is in accordance with the Sacred Scriptures, the Tradition of the Church, the examples of the Saints, and the life of JESUS CHRIST, not what is frivolous, useless, &c. It moves to self-abnegation, mortification, patience in adversity, imitation of CHRIST, giving up of the will, subjection of one's own judgment, perfect obedience, humility and contempt of the world, escape from honours, &c.: to labour with the due end, that is with a view to God's glory: in short, to labour with a right intention. It is discreet, and proceeds with due order, so that when It brings the soul into the wine-chamber of holy affections, It orders all with charity. Hence It only moves ordinarily to common things suited to the powers of the individual, leading them by straight and level roads. For God is the author of this ordinary road to heaven; sometimes however He gives extraordinary inspirations, but only in such as are well grounded in humility and free from the onslaughts of vain-glory, lest man should be hurried on to destruction. In extraordinary inspirations the end should be carefully attended to. It is a sign of the Good Spirit if the superior part of the soul only, such as the understanding and will, be the spring or seat of its operations, though it may gush forth to the inferior part, such as the fancy or sensitive appetite. For God alone can act directly upon the superior part, but the devil can only excite the inferior, and by means of this act indirectly upon the superior, producing the effects such as tears, sensible devotion, &c., which depend upon the power of the body; so that as God often makes use of man's constitution to excite true devotion, the devil does the like to excite false. Hence it appears that there are two kinds of consolations and inward joys; the one commencing in the superior part of the soul and descending to the inferior, the other commencing in the inferior, which may arise from the evil spirit, since he often sports more easily with melancholic and too impulsive persons than he does with manly, calm and affable persons.

Those who have experience are able to distinguish between Divine and other inspirations, though unable to explain how, even as we distinguish friends by certain tokens or the taste of honey.

The sign of the HOLY GHOST is the sense and taste of humility in the recesses of the soul, as when a person does not desire extraordinary things, does not incline to exercises which cause the admiration of others, places holiness in doing common things well, counts himself unworthy of GOD's gifts, and does not on account of them exalt himself and prefer himself to others; when he is glad at being despised if his Priest decides that his illuminations are illusions; when he hides his gifts, when he flies to humility if some special visitation enlighten him, and only desires them in order to please GOD thereby, when he is penetrated with a sense of his nothingness, and the like.

It is a sign of the Evil spirit when the temptation tends to falsehood and vices, as when the devil suggests a manifest falsehood, but veils it under various arguments, and veneers it so as to appear true throughout: sometimes suggests truth but deduces a deceitful inference therefrom. Thus the devil allows Acatholics to believe the Scriptures to be true, but only on condition that they be interpreted by every one according to his own way: sometimes he suggests truths in order to send man to sleep in security, as though conscious of being under the Good Spirit's inspirations, and then superadds error and enticement to sin. If the Evil spirit be perceived to urge to some good act, it is not to be omitted on that account nor to be carried out because he inspires it, but because either faith or right reason or morality counsel it. Thus the devil may advise you to give alms: you should give alms with a right motive, and your reward will be unaltered. If some falsehood or evil be interspersed with some good suggestion, it is a sign that the devil is sowing tares with the wheat; and this is no reason for thinking all one's inspirations to be from him, since he often does this to throw suspicion on holy desires and intentions that they may be rejected. In this case GOD must be intreated not to allow us to be deceived, and we must without mental perturbation and with a right intention towards GOD do that which right reason and grace dictate. If a suggestion tend to novelties and singularities, and such as beget the world's admiration and fame of sanctity, it is from the Evil spirit. The like may be said when it excites pride, vain-glory, presumption, despair, or any other less well-ordered affection, or concealment from the confessor.

If the Evil spirit approach pleasantly but leave behind sorrow, desolation, perturbation and darkness, it is a sign of the Evil spirit: for as it is a sign of the Good Spirit to console and tranquillize the mind, so it is a sign of the Evil spirit to leave these disorders behind.

Hence it follows that they are miserably deceived who think they have special Divine illuminations and impulses, when they wish for extraordinary things, and on that account undervalue others and exaggerate their own importance: talk lightly of their own experience, as if for the benefit of others: if they be dejected when contemned; if they yield to the temptations of pride and boast of the grace of devotion: indulge self-complacency and persuade themselves of their immeasurable superiority over others in their possession or use of the same: especially if such feelings last any appreciable amount of time.

The marks of the Divine inspiration are,—sudden and supernatural change of mind from lukewarmness to heat, darkness to light, cowardice to boldness, knowledge of GOD, or of some truth with fresh light, or unwonted hatred of some vanity, generating calmly and sweetly special motion towards GOD or virtue. So also if the mind suddenly expand with a desire of perfection, love of purity, mortification, imitation of CHRIST and perpetual union with GOD :—if the soul rest upon GOD, divine things and virtues, be sweetly raised to praises and embraces of GOD :—if there be an unwonted deeper sense of humility :—if contempt or trouble for GOD's sake be willingly received :—if it despise all worldly things which cannot fill the heart whenever it is expanded.

(98) *How to act in times of spiritual consolations.*

At such times man must encourage feelings of humility, ascribing all to GOD: with the intention of using them not for his own enjoyment, but for closer union with GOD, to His praise and glory, accounting himself unworthy of every gift of GOD and beseeching Him to aid him in making a right use thereof. He should therefore think how miserable he is wont to feel when GOD's consolations are absent, and prepare himself for desolations: for the visits and consolations of GOD are never constant nor alike to all: but GOD gives them only to prevent our being cast down, and withholds them lest we should abuse them and turn them into mischief or injury to health: that we may recognize them as His gifts alone, long for them, use them discreetly, and not fall into the snare of pride: not neglect the exercise of our calling: exercise our wonted virtues and labour as it were on our own account and expense. Hence the novices in the spiritual life are as it were in winter when the sun is usually hid: the advancing are in spring, when there is more variety: the perfect are in summer, when there is more constant heat and sun: but there are at times storms and clouds and tempests, which do not last: for consolations are to be waited for, not forced from GOD.

Should the soul be as it were inebriated so as scarcely to contain itself, it should repress its ardour, nor wish to penetrate the divine counsels, nor anticipate nor add to the divine work by its own powers and as it were get beyond the aid of divine grace.

It must be observed that true devotion consists in prompt, bold, and constant will to do whatever we know pleases GOD, and in avoiding whatever we know displeases Him: not in sensible sweetness of heart, which sends forth tears and sighs, and engenders a sort of spiritual taste, all which are not the essence of devotion, but often dangerous, and are false consolations originating with the devil or with nature. Hence many souls enjoy these affections but have no true devotion, though touched by discourses of the Passion, while they refuse to make restitutions, to give up any advantage or to bear any disadvantage for CHRIST's sake.

(99) *How to deal with sensible devotion.*

We may judge that this comes from GOD, if its effects are discernible in humility, patience, gentleness, mercy, mortification, &c., and we may humbly use it for its due end: but we must correct or reject it if it proceed from the devil, as when it is absorbed in self, or has for its end the pleasing of men: is in public lively, in private stale: if praises delight, and contempt deject: if it be anxiously and restlessly sought for: if when taken away or deferred perturbations and murmurs arise: if arrogance, presumption, sharpness towards others manifest itself. Nay, true sensible devotion is exposed to the crafts of the devil, who labours to turn the love of spiritual things into sensual, and impel to some intemperance or spiritual gluttony, to inordinate complacency, and when it finds a soft nature to crocodile tears. Hence women are more prone to illusions, so that they need special warning to act from supernatural motives.

(100) *How to deal with desolations.*

GOD sends consolations to abstract the mind from earthly delights, that they may become insipid, and that it may be excited to aspire to difficult virtues: that just as children are fed with milk till they are able to bear strong meat, He takes these consolations away by degrees and withdraws Himself in a certain manner, that they may learn to abandon themselves and serve Him for Himself. Often He does not give or withdraws consolations from the more advanced, either because they are not expedient for them, as being likely to do them harm, or because they have abused them for vain-glory, pride, self-esteem, spiritual indulgence, idleness in self-recollection, imperfection in ordinary exercises: or because they are unmortified, undetached from creatures, still given up to their own comforts, &c. GOD however does not allow these desolations ordinarily to be unceasing, but as He subjects the world to different changes of seasons and climates, so He governs His elect, now sending prosperity, now adversity, now consolations, now desolations. Hence man must adapt himself to the divine dispensations, as to those of a Father for the good of His children and for His own glory, so as not to be elevated by prosperity nor dejected by adversity. Sometimes temptations and drynesses arise in the midst of desolations, and such various and even foul thoughts, that men seem to themselves as if they only went to prayer in order to be tormented with all kinds of temptations, and as if they could not even dwell on the Passion, or if they could, yet without being moved thereby. Hence comes sometimes the feeling that GOD has forgotten them, and that it is of no use to pray.

(101) *Rules to be observed in desolations.*

(1) Never to despair, always resign thyself to the will of GOD, knowing that as cold and heat are needful for plants, so desolation is as necessary as consolation to purge out self-love, and lead thee to solid virtue.

(2) During dryness examine if it be owing to any

fault of thine. If not, thank GOD, and humble thyself before Him, acknowledging that thou art unworthy of His gifts, and confess that He deals with thee rightly in thus punishing thee for past sins, and desire not to have thy trouble removed. If thou feelest overcome, beseech GOD to take this cup from thee with full resignation to His will. But if the dryness be thine own fault, have a sincere grief for thy fault, ask pardon and receive the desolation as thy just punishment, in the full trust that GOD will be gracious to thee in a short time.

(3) Be persuaded that thus to suffer for the love of GOD is the nearest way to perfection, since thereby the soul is abstracted from all creatures.

(4) Be careful at such times to omit no customary devotion, but rather increase thy ordinary exercises, since they are the more acceptable to GOD and disappointing to the devil. Not to be able to go on without consolations is a sure sign of self-love. If even unable to pray, nevertheless be content that GOD allows thee to remain in His family, and wills to purify thee by such temporary chastisement. Represent to thyself JESUS abandoned on the Cross. The best prayer is patience and resignation.

(5) Should the desolation be due to physical causes, it is best to seek the aid of bodily exercise, and to exercise the will in different acts of virtue, as by praising, adoring, thanking, &c.

(6) The spiritual director should be freely consulted and followed.

(102) *How to deal with Communicants.*

Communicants should not be dissuaded from frequent or daily Communion, but only exhorted to more diligent preparation and thanksgiving. The Priest should inquire of persons anxious for more frequent Communion (1) how they prepare and are able to prepare and give thanks: (2) with what view they wish to increase their Communions, since the object should not be sensible devotion, or self-satisfaction, or the example of others, but progress in virtue, especially in charity: (3) how much spiritual progress they have made, whether they indulge old bad customs, and passions, or mortify them? Some have said that weekly Communion is for such as are free from mortal sin, daily for such as are not inclined to venial. And should a person commit a venial sin and have no opportunity of going to confession, he should not deprive himself of Communion, but strive to attain to such feelings of contrition and love as suffice for a good preparation. Nay, sometimes fervent acts of repentance, humility, confidence in God, and the like, evoke better dispositions for Communion than even confession. S. Thomas Aquinas says that venial sins, so far as increase of grace is concerned, do not hinder the effect of the Sacrament, provided they are not committed during reception, since Communion produces an act of love which effaces venial sins. If love to God increase *by means* of Communion without diminishing veneration thereunto, daily reception should not be disused. Much depends in giving permission to communicate whether the penitent desire it during a great festival, or be more than usually tempted and needs unusual strength. For though it is clearly a mistake to grant Communion to persons who are often falling into mortal sin without taking pains to amend, or who go to the Holy Table with attachment to venial sins without any effort to give them up, yet it is sometimes useful to allow persons to communicate who are in danger of mortal sin but powerless to resist it. But persons who go on committing venial sins deliberately without any apparent desire to amend, should be precluded from communicating oftener than once a week, in order that they may entertain greater horror of their faults and more veneration for the Blessed Sacrament. No doubt it is well to abstain from Communion out of veneration on a certain day. Yet it is best to communicate daily out of love than to abstain out of veneration.

Two sorts of persons need frequent Communion, the perfect and imperfect,—the one to continue perfect, the other to become so: the strong not to degenerate into feeble, the feeble to become strong: the sick to become healthy, the healthy not to fall sick. Those who are busy should communicate because they need it: those who are not busy because they are at liberty to receive it. The more feeble one is the more he needs the food of the strong. Frequent Communion should be restrained in the case of such as do not seem to advance by its means, in not correcting deliberate venial sins, such as of the gratification of the senses in eating and drinking, looking, listening, dressing, &c., were it only to make them more careful to amend. And though they ought to receive with great devotion, yet this is not required to be of the highest possible kind or sensibly manifested. It is enough that the penitent exhibit a firm and unchanging purpose to do the will of GOD. Else to abstain from Communion through lack of great fervour, would be like a man who though cold refused to warm himself at a fire through fear of feeling the heat. Hence many weak-minded persons through an overweening sense of their unworthiness by keeping from frequent Communion injure their spiritual progress. It is unnecessary that the soul be always conscious of increased fervour, for the Sacrament often effects this in us imperceptibly. Sometimes it is good when drawn very much to Communion to mortify oneself by abstaining, especially if disquietude, which is a mark of pride, result therefrom, and sometimes when lukewarmness or dryness is felt to communicate the oftener in order to obtain fresh strength. JESUS CHRIST would be more loved than He is if souls, who might be esteemed by some wanting in veneration and rash, entertaining horror of even slight faults, did seek frequent and even daily communion with the view of amendment and progress in Divine Love. The Priest should advise all who he knows have a real desire of Communion and strive to advance in holiness, to communicate often. They should be exhorted to acts of thanksgiving lasting for an hour if possible: remembering that in Communion JESUS comes and sets up His throne as King in the heart to grant all our requests. Spiritual Communion should be also recommended, as exhibiting to the SAVIOUR a proof of our love to Him, specially when debarred from actual.

(103) *Dispensations.*

These are acts of jurisdiction, whereby obligations to obey the laws of the Church are relaxed in special cases.

In regard to Festivals:

The Bishop has primarily right to dispense from the obligation to observe Festivals: secondarily Parish Priests, even when the Bishop is at hand, particularly so far as concerns servile work. Superiors of religious orders can dispense in the case of those who are under their obedience.

In regard to Ecclesiastical Fasts:

Primarily the Bishop, secondarily Parish Priests may dispense, as well as Superiors of religious orders in regard to those who are under them. The reasons for dispensation are chiefly inability, infirmity, and labour. A morally certain reason is required for a general dispensation from fasting. Hence for a general dispensation it is not enough to plead scarcity of fish: yet it would be enough to urge a danger of the fish being poisoned. Fasting may be commuted into prayer or alms. If the dispensation be granted on account of sickness at the beginning of Lent, should the sickness cease during Lent, the dispensation ceases also, unless there be any danger of the recurrence of the sickness through fasting.

In regard to Marriage:

The Bishop may dispense with the obstacles to marrying in Advent and Lent.

No dispensation can be granted in order to validate a marriage void by the law of nature, as when contracted in error, after consummation, where the parties are under age, where impotence exists, or where the first degree of consanguinity in the direct line has been infringed.

But after a marriage which does not come under the above heads, has been invalidly contracted, the Bishop may dispense when the following points concur: (1) if the marriage have been publicly performed; (2) if the impediment be secret so that it cannot be proved by the testimony of more than one witness; (3) if the marriage have been contracted in good faith and in ignorance of the impediment; (4) if scandal would result from separation. This applies to such cases in which a man may have cohabited with a mother and then married her daughter, or with a daughter and then married her sister. And this because one or the other may have married in ignorance of such facts, and the wickedness of one ought not to cause suffering to the innocent. But if both were aware of the impediment existing, no dispensation can be granted.

It must be borne in mind that all dispensations of this sort must be confined to the court of conscience, and cannot hold good in the courts of law of England, when not recognised by them.

(104) *Of Penances.*

On the part of the penitent three things are required —*contrition, confession,* and *satisfaction:*[1] and one on the part of the Priest, Absolution. Of those on the

---

[1] So in the Commination Service: *Bewailing and lamenting, confessing and acknowledging,* seeking to bring forth *worthy fruits of Penance.*

part of the penitent contrition is indispensable; for Confession and Satisfaction, the desire and intention suffices in case of necessity.

Contrition is an inward sorrow, sincere regret for sins committed, a detestation of them, and a resolution never to commit them anew.

It is natural and supernatural; proceeding from reason and faith respectively.

Supernatural is perfect and imperfect.

Perfect when the love of GOD makes us detest and loathe sin as an injury and outrage to His Majesty and Benevolence, and renders all acts of contrition, prayers, alms, and good works also perfect; imperfect when love is wanting.

Perfect contrition, in which is included a willingness to confess, blots out sin even before Absolution.

It should be inward, universal, supernatural, sovereign, loving, and perpetual.

Confession should not be delayed, lest there be difficulty of feeling perfect contrition: should consist of an avowal of all sins weighing on the conscience, of the circumstances which exaggerate their sinfulness, of the frequency of occurrence, and of whatever changes their character for the worse.

Satisfaction consists chiefly in prayer, alms and fasting, and endurance of sufferings sent from GOD. It should be imposed (1) according to the kind of sin as far as prudence allows, having regard to the ability and other circumstances of the penitent; (2) in order to punish the sinner, and preserve him from relapse, correct his bad propensities, and introduce him to a new course of life; (3) with the view of making his repentance manifest to the neighbours or congregation which he has scandalised, and inspiring penitence in such as have imitated his bad example. Thus the impure should be bidden fast, wear sackcloth, and endure suchlike mortifications: the covetous almsgiving and restitutions: the ignorant hearing sermons and catechising, &c. : but these require alteration and adaptation, as when the covetous is poor, the impure engaged in hard labour, &c.

The Priest may commute such penances on necessary occasions, even those which have been enjoined by another Confessor, according as they were penal or medicinal.

(105) *Example of Satisfactions ordained by Ancient Penitential Canons in the most common cases.*

This is given not to be followed strictly, but in spirit only.

For falling away from the Catholic Faith, ten years.

For exercising magic, divination, &c., seven years.

For consulting magicians, diviners, &c., five years.

For knowingly perjuring oneself, causing another to do so, forty days on bread and water and seven following years.

For blasphemy, seven Fridays on bread and water, the seven following Sundays to stand at the door of the church in penitential dress, and to feed two or three poor according to means, each Sunday.

For having done laborious work on Sundays or Great Festivals, to fast three days on bread and water.

For having danced in public before a church or on a Festival, three years of penance.

For having talked in church during the Divine Offices, six days on bread and water.

For having broken one of the fasts, twenty days.

For having wilfully caused abortion, three years of penance.

For infanticide to conceal sin, ten years.

For negligently allowing a child to die unbaptized, three years, one of which was to be on bread and water.

For wilful homicide, never to enter beyond the porch of the church, and only to communicate when death is at hand.

For killing a person in passion, three years of penance.

For advising another to commit homicide, forty days on bread and water, and seven years of penance.

For a robbery which deserves the greatest punishment inflicted by the law, five years of penance.

For a petty larceny, one year.

For taking usury, three years.

For keeping any valuables which one has found, the same as for larceny.

For fornication, three years of penance.

For having sinned with a married woman, seven years of penance, and the woman five.

For a maiden who has sinned with a married man, ten years of penance, and the man five.

For other sins against purity of a graver kind heavier penances.

For having borne false witness in a court of justice, or falsely charging another person with some crime on any occasion, seven years.

For having sold by false weight or measure, twenty days on bread and water.

For having coveted to obtain unjustly another's goods, three years.

For giving way to the desire of committing impurity, two years.

During the time assigned for penance acts of mortification were assigned on certain days, such as fasting and abstinence, fasting on bread and water twice or thrice a week, or abstinence without fasting. Such as could not endure fasting or abstinence were ordered to make up for it by alms, prayers, and other works of charity and piety.

(106) *Directions as to the assignment of Penances.*

Penances should be imposed not only in regard of the disease but also in regard to the patient. Hence the Priest must be careful both as to the quantity and quality of the penance which he prescribes, proportioning them so as not to increase one ill when he diminishes another. In some cases he must be content to effect by many doses the cure which the patient will not suffer him to perform by one. Beginners in the spiritual life must not be frightened away by too severe remedies, but drawn on gently till they of themselves ask for increase of penance.

Care should be taken not to impose too heavy or unsuitable penances lest they should be omitted. It is often best to give simple counsel or conditional penance. The Priest should guard against imposing such things as may lead to a discovery of the subject of confessions. Hence there is less risk in enjoining the recitation of so many " Our FATHER's," or Psalms, than the attendance at the Holy Sacrifice, or reading or meditation. It is better to select a penance for two or three days in a week than a whole week, and for the sake of easy recollection to appoint the same number of times, such as five times such a prayer, five psalms, five texts, &c. Penances should be such as neither provoke contempt by their easiness, nor cause danger of omission by their difficulty. They should be both satisfactory for the past and preservative for the future.

In delicate people the Priest should choose only such corporal austerities as are likely to suggest good thoughts and holy affections, and those acts which have a special power in obtaining the aid of GOD, such as spiritual reading and meditation, attendance at the Holy Sacrifice, devotions to the Passion of JESUS CHRIST.

To go often to Confession and the Holy Eucharist is one of the best penances which can be enjoined in order to obtain grace. But of course only in their case who use them with proper dispositions. This is especially the case in regard to relapsing sinners, who need great encouragement to come often. They should come, however, though not duly disposed, in the hope of becoming so, if it be merely to announce that the fever has broken out anew. The Priest should take special heed not to give such any rebuff by manner, tone or behaviour. Penance should be imposed afresh, if the penitent reveals something he had forgotten before Absolution. And penance should be always given before absolution since the mode of acceptance thereof by the penitent often is a key to the state of his contrition.

Penances may be diminished (1) if the penitent show deep contrition or have performed works of satisfaction:

(2) if the penitent be sick: (3) if the penitent be a person of little piety and be not likely to perform a severe penance. It is well to show the penitent what penance he has deserved. Sometimes it is necessary to consult the penitent as to his ability to fulfil such a penance, if the proper penance were disproportioned to the capacity of the penitent, lest a fresh sin be incurred by his omissions. (4) In regard to the quality of penances, perpetual or very difficult penances should be avoided: and vows, even not to relapse, should be discouraged, except for a short period, and in the case of a self-imposed vow when a short trial has been made of the probability of perseverance. Conditional penance may be imposed,—such as almsgiving and rendering help. Public penances must not be assigned for secret faults, except when they have been the cause of notorious injury to one's neighbour, and even in this case it is not always possible to prevail on the penitent to consent, and other penances must be substituted.

Penances must not only be medicinal and preservative, but also punitive. These are comprised under the heads of prayer, fasting, and alms. *Prayer* includes all religious and sacramental acts; *fasting* all acts of mortification; *almsgiving* all charitable actions.

Prayers are imposed for blasphemy, mortification for sensuality, &c.; alms for avarice, &c. Yet these if unsuitable to the case, may be injurious. The simplest and best for general uses are to make every night an act of contrition: renew resolutions every morning: to say some special prayer in church daily, such as for perseverance; three " Our FATHER's;" to say on going to bed, "I deserve to be now in hell," or, "One day perhaps I shall die on this bed:" for people who can read to take every day some portion of a religious book. But penances must not be multiplied lest the penitent be bothered and frightened. Light penances ought not to be assigned for heavy sins, such as one Our FATHER for impurity, or a Miserere for slander. They should not be too heavy in regard to the sinner, nor too easy in regard to the sin; and thus the same medicines cannot be administered to all alike. The Priest must avoid extravagance or imprudence in assigning penances,—such as to domestics churchgoing, and such things as interfere with their household duties: to women with child severe fasting: to young females to go to a remote and unfrequented church: to married women such austerities as may displease or rouse suspicions in their husbands: and to all whatever ill accords with time and place, age, condition of life, or bodily powers. In general, such penances should be chosen as are most antagonistic to the sins confessed, such as alms to covetous, mortifications to sensual, and so on. Relapsing persons should have their penances prolonged, "not only," as S. Chrysostom observes, "for healing the wound, but also to cure the scar." In short the disease is healed more easily by repeating the remedy. Penances may be given for several years in very rare cases: for many days or months according to the need of the penitent. In order to make him feel the enormity of his sins the Priest should exhort briefly and earnestly, pointing out what the Ancient Canons would have enforced for even one of the sins which he has committed. Then he may add with kindness, "It is true you have deserved a heavier penance, but I content myself with giving you a lighter."

(107) *Different kinds of Penances.*

(1) If the penitent have committed a great number of deadly sins he should be ordered to say the Penitential Psalms[1] during a week or fortnight, reciting them with contrition, with prayer to GOD for pardon and grace: if he be an habitual sinner, this penance may be prolonged according to the kind of sin. By this means the penitent may learn to say the Penitential Psalms by heart to his great benefit at any time.

(2) To say morning, noon, and evening three Our FATHER's with an act of contrition: and accompany them in the morning and midday with a firm resolution against sinning through the day: and in the evening,

[1] One ready way of saying the Penitential Psalms daily, is to repeat three in the morning and evening respectively as in the Ash Wednesday Matins and Evensong, and the 51st at midday. Gerson compares true penitence to a flight of seven steps, whereby the sinner who has *gone down* from Jerusalem to Jericho again returns to the Vision of Peace, the true Jerusalem. These correspond with the seven Penitential Psalms. The 6th is the fear of punishment, "*Domine, ne in furore:*" the 32nd, sorrow for the faults, "*Dixi, Confitebor:*" the 38th, the hope of pardon which was preceded by fear, "*Quoniam in Te, Domine, speravi:*" the 51st, the love of purity, "*Amplius lava me:*" the 102nd, the longing for heaven, "*Filii servorum tuorum habitabunt:*" the 130th, the distrust of oneself and trust in GOD, "*De profundis:*" the 143rd, the happiness of spiritual joy in prayer, "*Domine, exaudi.*" Gerson also observes that this appropriateness does not apply to the whole of the Psalms, and that there is occasionally a transition from one affection to the other.

against sinning through the night. This is a salutary penance in many cases, specially of unlearned persons.

(3) To go to church, specially at the time of Celebration, provided no duties are thereby hindered.

(4) Every morning to offer up the labours, trials, and difficulties of the day, or any spiritual exercise which includes acts of faith, hope, and charity; and every evening an examination of conscience, together with a meditation on death, taking care at the same time to fix the period of all or any of these devotions.

(5) To recite daily during a specified time five Our FATHER's in union with the five Blessed Wounds, stopping to dwell upon each thought of our LORD's Passion: to attend some church a certain number of times: read for a definite period a devotional book. At the same time lest their consciences be ensnared they should be advised that if they happened to forget to perform them as arranged, they may make up for their forgetfulness on another occasion, and even if hindered from doing this they need not entertain any scruple about it as if they had committed a grave fault.

Such as are capable of doing so—ecclesiastics, &c.—should be bidden to meditate on certain days for half an hour or more, or to read portions of a religious book: healthy and strong people to fast for a certain period: masters of households to say prayers with their family every evening at least: blasphemers to sign the earth with their tongues: drunkards to abstain for a fixed term, or have their drink watered: ignorant people to say certain Our FATHER's at a grave, with the thought that they may soon die: proud persons, to say prayers, acts of humility, &c.

Some may ask whether it is best to give heavy or light penances? Generally speaking, it is best to assign mild penances, especially where the penitent is not likely to fulfil a heavy one, or thinks that he is unable to perform it. In such cases the penance may be changed, except in that of relapsing or habitual sinners, when it is better to run the risk of their omitting it, than of their thinking less of sin. In their case it is necessary to deal severely, and even run the risk of imposing what they may not carry out, lest through the lightness of the penance imposed they imagine that the sin is less enormous than it is. The Priest may lessen the penance where the penitent shows great contrition and horror of his sins, and even fears that the penance is too slight. It is good sometimes to assign only a meditation on the Passion, since it, as has been well said, if devoutly exercised for a brief period, is more profitable than a long fast on bread and water or a sanguinary discipline. In the case of a reiterated general confession, the Priest need not trouble about devising a duly proportioned penance, since the sins have already been confessed. Some impose almsgiving or fasting upon every relapse, but this must be done with two cautions,—(1) Not to let them be too severe or difficult, lest the penitent omit them and be discouraged at omitting them: (2) not to allow them to be performed as equivalents, lest the penitent indulge his sin with this sop to his conscience.

Poor persons should not be enjoined almsgiving, nor labouring people fasting, nor busy people long prayers or psalms. Notorious sinners should be enjoined public penances. If money is offered the Priest, and he thinks it may be wisely accepted directly by himself, he must always apply it to some charitable work, and not to his own wants or pleasures.

The penitent should be persuaded to undertake his penance voluntarily; should have lighter assigned if he make reasonable objections: the penances should not be mixed, such as acts, and prayers, and psalms; but of one kind—not alms and fasting, fasting and prayers, prayers and psalms, and different religious books: but one thing or one book at a time. Sometimes the Priest has to force, sometimes to persuade, but always in the spirit of love for souls.

(108) *Secrecy of Confession.*

The English Church (Can. CXIII.) ordains that if any man confess his secret and hidden sins to the Priest for the unburdening of his conscience, such confession is not to be revealed or made known to any person whatsoever except in the case of such crimes as if concealed by the laws of the realm might call his life in question. This secrecy extends to all who are accomplices in or occasions of the sins which the penitent confesses, and to the faults, imperfections, and vices which he acknowledges.

Hence Priests are bound to abstain even from doing or saying anything which would hint at the faults of their penitents. This applies even to those who have overheard, or read, or been told the confessions of others.

The secrecy of Confession may be violated either *directly* or *indirectly*.

I. *Directly.*

(1.) By saying that a penitent has confessed such

and such a sin; that he has confessed mortal or venial sins; that he is in the habit of committing such and such a sin; that he is unworthy to communicate; that he is a bastard, illtempered, unfit for certain ecclesiastical offices, or for orders, or for a convent; by communicating in short to others what the Priest has learned in confession about his penitents.

(2.) By one Confessor talking to another about the sins of a penitent who has confessed partially to both, unless the penitent has wished them to confer together.

(3.) By speaking out of confession to a penitent about the sins which have been confessed, unless the penitent wishes to confer with the Confessor.

(4.) By saying of a parish, community, town, &c., that certain sins prevail therein, the knowledge of which is due to confession.

(5.) By giving a Bishop, or any other head in Church or State information that certain scandals and disorders prevail in their departments, which are known only in confession.

(6.) In denouncing, when preaching, certain sins as prevailing in the parish, when the sole source of information is confession.

II. *Indirectly.*

(1.) By saying that a penitent has been refused absolution, or been deferred, or that a heavy penance has been given.

(2.) By comparing one penitent to another, and saying that he is not subject to such and such sins.

(3.) By making certain movements or sounds while hearing confessions, so as to give an idea that the penitent confesses grave sins.

(4.) By behaving to a penitent out of confession so as silently to reproach him for his sins.

(5.) By refusing absolution when sins, which are only known by the confession of accomplices, are concealed by the penitent.

(6.) By telling a Judge not to be uneasy about the condemnation of a criminal.

Hence if Priests need to confer on the subject for the purpose of mutual instruction, they should take care not to do so in the presence of lay folk, and to do it with great precaution, and not to drop any hint whereby the penitent may be recognised. The smaller the town the greater the danger.

(109) *Restitution*

Is reparation for the wrong or loss inflicted upon one's neighbour which ought to be equivalent to the injury sustained.

The Priest must understand,—

1. In what things and ways one may wrong his neighbour.

2. What persons are bound to make restitution.

3. What rule should be observed by those who are bound to restitution.

4. What must be regarded in order to make restitution equal to the loss.

5. What reasons exempt from the necessity of restitution.

In what things and ways one may wrong his neighbour.

There are four things in which one's neighbour may be wronged,—*spiritual, natural, civil,* and *possessive.*

Spiritual.—Those which regard his salvation and sanctification, Sacraments, prayers and good works. Bishops and Clergy run the greatest risk in these respects, and are bound to repair the wrong done by giving instruction more frequently, ministering the Sacraments more diligently. This applies also to cases in which a Priest has set a bad example and led others into error. Also those who have misled or forced others into sin, hindered them from doing their duty, from accomplishing any good work, &c. They are bound to undeceive the victims of their delusions, to lead them to penitence, &c.

Natural.—Such as of body and soul, breath, life, use of reason, senses, liberty, &c. Those who wrong others in these respects are bound to replace what they have caused others to lose, or to repair as far as possible the evil consequences.

Civil.—Such as good character, and public or private esteem, friendship, honour and respect. Those who wrong others in this respect are bound to unsay what has been said, reconcile those who have been disunited, and do all they can to give back the esteem which has been taken away.

Possessive.—Personal and real estate.

Persons wrong their neighbour by (1) taking away openly or secretly; (2) by unjust exactions, or receipts, overcharges, &c.; (3) by holding back what is due, what they have found, or what has been entrusted to them; (4) by preventing payment of what is due, or hindering advancement, advising people to elude their creditors, or shielding them in doing so; (5) by injuring a neighbour's property.

Restitution is rehearsed in the following verses,

> Jussio, consilium, consensus, palpo, recursus,
> Participans, mutus, non obstans, non manifestans.

Or in other words, that those who give *orders* to others are responsible for the results, unless they have previously revoked them. In like manner those who give *advice*, unless they have effectually destroyed the grounds of their advice in time to prevent the results. This does not apply in cases in which the adviser does not pretend to knowledge of the subject, and does not intend to deceive. There is difference also when one advises if consulted, according to the most probable grounds, or shows that his advice is given with some degree of doubt, and does not urge any one to take his advice.

So also they who *consent* to any injustice, whether as individuals, or as a community; they who *applaud* or *approve* of the same; they who *shield* or *abet* others in the same; who are *accomplices in* or *after* the fact; who *keep* and *enforce silence* to the loss of their neighbour; who do not *withstand* or *hinder* the same; and who do not *inform* and *disclose* the wrong done to their neighbours. All these lie under the obligation of restoring to their neighbour what they have directly or indirectly caused him to lose.

(110) *Order to be observed in regard to those who are bound to make restitution.*

Persons who derive benefit from wrong done to their neighbour are bound to restitution, though they had no share in the act which caused the wrong.

There are two classes which are bound to restitution.
(1) Those who knowingly profit by injustice.
(2) Those who unknowingly profit by injustice.
The first must restore all.

The second only that which is in their hands when they have come to know it.

After these two classes we may rank those who have acted by the commands, prayers, promises, or menaces of others: noting that the person who supplies the motives for action is held to restitution before those who have aided in carrying it out. Those who *consent*, approve, and abet, are bound to restore in equal parts. Next to them the *silent*, the *non-resisting*, and the *non-informing*. When the first class have entirely restored, the last are free: but if the last restore, the first are bound to restore to them unless any special circumstances change that order.

When one bound partially to restore has restored entirely, the others are bound to restore to him their parts.

When many have agreed to commit some injustice, and one has carried it out on his own behalf and on that of others, he is only bound to restore on his own account; and if he restore the whole, the rest are bound to restore to him their part.

When the Priest meets with a penitent who is bound to make some restitution, and if the penitent is not primarily bound, the Priest ought before he compels restitution to learn whether the restitution has not been made by the person primarily bound; and so long as it has not been so restored, he must tell him that the person who is primarily bound ought to restore him what he is going to restore: and when he is only obliged to restore a part, he must tell him that all who are bound with him to restore must restore him their portions of the obligation. When he is primarily bound he must apprise the rest that the restitution is completed, that they may know that they are discharged from all obligation.

(111) *What must be done to make the restitution equivalent to the loss.*

Anything which has been wrongfully taken must be restored, and if depreciated in value by the fault of the detainer, the loss must be made up. Or if the thing be lost, its value must be substituted. Or if loss be incurred by its detention, it must be made up.

In order to know better how to make the restitution balance the loss, we must distinguish *four* kinds of fruits which may be derived from anything—*natural, industrial, mixed,* and *civil.*

Natural, which spring spontaneously.

Industrial, acquired by labour and care.

Mixed, partly natural and industrial.

Civil, barren of themselves, and fruitful only by the use made of them.

(1) *Natural* fruits must be restored, and nothing can be deducted but the expenses which the rightful proprietor must have laid out in any case.

(2) *Industrial* need not be restored, so long as they restore the original value of what they possess unjustly, and reimburse the rightful possessor in all loss that detention has caused him.

(3) *Mixed* fruits must be restored, so far as concerns the natural element, while retaining the industrial, and deducting all just expenses, such as for improvements and working, but not such as were for pleasure. But if any loss has accrued by bad management, it must be reimbursed to the proprietor. If no profit has been derived, nor would have been had the proprietor himself managed his own property, then the unjust occupant is not bound to make any restitution.

(4) Some hold that no restitution is required in the case of *civil* fruits, but that the simple restoration of the thing itself is sufficient. On the other hand, as by utilising what is in itself barren, the non-rightful owner may derive some fruit, he ought to pay to the rightful owner something out of what he has gained by possession and use. But the Priest must, to speak generally, be guided by the laws and customs on this head of the country where he exercises his office.

(112) *Causes of Exemption.*

They are *four*.

(1) *Inability to restore:* twofold, physical and moral.

When *physical* inability arises from want of funds, the obligation is suspended until he earns or receives money: when from want of meeting with the person wronged, the restitution must be made in almsgiving: when from the injury being such as cannot be repaired in kind, such as life, character, &c., by money payments, prayers, &c.

When *moral* inability arises on the part of the person to whom restitution is due, such as when money is due to a debauchee, arms to a mad or passionate man, restitution may be and should be delayed. So also when the person who owes restitution, cannot raise money or restore what is due without suffering great loss. But not if the injured person lose by delay or thereby lose more than the injurer. At all events, the injured person must be indemnified for such delay if it add to his loss.

(2) *Remission on the part of the injured person,* provided it be not done in ignorance of the amount or of the circumstances of the case and by compulsion.

(3) *When restitution is avoided on the ground of what is due from the injured party:* and then six things are necessary—1, Being sure that a particular amount is due; 2, and that in strict justice; 3, and can only be so recovered; 4, that more is not retained than ought to be; 5, that it can be done without scandal, and without risk of incurring legal penalties; 6, that proper means are taken to prevent the compensation being made twice over.

(4) *Prescription* avails—1. When what can legally be acquired by prescription may be legally retained by the same.

2. When the laws do not protect the owner against prescription.

3. When one has possessed as his own what he holds by prescription.

4. When he has himself believed it to be his own.

5. When this possession has been held during the legal period.

6. When there has been a title of sale, or donation, and the like, and the possessor has believed it to be good and legal.

Such exemptions do not avail for those who inherit anything wrongfully possessed at the first. It is otherwise when they obtain possession from a wrongfully possessed vendor or donor. But if doubt arise at the time of coming into possession, the prescription is invalidated.

(113) *To aid pious persons in their desire for perfection.*

In regard to *women*, the Priest should

1. Meet their natural inconstancy by striving to strengthen their judgment and stay their will.

2. Exercise them more in the practice of virtues than in contemplation: make them serve GOD a long time in the life of Martha ere he admit them to the life of Mary: approach JESUS before they unite themselves to Him: serve Him, wash His feet with their tears and dry them with their hair, before they are admitted to rest upon His Bosom and repose with Him in the union of holy love.

3. Drive away all that can render devotion ridiculous or repulsive, since GOD and goodness cannot be in a soul without its neighbour perceiving some sweetness. If the Priest allow tears when the heart is full of holy love, let them flow only gently, and like the rain which descends by night, cease with the morning sun, or only fall imperceptibly.

4. Encourage great simplicity in opposition to dissimulation or intrigue, but suffer it not to degenerate into folly so as to mistake dreams for revelations.

5. Bid them strive to be in the world like rocks in the midst of waves, so as to be immoveable against its

assaults and temptations, and living with mankind have its tongue and heart with GOD and the holy Angels.

6. Warn them against too great curiosity in acquiring useless knowledge.

7. Warn them against that false piety which is characterised by indolence, and that true devotion consists in passing time usefully, employing it with holy adroitness and to extract from it a profitable interest for eternity.

8. Exhort them to cultivate purity and modesty in the very soul of their life, without which they are but living sepulchres.

9. Let them not lead the life of recluses, but to mix in society according to their condition, and enjoy the recreations of their quality; and if they become attached to any creature, let it be only as a step towards resting in GOD and abiding in Him.

10. Recommend them, if his knowledge of their case authorize him to do so, to communicate at least weekly.

11. Never hinder their going to another Confessor, but rejoice at it and even send them sometimes to him, except when he believes it will be hurtful to them to go elsewhere than to himself. Never manifest any wish to become a director to any one. Never speak ill of other directors, but rather excuse their faults. Never take on him the burden of the children of other confessors without some urgent reason. Mere dislike or want of confidence are insufficient grounds of changing confessors. Nothing suffices but want of holiness or knowledge.

12. Avoid all partiality in devoting his attention more to one penitent than to another, so as to neglect

one for the other. One needs more aid than another, but attachment is one thing, and aid is another. It is best to manage so as not to give umbrage, by giving those who need more aid than others special days and hours, when he can give them more time without taking it from others. Let not young pious women cut their hair short or wear a religious habit too readily, before they have had some time to advance in religion and virtue, lest they hereafter give up their dress and marry to the great scandal of the world. Let not such young women learn accomplishments, &c., of male teachers, nor frequent churches and spend much time there to the annoyance of their parents. The Priest must beware of too great familiarity with them.

13. Be not content with rooting up vices, but plant virtues in their place. He can never get rid of sinners, but he may cultivate and train some souls to be entirely His. Therefore when he meets with a soul exempt from deadly sin, he should do his best to lead it into the way of perfection and Divine love : represent to it the numberless reasons which we have for loving GOD, Who is infinitely loveable, and the gratitude which we owe to JESUS CHRIST, Who has loved us unto death : make it understand all the peril of souls which, after having been called by GOD to a more perfect life, remain deaf to His voice. Now the direction of pious souls by their Confessor consists mainly in these things, meditation, contemplation, mortification, and frequenting the Sacraments.

14. First of all, the Priest should instruct them in *mental prayer*, i.e. meditation on the eternal truths and goodness of GOD, which though not necessary to salva-

tion, is necessary to preserve souls in the grace of GOD. Sin is compatible with other pious exercises, but not with meditation, which casts it out at last. As love is the surest bond of the soul with GOD, so meditation and prayer is the furnace of love.

15. The soul should be urged to spend half-an-hour a day in this manner, and to increase this period as fervour is augmented. Let it not excuse itself on the ground that it lacks time and place. The Priest should bid it select early morning, late at night, or midday, or during work and employment; if unable to do so otherwise, lift itself up to GOD, think of the verities of faith, of the last ends, especially in the case of beginners, or of the Passion of CHRIST, which is suitable for all: or if scholars, bid them read a book of devotions to help them to meditate, choose such subjects as aid them most to pray, stop when they meet some good sentiment, and follow up reflections by acts, prayers, or resolutions: (1) *acts* of humility, gratitude, faith and hope, of contrition, charity, and entire submission to the will of GOD: (2) *prayers*, upon which their entire perfection depends, and to which GOD ordinarily concedes His graces, especially of perseverance and of His love: for they who meditate not pray seldom and pray ill: (3) *resolutions*, so that meditations may not continue barren, for they ought never to pray without making some good resolutions either of avoiding some habitual fault or of practising some needful virtue. Want of thought it is which fills hell, want in short of mental prayer or meditation.

16. He should teach them how to meditate in three divisions, preparation, meditation, conclusion. In *pre-*

paration there are three acts : (1) entering into the Presence of GOD ; (2) humiliation of self; (3) invocation of the HOLY GHOST for enlightenment. As for *meditation,* persons who can read, very easily select what does them most good, passing like bees from flower to flower collecting the honey : those who cannot read may dwell on the last ends and on the Passion of our LORD, the best book for pious souls, which most shows the love of GOD for souls and the malice of sin. They must not however be content with meditating, but go on to form affections, prayers, and resolutions, the three fruits of prayer. Then is the time to make the acts (as above) especially of love or contrition, which are the same things, and to offer themselves to GOD. Then is the time to multiply prayers asking of GOD light, pardon, perseverance, the gift of a good death, paradise and the gift of His holy love, aid and comfort in desolations : and to make resolutions, as we have said, of amendment, such as to bear with the ill humour and ill temper of such a one : obey more exactly a superior or a rule, or mortify self in such a way. He should urge them never to leave meditation without making some such special resolution. The *conclusion* is composed of three acts—(1) thanksgiving for light vouchsafed in the meditation ; (2) promise to keep resolutions just made; (3) prayer to GOD for fidelity to them. It is good here to collect a nosegay for recollection throughout the day, by taking away with it some thoughts in which the soul has felt most unction, thus reviving its fervour even till night. The soul must try to practise some of the resolutions then made on every occasion great or small, to calm by gentleness the passion of some one who is vexed, or mortify eyes, ears, tongue, &c. : above all preserve by silence the affections which have been stirred up. Nor should penitents ever give up meditation amidst aridities and desolations: like courtiers waiting patiently on their king whether he show graciousness or otherwise. The Confessor should make his penitents give an account of their meditations, whether neglected, or made ill: and elicit whether they have only made them well so long as they enjoyed sensible consolations.

17. When he meets with a soul which has the gift of *contemplation*, he must find out how to conduct it and preserve it from illusions. As in meditation man seeks GOD, so in contemplation he sees without trouble GOD already found. In the one the soul acts by its own power; in the other it is GOD Who directs while the soul is passive and receives His gifts in it.

18. Before granting the gift of contemplation the LORD ordinarily introduces souls into the state of *recollective* or *contemplative repose;* the difference between these being that the soul is in the one case occupied with one holy thought, while in the other a general converse with GOD arrests and attracts lovingly towards Him. So long as the soul is in *active* contemplation it may take the opportunity of making acts of the will, but in *passive*, the soul becomes silent and suspends its own operations, yielding itself wholly up to the Divine.

19. Before entering into contemplation GOD usually tries the soul by *supernatural dryness* to purify it from its imperfections, which are obstacles to contemplation. This *dryness* is *sensible* or *substantial*. When the *sensible* dryness is natural it is accompanied with distaste for the things of GOD, and with darkness some-

what thick and lasting. When it is supernatural, it casts the soul into very deep obscurity more lasting and ever increasing. Nevertheless in this state the soul becomes more and more disengaged from creatures, and more occupied with GOD, Whom it desires ardently and constantly to love in a perfect manner. On the other hand it finds itself in a state of powerlessness to realize its desire by reason of its imperfections, which seem to provoke the anger of GOD, but nevertheless it never ceases to practise virtue courageously. While the soul detaches itself from the sensible, corporal or spiritual pleasures, which it perceives hinder its growth, it learns its own natural misery and helplessness out of GOD. It must be taught to humble itself, offer itself to GOD, and resign itself to the ever benevolent disposition of His all-loveable will.

20. Having thus purified the soul from all sensible affection, the LORD is wont to communicate to it the gift of contemplation, of *supernatural* recollection, of repose and union. But before union and after recollection GOD tries the soul by *spiritual* dryness, called on that account *substantial* dryness. GOD wills thereby that the soul should reduce itself to nothing, and learn its own nothingness. Then it is that it seems as if GOD rejected it entirely because of its ingratitude and imperfections; as if its devotions and communions only made it more odious to GOD, as if it hated GOD, as if it were reprobate already, and as if this desolation were accompanied with the most hideous temptations to sin. Not being able to distinguish consent from resistance men think they are abandoned by GOD. The Priest in such cases must not be alarmed, or seem to be so. He must

bid the soul fear not, but trust in GOD more than ever, since no one ever loves GOD without knowing it. He must console it by assuring it that its dire temptations are not acts of consent on its part, but only trials, which if borne with resignation render its union with GOD all the closer. It is the way of the Cross by which GOD leads the souls which are dearest to Him: though it should last a life, their reward is sure. They must be exhorted (1) to self-humiliation and acknowledgment of their deserts; (2) to resignation to the Divine Will, offering themselves to suffer even more if it be GOD's pleasure; (3) to abandon themselves, as if dead, to the embrace of the Divine goodness.

21. When the senses are purified, and the sensible dryness ended, the soul is admitted to contemplation, though the dryness may return to prevent negligence and conviction of its own nothingness. This contemplation is affirmative or negative. It is *affirmative* when it by the Divine light alone beholds some created truth, as of hell or heaven, or some uncreated truth as the love of GOD. It is *negative* when it views the Divine perfections in general and not in portions.

22. The first degree of contemplation is *supernatural recollection*, which differs from *natural* in that this last is active, and energises with the aid of ordinary graces, and the first is passive, and energises with the aid of extraordinary. In this *supernatural* recollection the soul must do nothing to interrupt the sweet converse with GOD, nor reflect on individual acts or things.

23. The second degree is *repose*. In recollection the force of love is communicated to the external senses; in repose immediately to the inmost recesses of the soul;

love is most ardent, and makes itself felt in the senses themselves. All the powers of the soul however are not suspended, the will is bound, because it can only love GOD Who attracts it to Himself, but the intellect, memory, or imagination remain free.

24. The *negative* contemplation may be called *clear obscurity*, because the abundance of light obscures the understanding. Just as one who gazes at the sun is dazzled by its splendour and sees nothing; so the soul in thus contemplating GOD sees nothing distinctly, but learns that His perfection is incomprehensible. Here the soul has all its interior, and even exterior powers suspended so as to enter sometimes into a sort of spiritual intoxication, which manifests itself by acts of an unrestrained love, charity, tears, &c.

25. After this the soul is conducted to *union*. It is not necessary to arrive at a *passive* union, *active* is sufficient. *Active* union is perfect conformity to the Divine will, in which all the perfection of Divine love consists. In the *passive* union all the powers of the soul are suspended; the soul must only remember GOD; the will is so one with GOD as to love nought else; the understanding so enlightened as to think of Him alone. In short the soul possesses a clear and experimental knowledge of GOD's presence, which unites it closely to Him. In other contemplations GOD is nigh,—in this He is present. The Priest must warn such a favoured soul of the necessity of humility and detachment, of loving the Cross, of being full of conformity to the decrees of Providence, of fearing greater punishment, if unfaithful on account of its ingratitude.

26. There are three kinds of union,—*simple*, of *es-*

pousals, of *consummation*, called *spiritual marriage*. We have just spoken of the first. The second is generally preceded by *substantial* dryness. In this union are three degrees, *ecstasy*, *ravishment*, and *spiritual flight*. In *simple* union the soul's powers are suspended, but not the body's. In *ecstasy* the use of the body is lost,—one sees not, hears not, feels not. In *ravishment* the soul is carried away suddenly and violently. In *spiritual flight* the soul seems carried out of the body, and ecstasy and ravishment are included. The *consummated* union is the most perfect, and the closest which GOD vouchsafes her. The soul is transformed into GOD, and becomes one with Him. The powers of the soul are not suspended here, but only purified. Hence the will loves GOD with supreme happiness, and the understanding knows and reflects on this close union. It is like seeing the sun without being dazzled by it, and knowing all its brightness. It is not transitory like the rest, but endures. In the midst of passions the soul is tranquil like a man on a rock above the waves.

27. In regard to *visions* the Priest may decide that they are false, and the work of the devil, (1) if they do not come suddenly and without any previous thought of the soul; (2) if they do not begin by causing alarm, nor end by giving rise to peace; (3) if they be not rare and return often; (4) if they last a long time; (5) if they do not leave the soul in peace and a living knowledge of its own misery combined with a great desire of perfection, but produce only passing impressions, and leave behind in the soul dryness, restlessness, and motives of self-esteem, and a sensible taste for this kind

of thing. As to *colloquies* and *revelations*, the Priest must decide on their reality by the facts whether what is expressed or commended, and what results is in accordance with Christian prudence and with the faith.

28. The Priest however (1) should repress all curiosity to learn what his penitent professes to have heard or seen, and all speaking to others about them; (2) all showing of special regard to a soul so privileged, as to exalt her own opinion of herself by sending others to consult her; (3) aid the soul which seems humble and timid in the midst of her privileges by confirming her in her belief of what she has seen and heard : and bid her ask of GOD the true ecstasy which is her complete detachment from all earthly goods and of itself. Attachments, self-esteem, and pride accompanying such gifts show that they are not of GOD but of the Devil. Any way the soul must be exhorted to meditate always on some point of our LORD's Life and Passion, at any rate at first. Souls which are beginners meditate on His Passion by reasoning, the contemplative no longer reasons upon but marvels at the mysteries of GOD, His goodness and mercy and love, whence He raises them when He will to the contemplation of His Divine Nature.

29. When pious women wish to consecrate themselves to GOD by becoming Sisters of Mercy or Nuns, the Priest must satisfy himself that they are willing to offer themselves a sacrifice exclusively to the honour of GOD by making a public and perpetual profession of their intention to adore Him perfectly, and of being entirely His, after the example of the Divine pattern of charity, poverty, obedience, and chastity in the GOD-

Man. They must be ready to embrace the religious life of JESUS CHRIST in all its devotion and sacrifice, to accept the evangelical counsels as their daily rule of life, to quit all and sacrifice all. While preserving their family affectionateness they must find in the sovereign love of JESUS power to sacrifice all earthly joys to the chief of all love, the Divine. All goods of this life must seem nothing in comparison of JESUS the eternal treasure, all bliss of human love and human ties nothing in comparison of union and espousals of JESUS. They must be ready to renounce their own will for the will of JESUS as manifested to them in the wills of their Superiors. They must look on to a perpetual service of GOD in good works, or to worship with joy and gladness in imitation of the life of JESUS CHRIST on earth; to the influence of good examples, the aid afforded by the rule of their community, their common employments, their choir offices, the readings at meals; to the sweet and calm recreations, wise, joyful, hearty, and truly sisterly, the spiritual conferences, the close and abiding directions, the loving counsels, the daily austerities of the life with its thousand little privations, the habitual silence, and all that tends to unite the soul to JESUS.

30. The notes of *vocation* in ordinary communities are according to S. Thomas, four. (1) Not being necessary at home for maintenance of or help to parents; (2) not being in debt; (3) having a pious purpose to follow after perfection and Paradise; (4) absence of all eccentric propensities which trouble a community life and hearty union. It is a supernatural life, and they who embrace it as they ought are the heroines of Christianity. They whom GOD really calls will receive the

necessary grace, but they need not extraordinary qualifications beyond the single and honest determination to follow faithfully and courageously the attractions of grace and perfection.

31. It is true there are two kinds which are found in the religious life,—those who are the cream, and those who are the milk of the community. The one comprises choice souls who go on courageously to perfection, and are the soul, life, and salt of the community; the other those who enter it for safety against the temptations of the world, who are saved instead of lost, and are holier and better than they could be in the world. The first sustain and carry the second. In deciding on the vocation of a Sister or Nun the Priest has to bear in mind most of these considerations.

www.ingramcontent.com/pod-product-compliance
Lightning Source LLC
Chambersburg PA
CBHW032140010526
44111CB00035B/682